BEST *of the* BEST
from
GEORGIA
COOKBOOK

◆

Selected Recipes from Georgia's
FAVORITE COOKBOOKS

The most significant architectural style in Georgia and all of the United States during the 1800s was Greek Revival. A classic example of this antebellum style is Oak Hill, home of the founder of Berry College. The estate was home to Union troops during the Civil War.

BEST *of the* BEST
from
GEORGIA
COOKBOOK

◆

Selected Recipes from Georgia's
FAVORITE COOKBOOKS

EDITED BY
Gwen McKee
AND
Barbara Moseley

Illustrated by Tupper England

QUAIL RIDGE PRESS
Preserving America's Food Heritage

Recipe Collection ©2006 Quail Ridge Press, Inc.

Reprinted with permission and all rights reserved under the name
of the cookbooks, organizations, or individuals listed below.

Atlanta Cooknotes ©1982 Junior League of Atlanta, Inc.; *Best of the Holidays* ©2001 Dot Gibson Publications; *Bevelyn Blair's Everyday Cakes* ©1999 by Bevelyn Blair; *Bevelyn Blair's Everyday Pies* ©2000 by Bevelyn Blair; *The Blue Willow Inn Bible of Southern Cooking* ©2005 by Billie and Louis Van Dyke; *Bread of Life* ©2003 Salem Baptist Church; *Breads and Spreads* ©1992 Carol Rees Publications; *Confessions of a Kitchen Diva* ©2003 Happicook, Inc.; *Cook and Love It* ©1976 The Mother's Club, The Lovett School; *Cooking with Herbs Volume I* ©1996 The Garden Patch Company.; *Cooking with Herbs Volume II* ©1996 The Garden Patch Company; *Delightfully Southern* ©1996 River Oaks Publications; *Eating from the White House to the Jailhouse* ©2004 by Louise Dodd; *Family Collections* ©1993 St. Matthew's Episcopal Church Women; *Famous Recipes from Mrs. Wilkes' Boarding House* ©1976 by Mrs. L. H. Wilkes; *Fine Dining Georgia Style* ©2005 by John M. Bailey; *First Come, First Served...In Savannah* ©2001 St. Andrew's School; *Flavors of the Gardens* ©2000 Callaway Gardens Resort, Inc.; *The Foxfire Book of Appalachian Cookery* ©1984 Foxfire Fund, Inc. / ©1992 The University of North Carolina Press; *From Black Tie to Blackeyed Peas* ©2000 by Irving Victor, M.D.; *From Our House to Yours* © Habitat for Humanity International; *Georgia National Fair Blue Ribbon Cookbook* ©2004 Georgia National Fair; *A Gift of Appreciation* ©2004 Dixie Aerospace Employees; *The Gingerbread House Cookbook* ©2000 The Gingerbread House; *Gone with the Grits* ©1992 by Diane Pfeifer; *Heart & Soul* ©2001 Clinch Chapel United Methodist Church Youth Choir; *Holiday Delights* ©1997 River Oaks Publications; *Holiday Favorites* ©1991 Dot Gibson Publications; *Home Sweet Habitat* © Habitat for Humanity International; *It's the People; It's the Food* ©2001 St. Matthew's Episcopal Church Women; *The Lady & Sons, Too!* ©2000 by Paula H. Deen; *The Lady & Sons Just Desserts* ©2002 by Paula H. Deen; *The Lady & Sons Savannah Country Cookbook* ©1997 by Paula H. Deen; *Mother's Finest: Southern Cooking Made Easy* ©2002 Mother's Finest; *Mountain Folk, Mountain Food* ©1997 by Betsy Tice White; *My Best to You* ©1991 by Carolyn Jackson; *The One-Armed Cook* ©2004 by Cynthia Stevens and Catherine Fliegel, RN, CCE; *Our Best Home Cooking* ©2001 by Judith C. Dyer; *Our Favorite Recipes* ©1996 The Garden Patch Company; *Out On Our Own* ©1993 River Oaks Publications; *Par 3: Tea-Time at the Masters®* ©2005 Junior League of Augusta; *Paula Deen & Friends* ©2005 by Paula Deen; *Peachtree Bouquet* ©1987 The Junior League of DeKalb County; *Perennials* ©1984 Junior League of Gainesville-Hall County, Inc.; *Puttin' on the Peachtree* ©1979 The Junior League of DeKalb County; *Savannah Seasons* ©1996 by Elizabeth Terry and Alexis Terry; *Second Round: Tea-Time at the Masters®* ©1988 Junior League of Augusta; *Simple Decent Cooking* © Habitat for Humanity International; *Some Assembly Required* ©2004 by Lee J. Chadwick; *The South's Legendary Frances Virginia Tea Room Cookbook* ©1981, 1996 by Mildred Huff Coleman; *Southern Bread Winners* ©1996 Dot Gibson Publications; *A Southern Collection: Then and Now* ©1994 Junior League of Columbus, GA, Inc.; *Southern Manna* ©1988 Dot Gibson Publications; *Strawberries: From Our Family's Field to Your Family's Table* ©2005 Calhoun Produce, Inc.; *A Taste of Georgia, Another Serving* ©1994 The Newnan Junior Service League; *A Taste of the Holidays* ©1988 Dot Gibson Publications; *A Taste of Georgia* ©1977 The Newnan Junior Service League; *Tea-Time at the Masters®* ©1977 Junior League of Augusta; *Traditions* ©1992 Carol Rees Publications; *A Traveler's Table* ©2002 by John Izard; *Tried & True Recipes* ©2005 Covington, Georgia East Metro Christian Women's Connection; *Tried & True Recipes* ©2005 Wild Timber Social Committee; *True Grits* ©1995 Junior League of Atlanta, Inc.; *Vidalia Sweet Onion Lovers Cookbook* ©1996 Bland Farms; *Wanted: Quick Draw's Favorite Recipes* ©2003 by Quick Draw Finch.

Library of Congress Cataloging-in-Publication Data

Best of the best from Georgia cookbook : selected recipes from Georgia's favorite cookbooks
/ edited by Gwen McKee and Barbara Moseley ; illustrated by Tupper England.
p. cm.
Includes bibliographical references and index.
ISBN-13: 978-1-893062-81-8 (alk. paper)
ISBN-10: 1-893062-81-3 (alk. paper)
1. Cookery, American—Southern style. 2. Cookery—Georgia. I. McKee, Gwen.
II. Moseley, Barbara.

TX715.2.S68B465 2006
641.59758–dc22   2006007231

Copyright ©2006 by Quail Ridge Press, Inc.
ISBN-13: 978-1-893062-81-8 • ISBN-10: 1-893062-81-3

First printing, May 2006 • Second, October 2007 • Third, September 2009

Front cover photo: The Fickling House during the Cherry Blossom Festival, Macon
Front cover and page photos courtesy of Georgia Department of Economic Development
Back cover photo by Greg Campbell
Design by Cynthia Clark • Printed by Tara TPS in South Korea

QUAIL RIDGE PRESS
P. O. Box 123 • Brandon, MS 39043 • 1-800-343-1583
e-mail: info@quailridge.com • www.quailridge.com

CONTENTS

PHOTO © GEORGIA DEPARTMENT OF ECONOMIC DEVELOPMENT

Located just south of Atlanta off I-75, Indian Springs is one of the oldest state parks in the nation. It became an official "State Forest Park" in 1927. Indian Springs was first visited by Creek Indians who believed the natural spring water had healing qualities.

The Quest for the Best

by Gwen McKee

I am frequently asked how the idea for the BEST OF THE BEST STATE COOKBOOK SERIES came about, and how it got started.

It all began with my love for cooking and entertaining, which I have been doing all of my married life. Having collected a variety of cookbooks, most of which have splatters or turned-down pages or notations on the recipes, one day it occurred to me that if I could compile all these earmarked favorite recipes, it would be an incredible cookbook! And wouldn't it be even more special if I could get favorite recipes from the best cookbooks from all over each state—the Best of the Best! Wow! The idea consumed me and became a passion. I knew I had to pursue this quest.

In the days before Internet, faxes, cell phones, or even inexpensive long-distance calling, the only way to gather everything I needed was to strike out and do my research in person. I started in my home state, and that is how *Best of the Best from Mississippi* became the first BEST OF THE BEST cookbook in 1982.

Completing the first cookbook was a lot of work, and I knew if I wanted to tackle Louisiana next, with all its cookbooks, I would need help.

My golfing buddy Barbara Moseley and I were always talking about food and recipes on the golf course, and I knew she was an excellent cook. Besides being my sounding board for all the decisions I faced with *Best of the Best from Mississippi,* she had a lot of office savvy and experience, and was not working at the time. So I asked her if she would be interested in helping me with the *Best of the Best from Louisiana.* Without a moment's hesitation, she replied, "When do we leave?" We left the next day, and we have been hitting the road ever since.

Until the distance to states far from our Mississippi home base necessitated flying and renting a vehicle, we traveled in our big van (we have worn out four) all over each state, our mission being to find out what people in that state liked to cook and eat. We tasted as we went, and talked to people everywhere about what they liked to cook and eat.

Invariably, local cookbooks captured the area's cuisine beautifully, and their creators were excited to share specific favorites.

From the very beginning, we established goals. We would search for cookbooks that captured local flavor with kitchen-friendly recipes that anybody anywhere could cook and enjoy. We would make the books user friendly, and edit for utmost clarity. Our criterion for including a recipe was threefold; it had to have great taste, great taste, and great taste!

Gwen McKee and Barbara Moseley

We went from Louisiana to Texas, then to other southern states that were in close proximity. After four years and four books, we began to say to each other, "Do you think we'll ever finish the whole United States?" Over the next 22 years of travel and research, we had poured through hundreds of thousands of recipes from more than 10,000 cookbooks, and had visited every state in the country.

In 2005, we were finally able to say, "We did it!" The BEST OF THE BEST STATE COOKBOOK SERIES now covers all fifty states. The result is more than 19,000 recipes gathered from every corner of our country. With more than two million copies sold, we are very proud that the series is known as the definitive source for state and regional cooking. (A free booklet entitled "We Did It!" that tells the story of how the series was developed is available upon request.)

Because it has become so much a part of our lives, and to further continue our motto of "Preserving America's Food Heritage," we have begun to revisit states, finding outstanding new cookbooks with more wonderful recipes to showcase and share. Journey with us to Georgia through the pages of this book, and you cannot help but catch the flavor and excitement of the Peach State as Barbara and I did. It will no doubt keep Georgia on your mind.

CONTRIBUTING COOKBOOKS

At the End of the Fork
Atlanta Cooknotes
Best of the Holidays
Bevelyn Blair's Everyday Cakes
Bevelyn Blair's Everyday Pies
The Blue Willow Inn Bible of Southern Cooking
Bread of Life–Chef Curtis Watkins and Friends
Bread of Life–Salem Baptist Church
Breads and Spreads
Collard Greens and Sushi
Confessions of a Kitchen Diva
Cook and Love It
Cooking with Herbs Volume I
Cooking with Herbs Volume II
Cooking with Watkinsville First Christian Church
Culinary Classics
The Day Family Favorites
Delightfully Southern
Down Through the Years
Eating from the White House to the Jailhouse
Family Collections
Famous Recipes from Mrs. Wilkes' Boarding House
Fine Dining Georgia Style
First Come, First Served...In Savannah
Flavors of the Gardens
The Foxfire Book of Appalachian Cookery
From Black Tie to Blackeyed Peas
From Our House to Yours
Georgia National Fair Blue Ribbon Cookbook
A Gift of Appreciation
The Gingerbread House Cookbook
Give Us This Day Our Daily Bread
Glorious Grass
Gone with the Grits
Grandma Mamie Jones' Family Favorites
Heart & Soul
Heavenly Dishes
Heritage Cookbook
Holiday Delights
Holiday Favorites
Home Run Recipes
Home Sweet Habitat
It's the People; It's the Food
The Lady & Sons, Too!

CONTRIBUTING COOKBOOKS

The Lady & Sons Just Desserts
The Lady & Sons Savannah Country Cookbook
Main Street Winder
Montezuma Amish Mennonite Cookbook I
Montezuma Amish Mennonite Cookbook II
Mother's Finest: Southern Cooking Made Easy
Mountain Folk, Mountain Food
My Best to You
The One-Armed Cook
Our Best Home Cooking
Our Favorite Recipes
Out On Our Own
Par 3: Tea-Time at the Masters®
Past & Present
Paula Deen & Friends
Peachtree Bouquet
Perennials
Puttin' on the Peachtree
Red Oak Recipes
Savannah Seasons
Second Round: Tea-Time at the Masters®
Sherman Didn't Burn Our Recipes, Bartow's Still Cooking
Simple Decent Cooking
Some Assembly Required
Southern Bread Winners
A Southern Collection: Then and Now
Southern Manna
The South's Legendary Frances Virginia Tea Room Cookbook
Special Treasures
Strawberries: From Our Family's Field to Your Family's Table
A Taste of Georgia
A Taste of Georgia, Another Serving
A Taste of the Holidays
Tastes for All Seasons
Tea-Time at the Masters®
Traditions
A Traveler's Table
Tried & True Recipes from Covington, Georgia
Tried & True Recipes–Residents of Wild Timber
True Grits
Vidalia Sweet Onion Lovers Cookbook
Wanted: Quick Draw's Favorite Recipes
What's Cookin'? in Winder, Georgia

BEVERAGES & APPETIZERS

Discover the history of Coca-Cola and see the world's largest collection of Coke memorabilia at the World of Coca-Cola in Atlanta. First served at a small pharmacy soda fountain, it is now served over a billion times a day and enjoyed in over 200 countries across the globe.

Southern Fresh Fruit Tea

5 family-size tea bags
1½ quarts water
1 (46-ounce) can pineapple
 juice
1 (6-ounce) can frozen
 orange juice

1 (6-ounce) can frozen
 lemonade concentrate
Sweetener of choice to taste

Boil tea bags in water for 5 minutes; let steep. Mix pineapple juice, orange juice, and lemonade in a gallon jug. Carefully pour in the tea; mix well. Add cold water to fill jug. Sweeten to taste; mix well. Serve cold.

VARIATION:
6–8 large lemons
4–6 large oranges
2 quarts water

1½ cups sugar
8 regular-size tea bags
1 cup diced, fresh pineapple

Peel lemons and oranges; carefully remove and discard the pith, reserving the rinds. Squeeze juice from lemons to measure 1½ cups juice; squeeze oranges to measure 2 cups juice. Set juice aside.

Bring water and sugar to a boil in large saucepan, stirring often; boil 1 minute. Pour over tea bags and rinds; cover and steep for 20 minutes. Discard tea bags and rinds, squeezing tea bags gently to remove all liquid. Be careful not to break the tea bags. Stir in juices and pineapple. Cover and chill at least 2 hours. Serve over ice. Garnish with lemon and orange slices. Makes about 3 quarts.

Tried & True Recipes from Covington, Georgia

Sparkling Cranberry Punch

1 (32-ounce) bottle cranberry
 juice cocktail
1 (6-ounce) can frozen orange
 juice, undiluted
1 (6-ounce) can frozen lemon
 juice, undiluted

2 cups water
Ice ring or cubes
2 (10-ounce) bottles ginger ale
Chilled orange slices

Combine fruit juices and water in punch bowl. Just before serving, add ice. Holding ginger ale bottle on rim of punch bowl, carefully pour in ginger ale. Garnish with orange slices.

Best of the Holidays

Kahlúa

Serve as an after-dinner liqueur, or over vanilla ice cream with whipped cream, nuts, and shaved chocolate.

2 rounded tablespoons instant
   coffee
1 cup water

3 cups white sugar
1 vanilla bean, finely chopped
1 fifth vodka

Boil coffee, water, and sugar. Stir until completely dissolved. Cool completely. Add finely chopped vanilla bean. Add vodka. Cork in airtight vessel. Store in a cool place for 30 days.

Puttin' on the Peachtree...

It's Almost Bailey's

1 cup Irish whiskey
1 (14-ounce) can sweetened
   condensed milk
4 eggs
2 tablespoons vanilla

2 tablespoons chocolate extract
1 tablespoon coconut extract
1½ tablespoons powdered
    instant coffee or espresso

Mix all ingredients in blender at low speed until thoroughly blended. Transfer to a bottle with a tight cover or good cork. Refrigerate 8 hours or until ready to serve. Shake well; serve very cold or over ice. Serves 6.

Peachtree Bouquet

Mulled Cider

Pour this winter treat over clove-studded orange wedges.

½ cup brown sugar
1 teaspoon whole allspice
1 teaspoon whole cloves
¼ teaspoon salt

Dash of nutmeg
1 (3-inch) cinnamon stick
2 quarts apple cider

Combine all ingredients in a saucepan and bring slowly to a boil. Cover and simmer for 20 minutes. Strain before serving. Serves 8–10.

A Taste of Georgia

Banana Strawberry Float

¾ cup mashed bananas
¾ cup mashed strawberries
¾ cup sugar
Dash of salt

5 cups milk, chilled
1 pint vanilla ice cream
6 whole strawberries

Blend mashed bananas and strawberries with sugar and salt. Add milk and stir to blend. Pour into 6 tall, cold glasses; top with ice cream. Garnish with whole strawberries. Serves 6.

Holiday Delights

After-Dinner Ice Cream Shake

½ gallon vanilla ice cream,
   softened
¼ cup amaretto

¼ cup crème de cacao or
   Kahlúa

Fill blender ¾ full with ice cream. Add liqueurs. Blend until smooth. Serve in oversized wine glasses.

Note: For a different flavor, substitute coffee ice cream for vanilla, increase crème de cacao to ½ cup, and omit amaretto.

Second Round: Tea-Time at the Masters®

Snappy Cheese Wafers

1 cup butter or margarine,
   softened
2 cups all-purpose flour
1 (8-ounce) package grated
   sharp Cheddar cheese

½ teaspoon cayenne pepper
½ teaspoon salt
2 cups Rice Krispies

Mix butter and flour until the texture of cornmeal. Add cheese, pepper, and salt, mixing with your hands until smooth. Stir in Rice Krispies. Pinch off small pieces and roll into balls. Place on ungreased cookie sheet and press down with fork. Bake in pre-heated 350° oven 15 minutes. Makes about 125.

A Southern Collection: Then and Now

Sesame Cheese Straws

½ pound sharp Cheddar
    cheese, shredded
1 (2-ounce) jar sesame seeds
½ cup margarine, softened

1¼ cups all-purpose flour
½ teaspoon salt
⅛ teaspoon cayenne pepper

Allow shredded cheese to reach room temperature. Toast sesame seeds in heavy skillet, stirring constantly over medium heat about 20 minutes or until golden brown; cool. Combine cheese, margarine, flour, salt, and cayenne. Work into dough until mixture is thoroughly blended. Add sesame seeds. Roll dough ⅛ inch thick. Cut into 4x½-inch strips. Bake at 400° for 12–15 minutes until golden brown. Cool on wire rack. Place in airtight container. Makes 5 dozen.

Past & Present

Cosmopolitan Cheddar Crisps

½ cup grated Parmesan cheese
1 pound extra sharp Cheddar
    cheese, shredded
1 stick salted butter, softened

½ teaspoon cayenne pepper
½ teaspoon water (optional)
2 cups flour
Kosher salt

Combine Parmesan cheese, Cheddar cheese, butter, and cayenne in mixing bowl; mix well. Add ½ teaspoonful of water, if needed, to moisten (some cheeses are wetter than others). Add flour, mixing until mixture forms a ball. Roll or press out by hand on a lightly floured surface. Cut into strips and place on a baking sheet. Bake at 350° for 15–20 minutes or until the edges begin to brown. Press in kosher salt crystals while hot.

These will last a week when stored in glass or metal—less in plastic.

Some Assembly Required

Colonized by James Edward Oglethorpe in 1733, Georgia was the last of the original thirteen English colonies. Named after King George II of England, Georgia became the fourth state to join the Union on January 2, 1788.

Bacon and Tomato Tarts

3 tomatoes, chopped and
  drained
1 pound bacon, cooked crisp
  and crumbled
1 cup mayonnaise
1 tablespoon Italian seasoning

1½ cups shredded Swiss
  cheese
1 Vidalia onion, chopped
2 (15-count) packages miniature
  phyllo shells

Mix tomatoes, bacon, mayonnaise, seasoning, cheese, and onion in a bowl. Spoon into phyllo shells. Arrange on a baking sheet. Bake at 350° for 15 minutes or until golden brown. Serves 30.

Par 3: Tea-Time at the Masters®

Crabmeat Bacon Fingers

½ cup tomato juice
1 egg, beaten
1 cup dry bread crumbs
½ teaspoon salt
Dash of pepper
1 teaspoon chopped parsley

1 teaspoon chopped celery
  leaves
1 (6½-ounce) can crabmeat,
  flaked
12 slices bacon, cut in half

Mix first 8 ingredients thoroughly. Roll into finger lengths and wrap each with one-half of a slice of bacon. Secure with toothpicks. Broil until brown on all sides 10–15 minutes, turning several times. Drain on paper towels. Serve immediately. Makes approximately 2 dozen.

Note: May be frozen and baked at the last minute.

Tea-Time at the Masters®

Confetti Crunch Spread

1 (8-ounce) package cream
  cheese, softened
3 tablespoons mayonnaise
¼ teaspoon salt

⅛ teaspoon garlic powder
½ cup chopped red pepper
½ cup chopped green pepper
½ cup chopped yellow pepper

Blend together all ingredients. Shape into a ball and chill at least 2 hours prior to serving. Makes one ball.

Breads and Spreads

Garden Patch
Herbed Cheese Spread

1 cup unsalted butter, softened
2 (8-ounce) packages cream
  cheese, softened
2 or 3 garlic cloves, minced
1 tablespoon chopped oregano

1½ teaspoons chopped thyme
1½ teaspoons chopped basil
1½ teaspoons chopped dill
½ teaspoon freshly ground
  pepper

Cream butter and cheese together. Add remaining ingredients and mix thoroughly. Cover and refrigerate overnight. (Will keep for a week if covered and refrigerated.) Serve at room temperature. Makes 3 cups.

Cooking with Herbs Volume II

Black Olive Spread

1 stick butter, softened
1 (8-ounce) package cream
  cheese, softened

4 green onions, diced
Chopped black olives to taste

Mix together and serve at room temperature. This is good served with crackers. Also good for finger sandwiches or other party sandwiches. To use as a tortilla spread, spread on a flour tortilla, roll up, chill, then cut into bite-size pieces. Secure with a toothpick and place on serving dish. Serve with salsa dip. (May be made ahead, covered with plastic wrap, and refrigerated.)

Home Run Recipes

Demorest's biggest attraction is the birthplace of a cat—the "Big Cat" that is. Now a member of the Baseball Hall of Fame, Johnny Mize, born January 7, 1913, lived in Demorest most of his life. His major league career included stints with the St. Louis Cardinals, New York Giants, and New York Yankees. Mize holds the Yankees' team record for being the only man to hit three home runs in a game six times. Mize died in 1993.

Gingerbread House Boursin

2 (8-ounce) packages cream
   cheese, softened
¼ cup butter, softened
¼ cup sour cream
2 tablespoons chopped chives

1 tablespoon chopped parsley
1 clove garlic, chopped
Salt and freshly ground black
   pepper to taste

Mix cream cheese and butter together until smooth in food processor; add sour cream and pulse a few seconds to blend. Add remaining ingredients and stir to mix. Use as a spread on crackers or as stuffing for celery or cherry tomatoes. Mixture may also be put in a decorative mold, chilled 4–5 hours, and served with crackers. Makes 2 cups.

The Gingerbread House Cookbook

The Gingerbread House in Savannah is considered one of the most outstanding examples of Steamboat Gothic gingerbread carpentry in the United States. When the home was built by the Asendorf family in 1899, people soon began calling it the Gingerbread House, because of the elaborate gingerbread arches and spindles adorning the front porches and side balcony of the house. Today, "Savannah's most photographed house" is a favorite site for weddings, receptions, parties, corporate functions, tour group dinners, and other events.

Crab Pâté

1 (10¾-ounce) can cream of
   mushroom soup
1 envelope unflavored gelatin
3 tablespoons cold water
1 (8-ounce) package cream
   cheese, softened

¾ cup mayonnaise
1 (6-ounce) can crabmeat,
   drained and flaked
1 small onion, grated
1 cup finely chopped celery

Heat soup in a saucepan over low heat; remove from heat. Dissolve gelatin in cold water in a bowl. Stir into heated soup. Add cream cheese, mayonnaise, crabmeat, onion, and celery; mix well. Spoon into a mold. Chill, covered, until firm. Unmold onto a serving plate. Garnish with parsley. Serve with assorted crackers.

Mother's Finest: Southern Cooking Made Easy

Salmon Ball

1 (1-pound) can salmon,
   drained and flaked
1 (8-ounce) package cream
   cheese, softened
1 tablespoon lemon juice
2 teaspoons grated onion

1 teaspoon horseradish
¼ teaspoon salt
¼ teaspoon liquid smoke
½ cup finely chopped pecans
3 tablespoons chopped parsley

Combine salmon with cream cheese, lemon juice, grated onion, horseradish, salt, and liquid smoke. Chill for several hours. Form into ball; roll in nuts and parsley.

Family Collections

Tina's Pineapple Cheese Ball

3 (8-ounce) packages cream
   cheese, softened
1 cup well-drained crushed
   pineapple (squeeze the juice
   out with your hands)

5 green onions, finely chopped
½ green bell pepper, chopped
½ cup chopped pecans
Dash of salt

Combine all ingredients. Shape into ball. Chill.

My Best to You

Hot and Spicy Cheese Dip

6 slices bacon
1 (8-ounce) package cream
  cheese
2 cups shredded Cheddar
  cheese

6 tablespoons heavy cream
1 teaspoon Worcestershire
¼ teaspoon dry mustard
¼ teaspoon onion salt
3 drops hot sauce

In skillet, fry bacon until crisp. Drain, crumble, and set aside. In double boiler, combine cream cheese, Cheddar cheese, cream, Worcestershire, mustard, onion salt, and hot sauce. Heat, stirring occasionally, until cheese melts and mixture is hot. Add bacon. Serve in chafing dish. Dip will hold for several hours. If dip becomes thick, stir in additional cream. Makes 2 cups.

By permission of American Dairy Association
Traditions

Apple Dip

Granny Smith apples (or other)
Pineapple juice to cover
1 (8-ounce) package cream
  cheese, softened
¾ cup brown sugar

½ cup white sugar
1 tablespoon vanilla
1 (8-ounce) package Heath
  Bits-O-Brickle

Slice and core apples. Soak in pineapple juice (this keeps apples from turning brown) overnight in refrigerator.

Mix next 4 ingredients together and whip until smooth. Stir in brickle. Place dip in a bowl. Drain apples and serve with dip.

Heritage Cookbook

White Bean Dip

¼ cup plain bread crumbs
2 tablespoons dry white wine or water
1 (15- to 19-ounce) can cannellini beans or Great Northern beans, rinsed and drained
¼ cup slivered almonds

1 teaspoon bottled minced garlic
2 tablespoons lemon juice
2 tablespoons olive oil
⅛ teaspoon ground red pepper
½ teaspoon dried basil
¼ teaspoon salt

In a small mixing bowl, combine bread crumbs and wine or water; set aside. Place remaining ingredients in a food processor or blender container and process or blend until almost smooth. Add bread crumb mixture. Process or blend again until smooth, stopping to scrape down sides. Place in a serving bowl, cover with plastic wrap, and chill 3 hours. Makes 1½ cups.

The One-Armed Cook

Peachy Lime Guacamole

1 medium Georgia peach
5 medium ripe avocados
1 cup chopped fresh cilantro
Salt and black pepper to taste

Garlic salt to taste
Cayenne pepper to taste
Juice of 1 lime

Peel peach and halve, removing pit. Chop into very small pieces. Peel avocados and halve, removing pits. Place avocado halves cut side down and slice thinly; rotate and slice into small pieces. Combine peach, avocados, cilantro, and seasonings in a large glass bowl. Add lime juice gradually, tossing gently. Chill 1 hour or longer. Toss before serving. Serve with blue corn tortilla chips or your favorite chips.

True Grits

The state song, "Georgia on My Mind" by Hoagy Carmichael, was originally written about a woman of that name, but after Georgia native Ray Charles sang it, the state legislature voted it the state song. Ray Charles sang it on the legislative floor when the bill passed in 1979.

Avocado-Feta Salsa

2 plum tomatoes, chopped
1 avocado, halved, seeded,
  peeled and chopped
¼ cup finely chopped red
  onion
1 clove garlic, minced
1 tablespoon snipped fresh
  parsley

1 tablespoon snipped fresh
  oregano
1 tablespoon olive oil
1 tablespoon red or white
  wine vinegar
4 ounces feta cheese, coarsely
  crumbled

In a medium bowl, combine tomatoes, avocado, onion, garlic, parsley, oregano, oil, and vinegar. Stir gently to mix. Gently stir in feta. Cover and chill 2–6 hours. Serve salsa with pita or tortilla chips. Makes 12 (¼-cup) servings.

Tried & True Recipes–Residents of Wild Timber

Watermelon Fire and Ice Salsa

3 cups seeded, chopped
  watermelon
½ cup chopped green bell
  pepper
2 tablespoons lime juice

1 tablespoon chopped cilantro
1 tablespoon chopped green
  Vidalia onion
1–2 jalapeños, seeded and
  chopped

Combine watermelon, bell pepper, lime juice, cilantro, onion, and jalapeños in a bowl and mix well. Refrigerate, covered, for 1 hour or longer. Yields 6 (½-cup) servings.

From Black Tie to Blackeyed Peas

Revered as the Watermelon Capital of the World, Cordele claims to grow watermelons bigger and more luscious than any place on earth. Cordele is also home to the fastest ⅜-mile paved oval speedway in the South, "Watermelon Capital Speedway."

Layered Nacho Dip

1 (16-ounce) can refried beans
½ (1.25-ounce) package taco
  seasoning mix
1 (6-ounce) carton avocado dip
1 (8-ounce) carton sour cream
1 (4½-ounce) can chopped
  ripe olives
2 large tomatoes, diced
1 small onion, chopped
1 (4-ounce) can chopped green
  chiles
1½ cups shredded Monterey
  Jack cheese

Combine beans and seasoning mix. Spread bean mixture evenly in 12x8x2-inch dish. Layer remaining ingredients in order listed. Serve with large corn chips or tortilla chips.

Main Street Winder

Georgia Brie Appetizers

1 (3-ounce) package cream
  cheese, softened
4 ounces Brie, room
  temperature
1 large egg
½ teaspoon almond extract
⅛ teaspoon salt
½ teaspoon pepper
2 (15-count) packages mini
  phyllo dough shells
1⅔ cups peach preserves
1 tablespoon amaretto liqueur,
  or ½ teaspoon almond
  extract plus 1 tablespoon
  orange juice
½ cup sliced almonds, toasted

Preheat oven to 350°. Thoroughly mix together cream cheese, Brie, egg, almond extract, salt, and pepper; mixture may be lumpy. (Can be made to this point and kept refrigerated one day.) Divide filling evenly among phyllo shells that have been placed on a cookie sheet; bake 10–12 minutes or until custard is set.

Mix peach preserves with amaretto. Remove shells from oven; top each with 1 teaspoon peach mixture, and sprinkle with almond slices. Makes 30 pieces.

Confessions of a Kitchen Diva

Jalapeño Cocktail Pie

Can be made several days ahead–just reheat.

3–4 jalapeño peppers, seeded
   and chopped
1 large onion, finely chopped
1 clove garlic, minced

1 (16-ounce) package shredded
   sharp Cheddar cheese
6 eggs, beaten

Sprinkle peppers, onion, and garlic in a well-greased 9-inch square pan. Cover with cheese. Pour eggs over cheese. Bake at 350° for 30 minutes or until firm. Cool and cut into 1-inch squares. Yields 6 dozen 1-inch squares.

A Taste of Georgia

Vidalia Sweet Onion Appetizer

1 cup finely chopped Vidalia
   sweet onions

1 cup shredded Swiss cheese
1 cup mayonnaise

Mix all ingredients together and pour into pie plate. Bake 20–30 minutes at 375°–400° until brown and bubbly on top. Remove from oven and serve with your favorite crackers or bread thins.

Note: This recipe can be halved or doubled. Just keep the proportions equal.

Vidalia Sweet Onion Lovers Cookbook

Quiche Antipasto

My friend, Kathy Hocevar, gave me this recipe in 1994 and that is about how many times I have made it since. Thank you, Kathy, for such a great appetizer!

2 (8-count) packages refrigerated crescent rolls
¼ pound provolone cheese (about 6–8 slices)
¼ pound Swiss cheese (about 6–8 slices)
¼ pound baked ham (about 6–8 slices)
¼ pound hard salami (about 12–14 slices)

1 (24-ounce) jar roasted red peppers, thoroughly drained, or 3–4 large red peppers, roasted
3 large eggs
¼ cup grated Parmesan cheese
⅛ teaspoon black pepper

Preheat oven to 350°. Lightly grease or coat a 9x13-inch baking pan with nonstick cooking spray. Unroll 1 package of rolls and cover the bottom of prepared pan, firmly pressing perforations to seal; stretch to fit as necessary. Layer with provolone, covering all of dough. Layer with Swiss cheese, covering the first layer. Lay ham over cheese; cover ham with salami. Pat peppers dry with a paper towel. Lay out flat over salami (if peppers were left whole, split open to lay flat).

Mix eggs, Parmesan, and pepper together. Pour ¾ egg mixture over peppers. Unroll remaining can of rolls and place over top of peppers and egg mixture (press perforations together to seal), stretching dough to cover roasted peppers. Brush top of dough with remaining egg mixture. Cover pan with foil; bake 30 minutes. Remove foil and bake an additional 10–15 minutes or until top is golden brown. Remove from oven and let cool slightly before cutting into squares. (For smaller servings, cut each piece into a triangle.) Can be made a day ahead, refrigerated, and served at room temperature. Serves 20.

Confessions of a Kitchen Diva

Stuffed Cherry Tomato Hors D'Oeuvres

30 good-size cherry tomatoes
1 (4½-ounce) can deviled ham
¾ cup grated Swiss cheese, divided

½ cup finely chopped pimento-stuffed olives
1 tablespoon minced onion

Rinse and dry tomatoes. Slice off tips, scoop out pulp, and drain shells upside down on paper towels. In a small mixing bowl, stir together the deviled ham, ½ cup cheese, olives, and onion. Spoon into tomato shells; sprinkle with the remaining cheese. Cover and refrigerate until ready to use. Best served shortly after making. Makes about 30 hors d'oeuvres.

A Taste of the Holidays

Sausage Stuffed Mushrooms

1 pound raw mushroom caps
¼ cup butter
1 pound sausage

1 (8-ounce) package cream cheese, softened
Parmesan cheese

Lightly sauté mushrooms in butter. Arrange on cookie sheet and set aside. Brown sausage and drain grease. Mix sausage and cream cheese until smooth. Fill mushroom caps. Sprinkle with Parmesan cheese. Bake at 350° for 10 minutes. May be made a day before and refrigerated.

A Taste of Georgia, Another Serving

 Athens is the birthplace of America's first garden club. Founders Memorial Garden, on the University of Georgia's North Campus, was established to honor the club.

Herbed Stuffed Eggs with Asparagus

6 large hard-cooked eggs
½ teaspoon salt
⅛ teaspoon ground oregano
⅛ teaspoon ground black
   pepper
¼ teaspoon garlic powder
2 tablespoons finely chopped
   celery

3 tablespoons finely chopped
   tomato
½ teaspoon fresh lemon juice
2 pounds fresh asparagus,
   cooked crisp-tender
3 tablespoons French dressing

Shell eggs and cut in half. Remove yolks and mash with the next 7 ingredients. Stuff the egg whites with this mixture. If stuffed ahead of serving time, put stuffed egg halves together, wrap in foil and chill. Serve with cold, cooked asparagus spears marinated in French dressing.

Glorious Grass

Herbed Eggs

A must for Garden Patch picnics!

6 hard-cooked eggs
2 tablespoons plain yogurt
2 tablespoons mayonnaise
½ teaspoon mustard
2 tablespoons chopped chives

1 tablespoon chopped dill
1 tablespoon chopped tarragon
1 teaspoon chopped chervil
Salt and pepper to taste
Fresh dill sprigs

Shell boiled eggs and cut in half lengthwise; remove yolks carefully. Mash yolks, moistening with yogurt, mayonnaise, and mustard. Season with herbs. Add salt and pepper to taste. Pile mixture back into egg whites. Arrange eggs on a platter and garnish with feathery sprigs of dill.

Cooking with Herbs Volume II

Sesame Appetizer Meatballs

1 pound ground beef	½ teaspoon salt
⅔ cup minced onion	⅛ teaspoon pepper
½ cup soft bread crumbs	1 tablespoon plus 1 teaspoon
1 egg	Worcestershire
¼ cup milk	2 cups beef broth

Combine all ingredients except beef broth. Mix well and shape into 1-inch meatballs; bake in 325° oven 20 minutes or until lightly browned. Drain in colander, then simmer on stovetop in beef broth for 10 minutes or until cooked through. Serve with Sesame Seed Sauce. Yields 3 dozen.

SESAME SEED SAUCE:

2 tablespoons butter	1 teaspoon Worcestershire
2 tablespoons flour	2 tablespoons sesame seeds,
¼ teaspoon salt	toasted
Dash of cayenne pepper	1 cup sour cream, room
½ cup beef broth	temperature
1 teaspoon soy sauce	

In a saucepan, melt butter over medium heat. Blend in flour, salt, and cayenne pepper. Heat, stirring, until bubbly. Add broth all at once and cook, stirring, until sauce thickens. Stir in soy sauce, Worcestershire, and sesame seeds.

Empty sour cream into medium bowl; gradually add sauce, stirring constantly. Return sauce to pan, fold in meatballs, and heat gently to serving temperature. Serve from chafing dish with toothpicks.

The Gingerbread House Cookbook

Munchies

An easy gift.

6 cups popped popcorn
1 (6-ounce) bag corn chips
2 cups bite-size pretzels
1 (3-ounce) can Chinese noodles

1 stick margarine
2 teaspoons Worcestershire
¼ teaspoon Tabasco
⅛ teaspoon garlic powder

Combine popcorn, chips, pretzels, and noodles. Melt margarine; stir in sauces and garlic. Pour over popcorn; toss to coat. Bake at 250° for 1 hour. Stir every 15 minutes. Cool and store in airtight containers. Yields 12 cups.

Best of the Holidays

White Trash

1 (12-ounce) box Golden
  Graham cereal
1 (12-ounce) box raisins
3 cups roasted peanuts, or
  1 (24-ounce) jar peanuts
2 cups peanut butter

1 (12-ounce) package semisweet
  chocolate morsels
1 stick butter
1 (16-ounce) box confectioners'
  sugar

Mix cereal, raisins, and peanuts in large container. Over low heat, melt peanut butter, chocolate morsels, and butter; stir well. Let cool and pour over cereal mixture; mix well. After cooling, place mixture in large paper bag. Pour in box of confectioners' sugar and shake until mixture is coated. Keep in airtight container. Great snack for a crowd, especially teenagers.

Note: This makes a large amount and it is easier to handle if you divide it into two batches when you do the shaking.

Southern Manna

Holiday Bourbon Brandy Balls

1 small box vanilla wafers,
   crushed
1½ tablespoons cocoa
2 tablespoons light corn syrup
1 cup powdered sugar

1 cup chopped pecans
¼ cup brandy
¼ cup bourbon
Powdered sugar for coating

Mix all ingredients thoroughly and roll into balls; balls will be quite moist. Sprinkle additional powdered sugar on wax paper; roll balls in it to coat. Store in an airtight container until ready to serve. Makes about 4 dozen.

The Gingerbread House Cookbook

Swedish Pecans

½ cup margarine
2 egg whites
1 cup sugar

Dash of salt
4 cups pecan halves

Melt margarine in metal baking pan. Beat egg whites until soft peaks form. Add sugar and salt. Beat a few more minutes. Mixture will be thick and heavy. Add pecans.

Spread mixture evenly in the pan in which the margarine was melted. Bake at 300° for 30 minutes or until coating is light brown. Margarine will be absorbed during the toasting. Stir every 10 minutes because it can brown very quickly. May only take 22–25 minutes in some ovens.

Home Run Recipes

BREAD & BREAKFAST

PHOTO © GEORGIA DEPARTMENT OF ECONOMIC DEVELOPMENT

A relaxing view of moss-draped magnolias from an inviting front porch is just one of the amenities at Fort Gaine's Sutlive House Bed and Breakfast, which was built in 1820. Guests enjoy true southern elegance and hospitality in this charming historic home.

Sweet Onion Cornbread

2 cups self-rising cornmeal
1 tablespoon sugar
1 teaspoon baking powder
2 cups milk
1 egg
4 tablespoons vegetable oil, divided
2 cups finely chopped sweet onions

Preheat oven to 350°. In a large mixing bowl, combine the cornmeal, sugar, and baking powder. Add the milk, egg, and 2 tablespoons of oil, mixing well (the batter will be quite thin). Stir in the onions and mix well. Grease a 10-inch iron skillet with the remaining oil, pour in the batter, and bake for 30–35 minutes or until light brown. Let cool 10 minutes before serving. Makes 8 servings.

Breads and Spreads

Mexican Cornbread Casserole

1 cup yellow cornmeal
½ teaspoon baking soda
½ teaspoon salt
1 cup milk
2 eggs, beaten
1 (17-ounce) can cream corn
2 cups shredded Cheddar cheese
1 (4-ounce) can mild green chiles, chopped
½ cup chopped onion
1 pound ground beef
1 (16-ounce) can kidney beans
½ (8-ounce) can tomato sauce
2 teaspoons chili powder
¼ teaspoon garlic powder
Yellow cornmeal for sprinkling

In a bowl, stir together cornmeal, baking soda, and salt. Stir in milk, eggs, and corn. Stir in cheese, chiles, and onion. Mix until well blended; set aside.

Cook ground beef until browned; drain. Stir in beans, tomato sauce, chili powder, and garlic powder. Cook together until heated through. Grease and sprinkle a thin layer of cornmeal over the bottom of a 9x13-inch baking dish. Pour in ½ the batter. Cover this with the meat mixture. Top with remaining batter. Bake in a 350° oven for 45 minutes or until top is browned.

Tried & True Recipes from Covington, Georgia

Sour Cream Cornbread

1 cup flour	1 teaspoon salt
¾ cup cornmeal	1 egg, well beaten
1 teaspoon baking soda	1 cup thick sour cream
1 teaspoon cream of tartar	4 tablespoons milk
2½ tablespoons sugar	2 tablespoons melted butter

Sift flour and cornmeal together; add baking soda, cream of tartar, sugar, and salt. Add beaten egg, sour cream, milk, and melted butter. Beat thoroughly. Pour into greased 9-inch square pan. Bake at 425° for 20 minutes. Serve with strawberries and milk, or beans (your choice) with a thin white sauce.

Montezuma Amish Mennonite Cookbook I

Corn Sticks

These authentic Georgia corn sticks are from a true southern restaurant, Pittypat's Porch.

5 eggs	5 cups plain cornmeal
5 cups buttermilk	2½ teaspoons baking soda
7½ tablespoons butter, melted	3 tablespoons cold water
2½ teaspoons sugar	7½ teaspoons baking powder
5 teaspoons salt	

Preheat oven to 450°. Beat eggs until light. Add buttermilk, butter, sugar, and salt; blend well. Carefully blend in cornmeal. Dissolve baking soda in water; add to cornmeal mixture. Sift baking powder; add to cornmeal mixture. Stir well. Pour into greased and heated corn stick pans. Bake for 10–15 minutes until lightly browned. Makes 4 dozen.

Peachtree Bouquet

Streets with "Peachtree" in the name are common in Georgia. As a matter of fact, there are about fifty-five streets that include the word. Peachtree in Atlanta is one of America's best-known streets. It winds north from downtown Atlanta through the heart of Buckhead, closely following the Chattahoochee Ridge route of the Indian-era Peachtree Trail. Downtown, it's Peachtree *Street*, but after it merges with West Peachtree and heads north, it becomes Peachtree *Road*.

Corn Cakes

2 cups cornmeal
1 heaping tablespoon flour
1 teaspoon salt
2 teaspoons baking powder

1 tablespoon melted butter
  or lard
2 eggs, beaten
Buttermilk

Sift together dry ingredients. Add butter and beaten eggs. Mix in enough buttermilk to make a thin batter, being careful not to let it get too thin. Pour out into a hot griddle and flip onto other side when brown. The amount of batter poured out depends on the desired size of cakes. Good with butter and syrup.

The Foxfire Book of Appalachian Cookery

Cornbread Dressing
with Sausage and Giblets

¼ pound pork sausage,
  browned and crumbled
1 package cornbread mix,
  prepared according to
  directions
1 large onion, chopped
1 rib celery, chopped

1½ ounces turkey giblets
½ onion, whole
½ rib celery, whole
¾ cup water
½ cup milk
2 large eggs, slightly beaten
7½ ounces chicken broth

Preheat oven to 350°. Butter a 9x13-inch baking dish. Brown sausage in a heavy skillet. Remove sausage from pan and crumble into a large bowl. Discard the fat from skillet but do not wipe out pan. Crumble cornbread and add to sausage. In same pan, sauté chopped onion and chopped celery until onion is transparent. Add to sausage mixture in large bowl.

Simmer the turkey giblets, ½ onion, and ½ rib celery in water. Cover and cook until tender, about 20 minutes. Discard onion and celery. Remove giblets, chop, and add to sausage and vegetables. Add giblet water. Stir in milk and eggs until well blended. Add chicken broth and stir until evenly moist. Pour into baking dish. Bake approximately 45 minutes until dressing is set and browned.

Bread of Life–Chef Curtis Watkins

Cornbread Dressing

3 cups crumbled cornbread
3 cups herb-seasoned stuffing
1 stick butter
1 large onion, finely chopped
1 cup finely chopped celery

3 cups turkey or chicken broth
  (enough to moisten mixture)
3 eggs, beaten
Salt and pepper to taste

Mix together cornbread crumbs and stuffing; set aside. Melt butter in heavy skillet and sauté onion and celery in butter until translucent. Add broth and pan drippings; pour entire mixture over crumb-seasoning blend. Work very lightly to blend (working this dressing too much ruins the taste and texture); more broth may be added to adjust to desired moistness. Add beaten eggs and mix lightly; add salt and pepper to taste.

Use part of this dressing for stuffing turkey or other poultry, if desired. Bake remainder in shallow pan for 30 minutes at 350°. Makes enough dressing to stuff 1 (18- to 22-pound) turkey with enough left for 8–10 servings.

The Gingerbread House Cookbook

Cornmeal Supper Biscuits

1½ cups self-rising flour
½ cup self-rising cornmeal mix
1 teaspoon sugar

⅓ cup shortening
¾ cup plus 2 tablespoons
  buttermilk

Heat oven to 450°. Lightly grease a cookie sheet. In medium bowl, combine flour, cornmeal mix, and sugar; mix well. With pastry blender or fork, cut in shortening until mixture resembles coarse crumbs. Add buttermilk; stir with fork until soft dough forms and begins to pull away from sides of bowl. On lightly floured surface, knead dough just until smooth. Roll out dough to ½-inch thickness. Cut with floured 2-inch round cutter. Place on greased cookie sheet. Bake at 450° for 10–12 minutes or until golden brown. Serve warm.

Georgia National Fair Blue Ribbon Cookbook

Buttermilk Biscuits

Be prepared to make more than one dozen; these have a way of disappearing—especially when there are hungry men present!

2 cups self-rising flour　　　**4 tablespoons shortening**
¼ teaspoon baking soda　　　**¾–1 cup buttermilk**

Mix flour and baking soda. Cut shortening into flour until mixture resembles cornmeal. Add buttermilk; mix to form soft dough. (May be done to this point in food processor, using steel blade.) Turn onto floured board; knead lightly several times until dough is smooth. Roll to desired thickness. Cut with floured biscuit cutter. Place on lightly greased baking sheet. Bake at 450° for 15 minutes or until golden brown. Makes 12 biscuits.

Variation: For whole-wheat biscuits, substitute 1 cup whole-wheat flour for half the white flour. Add 2 teaspoons sugar. Proceed as above.

Perennials

Herbed Butter

Excellent on French, Vienna, or Italian bread.

1 (8-ounce) tub margarine　　　**Cayenne**
1 teaspoon chopped parsley　　　**Basil**
¼ teaspoon oregano　　　**Marjoram**
¼ teaspoon dill　　　**Celery seed**
Garlic powder

Soften the margarine and blend with the parsley, oregano, and dill. The remaining ingredients should be added in small amounts to suit your taste or to make variations of the butter. Replace the mixture in the tub or butter mold, and chill. Makes 1 cup.

Breads and Spreads

Delicious Angel Biscuits

2 packages yeast
¼ cup warm water
5 cups self-rising flour
1 teaspoon baking soda

⅓ cup (scant) sugar
1 cup shortening
2 cups buttermilk

Dissolve yeast in warm water. Combine dry ingredients in bowl. Cut in shortening until crumbly. Stir in yeast mixture and buttermilk: mix well. Roll out on floured surface. Cut with biscuit cutter. Place on baking sheet. Bake at 500° until brown (about 10 minutes). May store dough in refrigerator for 1 week. Use as needed.

Cooking with Watkinsville First Christian Church

Sweet Potato Biscuits

The next time you prepare sweet potatoes, fix a little extra so you can make these moist, delicious biscuits.

2 cups all-purpose flour
2 teaspoons baking powder
1 teaspoon salt
¾ cup mashed, cooked
 sweet potatoes

½ cup margarine, melted
2 tablespoons brown sugar
½ teaspoon baking soda
¾ cup buttermilk

Sift together flour, baking powder, and salt. Combine mashed sweet potatoes, margarine, and sugar in a small bowl. Beat together with a wire whisk. Stir baking soda into the buttermilk. Combine all ingredients, and stir to form a soft dough. If the dough is too sticky, add a little more flour. Place on a floured surface and knead dough for a few minutes. Roll dough ½ inch thick, and cut with a floured biscuit cutter. Bake at 400° for 20 minutes or until lightly browned. Butter and serve hot with jelly. Makes 10 biscuits.

Southern Bread Winners

Pro Football Hall-of-Famer Francis "Fran" Tarkenton, who attended Athens High School and University of Georgia, set National Football League (NFL) records for most career touchdown passes (342) and most career passing yardage (3,686 completions for 47,003 yards), records held until 1995. In 1986, he was voted a member of the NFL Hall of Fame.

Dinner Rolls

3 potatoes, peeled
4 cups milk
3 sticks margarine
4 tablespoons yeast
1 cup warm water

2½ cups sugar
2 eggs
2 tablespoons salt
12–15 cups bread flour

Cook potatoes in water to cover until tender. Do not drain water; mash potatoes with water. Scald milk and margarine. Dissolve yeast in warm water. Cool milk mixture, then add yeast mixture. Mix together sugar, eggs, salt, and potatoes; add milk mixture. Add 5 cups flour to make sponge. Let rest ½ hour, then add remaining flour until smooth and elastic; knead. Let rise until light, about 30 minutes. Shape into rolls, then bake on greased baking sheets at 350° for 20–25 minutes. Makes 10–12 dozen rolls.

Montezuma Amish Mennonite Cookbook II

Butterhorns

This recipe does not require a leavening agent. The butterhorns are delicately flaky and delicious.

1 cup butter, softened
12 ounces cottage cheese
1¼ teaspoons vanilla

Dash of salt
2 cups all-purpose flour

Cream the butter and cottage cheese together. Beat in vanilla and salt. Add flour slowly to form a dough. Refrigerate the dough for 4 hours or overnight. Be sure to cover tightly so the dough will not dry out.

Divide dough into 3 parts. Place on floured surface and roll each part into a circle. Cut circles into 12 wedges. Roll each wedge, starting with the wide end. Place butterhorns seam side down on a greased cookie sheet; bake at 350° for 30 minutes.

GLAZE:

1 cup powdered sugar
1 tablespoon milk
½ teaspoon vanilla

1 tablespoon margarine,
   softened

Combine powdered sugar, milk, vanilla, and margarine. Frost the top of each butterhorn while warm. Makes 36.

Southern Bread Winners

Croissants

1 package active dry yeast
¼ cup warm water (115°)
2 eggs
1 tablespoon sugar

½ teaspoon salt
1 cup lukewarm milk
4 cups bread flour, divided
2 sticks butter

Sprinkle yeast into warm water and let stand until dissolved. In a medium bowl, beat eggs and stir in sugar, salt, warm milk, yeast mixture, and ¾ cup flour. Mix well and set aside. Reserve approximately ½ cup flour to use on breadboard while kneading. Cut butter into remaining flour until particles are the size of large peas. Pour in yeast mixture and mix lightly, just until flour is moistened. Cover bowl and chill for at least 2 hours.

Turn out onto floured breadboard and knead lightly, about 5 minutes. Divide dough into thirds and roll each piece into a 16-inch circle. With a sham knife cut each circle into 12 pie-shaped wedges. Starting at the wide end, roll up and shape into crescents. Place point down on a greased cookie sheet and set in a warm place to rise.

EGG GLAZE:
1 egg white   1 tablespoon water

Beat egg white and water together. When the rolls have doubled in size, brush with Egg Glaze. Bake in a preheated oven at 375° for 15–20 minutes or until golden brown. Makes 3 dozen rolls.

Breads and Spreads

Potato Bread

1 medium potato	1 package yeast
½ cup potato water	2 teaspoons sugar
1½ sticks margarine	1 teaspoon salt
6½ cups bread flour, divided	1 egg

Peel and cook potato. Drain, saving ½ cup potato water. Mash potato and set aside. In a saucepan, heat potato water and margarine until margarine melts. Combine 2 cups flour, yeast, sugar, and salt in a large mixing bowl and mix well. Add the warm but not hot (approximately 115°) liquid to the flour mixture. Add the egg and mashed potato and beat until all ingredients are thoroughly mixed, approximately 2 minutes on medium if you are using an electric mixer. Add remaining flour, 1 cup at a time, to form a soft dough, saving approximately ½ cup to use on breadboard while kneading. Turn out onto a lightly floured breadboard and knead hard for 5–10 minutes or until dough is smooth and elastic. Place the ball in a greased bowl; cover and set in a warm place.

When dough has risen to double its original size (about 45 minutes), punch it down and knead about 5 minutes. To make a round loaf, shape into a ball and place on a greased cookie sheet, or divide the dough in half and shape into two loaves and place them into 2 greased 9x5-inch loaf pans. In either case, cover the loaves with a dish towel; set them in a warm place to rise. When they have doubled in size, bake in a preheated oven at 350° for 40–50 minutes or until they have turned deep brown and sound hollow when tapped. Cool in pans 10 minutes. Remove from pans and finish cooling on rack. Yields 1 round or 2 regular loaves.

Breads and Spreads

Fan-Style Bread

The Cake Box, a Gainesville tradition, shares its most famous recipe.

8 packages yeast	6 cups bread flour
2 cups lukewarm water	¼ cup plus 1 tablespoon sugar
¾ cup lard or vegetable shortening	1 tablespoon plus ½ teaspoon salt
½ cup plus 2 tablespoons cake flour	Melted butter

Place yeast and water in large mixing bowl; stir to dissolve. Add shortening; stir to soften. Add all remaining ingredients except butter. Mix until dough leaves sides of bowl. Cover; let rise until doubled in bulk, approximately 1 hour.

Divide into 4 portions. Round up each portion; let rest (30 minutes). Cut each portion into 12 pieces; stand pieces on edge in 4 greased 9x4x3-inch baking pans. Brush with melted butter. Let rise until dough is even with top of pan. Bake at 425° for 15 minutes or until golden brown. Brush with additional butter; turn out on cooling rack. Yields 4 loaves.

The Cake Box Bakery in Gainesville, Georgia
Perennials

Cheesy Bread Ring

5 ¼ cups bread flour, divided
¼ cup sugar
1 ½ teaspoons salt
2 packages dry yeast
1 cup water

1 cup milk
½ cup margarine
2 eggs, beaten
2 tablespoons sesame seeds

In a large bowl, combine 2½ cups flour, sugar, salt, and yeast; stir to blend. In a small saucepan, heat water, milk, and margarine until very warm. Add warm liquid and eggs to flour mixture and beat on low speed 3 minutes. Stir in enough remaining flour to make a sticky dough. Grease a 10-inch tube pan and sprinkle with sesame seeds. Spoon half of batter into pan.

FILLING:
1 cup shredded mozzarella
   cheese
½ teaspoon Italian seasoning

¼ teaspoon garlic powder
¼ cup margarine, softened

Combine ingredients and mix well. Spoon Filling evenly over batter to within ½ inch of sides of pan. Add remaining batter. Cover and let rise until it doubles in size. Bake at 350° for 30–40 minutes to a golden brown. Loaf should sound hollow when tapped. Remove to a platter and serve warm. Makes 1 bread ring.

Southern Bread Winners

Erskine Caldwell was born December 17, 1903, near Moreland. As one of the first authors to be published in mass-market paperback editions, he is a key figure in the history of American publishing. By the late 1940s, Caldwell had sold more books than any writer in the nation's history. He is the author of 25 novels, 150 short stories, and 12 nonfiction books. The stage adaptation of Caldwell's *Tobacco Road* (which opened on Broadway on December 4, 1933) made American theatre history when it ran for 3,182 consecutive performances over a period of seven-and-a-half years. Three of Caldwell's books have been made into movies: *Tobacco Road* (1941), *God's Little Acre* (1958), and *Claudelle Inglish* (1961). The house in which he was born has been moved to Moreland's town square where it serves as a museum. Caldwell died in 1987.

Brunch-Time Sunburst

A prize-winning recipe.

2½–3 cups all-purpose flour, divided
1 teaspoon salt
1 package dry yeast
⅔ cup milk
⅔ cup sugar, divided

⅓ cup shortening
1 egg
1 teaspoon grated orange peel
⅓ cup margarine, melted
½ teaspoon cinnamon

In a large mixer bowl, combine 1 cup flour with salt and dry yeast. In a saucepan, heat milk, ⅓ cup sugar, and shortening until ingredients are dissolved. Add to flour mixture; stir in egg and orange peel. Beat with mixer on low speed for 2 minutes. Stir in as much of remaining flour as you can mix with a spoon. Turn onto lightly floured surface and knead dough 5 minutes. Place in greased bowl; turn once to grease top surface. Cover and let rise in a warm place until dough has doubled in size.

Punch down and roll dough into a 10x8-inch rectangle. Cut into 12 doughnuts; save holes. Dip each in melted margarine and arrange in a circle on baking sheet. Stretch centers with fingers to elongate. Cut additional holes (from excess dough). Fill center of pan with a cluster of doughnut holes that have been dipped in margarine. Mix ⅓ cup remaining sugar with cinnamon; sprinkle on center of sunburst. Let rise 45 minutes in a warm place. Bake at 375° for 25 minutes or until lightly browned.

GLAZE:
1½ cups confectioners' sugar
3 tablespoons orange juice

¼ teaspoon vanilla

Combine confectioners' sugar, orange juice, and vanilla. While sunburst is still warm, drizzle glaze in areas between the doughnuts and over stack of holes in center.

TOPPING:
¼ cup strawberry preserves   ¼ cup chopped nuts

Fill centers of doughnuts with the preserves. Garnish center with nuts.

Southern Bread Winners

Strawberry Nut Bread

Pretty and delicious.

4 eggs	3 cups flour
2 cups sugar	1 teaspoon cinnamon
1 cup cooking oil	1 teaspoon baking soda
2 (10-ounce) packages frozen	1 teaspoon salt
strawberries, thawed	1 cup chopped nuts

Beat eggs until fluffy; add sugar, oil, and strawberries. Combine flour, cinnamon, baking soda, and salt; sift together. Add to egg mixture and mix well. Stir in nuts. Pour into 2 greased and floured loaf pans. Bake at 350° for 1 hour and 10 minutes.

For that little extra, serve with strawberry butter. Mix 2 sticks margarine with ½ cup strawberry jam; blend.

A Taste of the Holidays

Ever-Ready Bran Muffins

5 cups all-purpose flour	1 (15-ounce) box raisin bran
3 cups sugar	4 eggs, beaten
1 tablespoon plus 2 teaspoons	1 quart buttermilk
baking soda	1 cup vegetable oil
2 teaspoons salt	

Sift flour, sugar, baking soda, and salt in a large bowl. Add raisin bran; stir to mix thoroughly. Make well in center of mixture. Add eggs, buttermilk, and oil. Stir just enough to moisten dry ingredients. Cover and store in refrigerator until ready to bake. Can be kept in refrigerator up to 6 weeks. To bake, grease muffin pan, spoon batter into tins (⅔ full), and bake at 400° for 12–15 minutes.

Heavenly Dishes

Georgia is the nation's number one producer of peaches, peanuts, pecans, lima beans, and pimiento peppers.

Carrot-Poppy Seed Muffins

½ cup flour
½ cup whole-wheat flour
¼ cup brown sugar
1½ teaspoons baking powder
¼ teaspoon salt
1 egg, beaten

½ cup milk
2 tablespoons butter or
   margarine, melted
⅓ cup shredded carrots
3 tablespoons poppy seeds

Combine flours, sugar, baking powder, and salt; stir to mix well. Combine in a separate bowl egg, milk, and melted margarine; add to the dry ingredients. Stir until moist and lumpy batter forms. Stir in carrots and poppy seeds. Spoon batter into greased muffin tins. Bake at 375° for 20–25 minutes or until a toothpick inserted into the center comes out clean.

Delightfully Southern

Orange Muffins

Delicious made ahead and frozen.

2 cups plain flour
1 teaspoon baking soda
1 stick butter, softened
1 cup sugar

2 eggs
¾ cup buttermilk
1 cup golden raisins
1 cup chopped pecans

Sift flour and baking soda together. Cream butter, sugar, and eggs; add buttermilk. Combine flour and buttermilk mixtures. Add raisins and pecans. Pour into small greased muffin tins and bake for about 15 minutes at 400°. Makes 3 dozen.

GLAZE:

Juice and zest of 2 oranges
   and 1 lemon

1 cup sugar

Stir ingredients together. Dip tops of muffins in Glaze while hot.

A Taste of Georgia, Another Serving

Homemade Pancakes

1 egg
1¼ cups milk
3 tablespoons melted butter
1½ cups sifted all-purpose
　flour
2½ teaspoons baking powder

2 tablespoons sugar
¾ teaspoon salt
½ cup fruit, or 1 cup chopped
　nuts (optional)
Margarine or bacon drippings

Mix egg and liquid ingredients together. Combine dry ingredients. Combine liquid and dry ingredients; mix only until dry ingredients are wet. If desired, add fruit or your favorite nuts to batter. Cook on hot griddle that is lightly greased with margarine or bacon drippings. Reduce to low heat and cook until rim of each cake is free of bubbles and brown on bottom. Brown on both sides. Turn only once.

Famous Recipes from Mrs. Wilkes' Boarding House

Buttermilk Doughnuts

1 package dry yeast
½ cup warm water
½ cup buttermilk
3 tablespoons shortening,
　melted
3 tablespoons sugar

2½–3 cups self-rising flour,
　divided
Vegetable oil
2½ cups sifted powdered
　sugar
¼ cup milk

Dissolve yeast in warm water in a large mixing bowl; let stand 5 minutes. Add buttermilk, shortening, and sugar. Add 1½ cups flour, stirring well. Add enough remaining flour to make a soft dough. Turn dough out onto a floured surface; knead several times. Roll dough to ½-inch thickness and cut with 2½-inch doughnut cutter. Place dough on lightly floured surface. Cover and let rise in a warm place, 45 minutes or until doubled in bulk. Drop doughnuts in hot oil and cook until golden brown. Drain on paper towels. Combine powdered sugar and milk. Dip each doughnut in glaze while still warm.

Give Us This Day Our Daily Bread

Deluxe French Toast

1 (8-ounce) loaf French or	4 eggs
Italian bread	½ teaspoon vanilla
4 ounces cream cheese, softened	½ cup water
½ cup chopped nuts	4 tablespoons margarine

Slice bread diagonally into 16 slices. Mix softened cream cheese and chopped nuts; blend well. Spread this mixture onto the top of 8 bread slices and top with remaining bread to make a sandwich. Beat eggs, vanilla, and water together with a wire whisk. Dip sandwiches into egg mixture coating each side. Melt margarine in a 10-inch skillet. Add sandwiches and brown on each side. Makes 8 servings.

Southern Bread Winners

Favorite French Toast

12 slices white bread, divided	¾ cup milk
¾ cup peanut butter	¼ teaspoon salt
¾ cup jelly or jam	2 tablespoons butter
3 eggs, beaten	Confectioners' sugar

Spread 6 slices of bread with peanut butter and 6 slices with jelly or jam. Put together to form sandwiches. Mix together eggs, milk, and salt. Melt butter in a large skillet or griddle on medium-high heat. Dip sandwiches in egg mixture; brown on both sides. Sprinkle with confectioners' sugar and serve immediately. Makes 6 servings.

Sherman Didn't Burn Our Recipes, Bartow's Still Cooking

On January 18, 1861, Georgia joined the Confederate States of America, and became a major theater of the American Civil War. In December 1864, a large portion of Georgia, from Atlanta to Savannah, was destroyed by fire during General William Tecumseh Sherman's "March to the Sea." On July 15, 1870, following Reconstruction, Georgia became the last former Confederate state to be readmitted to the Union.

Orange Toast

½ cup butter, softened
½ cup sugar

1½ tablespoons orange zest
1 loaf thin white bread

Preheat oven to 325°. Combine butter, sugar, and zest. Spread evenly over both sides of bread slices and place on a baking sheet. Bake 15–20 minutes or until lightly browned. Cut each slice into 3 strips or into 4 triangles. Makes 60 sticks or 80 triangles.

To freeze, place uncooked, coated toast on a baking sheet and freeze. Remove and place in plastic zipper bags and return to freezer until ready to bake.

First Come, First Served...In Savannah

Burr-grit-os

1 medium yellow onion, diced
3 cloves garlic, minced
2 tablespoons oil
½ cup grits
1 cup bulgur (cracked) wheat
3–4 cups water
1 teaspoon salt
2 teaspoons cumin
1 teaspoon chili powder

1 teaspoon garlic powder
¼ teaspoon cayenne pepper,
  or to taste
10–12 flour tortillas
1 (16-ounce) can refried beans,
  heated through
Optional: sour cream, chopped
  jalapeños, black olives,
  chopped tomatoes

In large skillet, sauté onion and garlic in oil over low heat until onion is translucent. Add grits and bulgur. Sauté briefly, stirring to coat grains well. Stir in 3 cups water and spices (as a shortcut, you may use 2 tablespoons packaged taco seasoning instead of dry spices). Cover and let simmer, stirring occasionally. Cook until grains are slightly chewy, adding more water if necessary. Heat large skillet. Place tortillas one at a time on skillet about 10 seconds on each side. Remove and cover with cloth to keep warm, or assemble immediately.

Spread ¼ cup grits mixture, ¼ cup refried beans, and 3 tablespoons of optional ingredients in center of tortilla. Fold bottom of tortilla up slightly, then fold sides to meet in center.

Vegetarians may use refried beans with no lard. Makes 10–12 burritos.

Gone with the Grits

Sunburst Sausage Brunch Bake

1 package puff pastry sheets,
  thawed
1 (16-ounce) package ground
  sausage, sage flavor
¼ cup diced bell pepper
2 tablespoons minced onion
3 cups shredded hash browns
½ teaspoon salt
Dash of coarsely ground black
  pepper

1½ cups Mexican blend cheese
  with jalapeños
¼ cup peach preserves
1 egg
¼ cup whipping cream
1 egg (optional)
1 tablespoon water (optional)
Peach Syrup (optional)

Preheat oven to 400°. Lay one puff pastry sheet in an 8- to 9-inch pie plate; cut off corners, and reserve. Brown sausage, bell pepper, and onion on high heat for 5 minutes; remove to paper towels. Sauté hash browns, salt, and pepper in same pan for 3 minutes. Layer in pastry the hash browns, half the cheese, then sausage and peach preserves. Mix together egg and whipping cream; pour over pie. Top with other half of cheese. Place remaining puff pastry atop pie, cutting off corners. Tuck in top crust. Place the corners around edge of pie to make a sun design, cutting the corners in half as needed. If desired, mix egg and water together and brush crust with egg wash. May be served with syrup, if desired. Bake in 400° oven till golden brown.

PEACH SYRUP:
½ cup peach preserves   2 tablespoons water

Mix together and heat for 1 minute in microwave.

Georgia National Fair Blue Ribbon Cookbook

Country Breakfast Pie

1 pound bulk sausage, cooked,
   crumbled, and drained
1½ cups grated Swiss cheese
1 (9-inch) deep-dish pie crust
4 eggs
¼ cup chopped red bell pepper

¼ cup chopped green bell
   pepper
2 tablespoons chopped onion
1 cup light cream
1 tomato, sliced (optional)

Preheat oven to 375°. Mix sausage and cheese and sprinkle in pie crust. Lightly beat eggs in a mixing bowl. Add bell peppers, onion, and cream to eggs. Pour mixture into pie crust. Top with tomato slices, if using. Bake 40–45 minutes. Cool on a rack 10 minutes. Serves 6–8.

First Come, First Served...In Savannah

Brunch Frittata

1 tablespoon butter
1½–2 cups hash brown
   potatoes, partially cooked
8 slices bacon, cooked and
   crumbled, or ½ cup
   cubed ham

8–10 eggs
¾ cup cream of mushroom
   or celery soup (optional)
1½ cups shredded Cheddar
   cheese

Melt butter in skillet over moderate heat. Add hash browns and top with bacon or ham. Beat eggs and pour over ingredients in a 10-inch skillet. Cover pan and turn heat to low. Cook 10–12 minutes, until eggs are set. Top with cream soup, if desired, and add Cheddar cheese the last few minutes of cooking. Cut into wedges and serve. Makes 8 servings.

Montezuma Amish Mennonite Cookbook II

 The Trackrock Archeological Area near Blairsville is a 52-acre preserve that contains numerous stone-embedded pictographs of bird, animal, and human tracks estimated to be over 10,000 years old.

Double Cheese Strata

10 slices bread
1 pound sausage
2 cups shredded sharp Cheddar
  cheese
2 cups shredded mild Cheddar
  cheese

¾ teaspoons dry mustard
3 cups milk, divided
6 eggs, beaten
½ teaspoon salt
Dash of white pepper

Remove crust from bread and cut into cubes. Fry bulk sausage to remove grease; drain. Place layer of bread pieces in well-greased 3-quart casserole. Top with layer of sharp cheese, sausage, another layer of bread, and mild cheese. Dissolve mustard in 2–3 tablespoons milk. Beat eggs with remaining milk, mustard, salt, and pepper. Pour mixture over casserole. Cover and refrigerate overnight.

When ready to cook, bake at 325° uncovered for 1 hour and 15 minutes.

Holiday Favorites

Crispy Parmesan Squares

½ teaspoon salt
4 cups water
1 cup grits
1½ cups grated Parmesan
  cheese, divided

2 tablespoons flour
½ teaspoon seasoning salt
½ teaspoon pepper
Butter or oil for frying

Bring salted water to a boil in medium saucepan. Slowly stir in grits; cover, reduce heat, and cook according to grits package directions, stirring occasionally until liquid is absorbed. Stir in 1 cup Parmesan cheese. Spread in 9x13-inch pan and let cool until firm. Cut into 2-inch squares. Combine flour, seasoning salt, pepper, and remaining cheese in medium bowl. Coat grits squares in breading mixture, turning until all sides are well-coated. Melt butter in large skillet. Fry grits until crispy on both sides. Serves 6–8.

Gone with the Grits

Crustless Ham and Grits Pie

⅓ cup quick-cooking grits
1 cup water
1 cup evaporated milk
¾ cup shredded Cheddar
  cheese
¾ cup chopped cooked
  lean ham

3 eggs, beaten
1 tablespoon chopped fresh
  parsley
½ teaspoon dry mustard
½ teaspoon hot pepper sauce
¼ teaspoon salt

Cook grits in water using package directions, omitting the salt. Mix grits, evaporated milk, cheese, ham, eggs, and seasonings in a bowl. Spoon into a greased 9-inch pie plate. Bake at 350° for 35 minutes. Let stand 10 minutes before serving. Serves 6.

True Grits

Surprise Grits

1 quart milk
½ cup butter
1 cup grits (regular)
1 teaspoon salt

⅛ teaspoon pepper
⅓ cup butter
1 cup grated Gruyére cheese
1 cup grated Parmesan

Bring milk to a boil. Add ½ cup butter; gradually stir in grits. Cook and stir until thick. Remove from heat and add salt and pepper. Beat with mixer at high speed until creamy. Pour into ungreased 9x13x2-inch casserole and refrigerate overnight.

When ready to bake, cut into squares and place like fallen dominoes in greased casserole. Pour ⅓ cup melted butter over squares and sprinkle with the grated cheeses. Bake at 400° for 35 minutes. Serves 6.

Cook and Love It

Grits, the breakfast-of-choice among southerners, became the official State Prepared Food of Georgia in 2002. The dish was chosen because it is made from corn, which is one of Georgia's main crops.

Made by grinding corn or hominy into bits, grits were first produced by Native Americans many centuries ago. Grits can be a simple breakfast dish or can be incorporated into gourmet cooking through countless recipes.

Savannah Cheese Grits with Breakfast Shrimp

2 cups milk	1½ cups grated sharp or
1 cup water	smoked Cheddar cheese
¾ teaspoon salt	2 eggs, beaten
1 cup quick-cooking grits	½ cup butter
¼ teaspoon garlic powder	Paprika for garnish
Dash of hot pepper sauce	

Combine milk, water, and salt in a 2-quart casserole dish. Microwave on HIGH 8–10 minutes or until boiling. Stir in grits. Microwave 2–3 minutes or until soft. Stir in garlic powder, pepper sauce, cheese, eggs, and butter. Mix well. Microwave on HIGH 4–5 minutes or until thickened. Sprinkle with paprika. Serves 8.

BREAKFAST SHRIMP:

3 tablespoons butter	1 teaspoon or less salt
1 medium onion, chopped	Dash of hot pepper sauce
¼ green bell pepper, chopped	1 teaspoon Worcestershire
2 tablespoons all-purpose flour	4–5 tablespoons ketchup
1 pound raw shrimp, peeled	2 tablespoons chopped
and deveined	fresh parsley
Water to cover	½ cup whipping cream

Melt butter in a medium skillet over medium heat. Add onion and bell pepper and cook until tender. Stir in flour; cook and stir until bubbly. Cook 1 minute. Increase heat and add shrimp. Cook and stir 2 minutes or until shrimp are pink. Add enough water to cover shrimp. Cook and stir until mixture thickens slightly. Add salt, pepper sauce, Worcestershire, ketchup, and parsley; stir. Simmer about 5 minutes. Adjust seasonings as needed. Stir in cream. Heat thoroughly, but do not bring to a boil. Serve immediately over plain or cheese grits. Serves 4. (You may double ingredients for shrimp.)

Variation: You may add sliced andouille or Lumber Jack sausage.

First Come, First Served...In Savannah

Grits-topher Columbus Herb Grits

1–1½ teaspoons salt
4 cups water
1 cup grits
2 tablespoons butter or
 margarine
1 tablespoon olive oil
½ teaspoon oregano

½ teaspoon basil
½ teaspoon marjoram
1 teaspoon garlic powder
1 teaspoon onion powder
½ cup grated Parmesan
 cheese

Bring salted water to boil in medium saucepan. Slowly stir in grits. Cover, reduce heat, and cook according to grits package directions, stirring occasionally until liquid is absorbed. Stir in butter, oil, oregano, basil, marjoram, garlic powder, and onion powder. Sprinkle with Parmesan cheese. Serves 6.

Variation: Pour mixture into 9x13-inch pan and chill 4 hours or overnight. Cut into 2-inch squares. Heat small amount of butter in skillet. Fry grits until golden and crispy on both sides. Serve lightly topped with warmed marinara sauce and sprinkle of Parmesan cheese.

Calorie cutter: Skip the olive oil and use diet margarine.

Gone with the Grits

Hawaiian Nut Sandwiches

¼ cup evaporated milk
2 (8-ounce) packages cream
 cheese, softened
¼ cup chopped pecans

1 cup pineapple, crushed and
 drained well
Homemade orange bread or
 raisin bread

Blend milk and cheese together well. Add nuts and pineapple. Blend well. Good on orange or raisin bread as well as white bread. (May cut crusts.) Cut in fourths. Makes enough for approximately 12 dozen party sandwiches.

A Taste of Georgia

PHOTO © GEORGIA DEPARTMENT OF ECONOMIC DEVELOPMENT

Carved into Stone Mountain are the figures of three Confederate heroes of the Civil War: Stonewall Jackson, Jefferson Davis, and Robert E. Lee. The monument was designed as a memorial to the heroic struggle of the South during the Civil War.

Basic Vegetable Soup

1 (3-pound) beef shank bone
with meat
3 quarts water
4 cups shredded cabbage
1 (16-ounce) can tomatoes
1½ cups chopped onions
1 cup chopped celery

1 cup sliced carrots
1 (10-ounce) package frozen
succotash
1 tablespoon salt
2 teaspoons sugar
¼ teaspoon pepper

Place beef bone in large stockpot. Add water, cover, and simmer 3 hours, or until beef falls off bone. Remove beef and bone from stock; set aside. Strain stock; add enough water to make 3 quarts. Return stock to stockpot and add all remaining ingredients except meat. Cover and simmer about 30 minutes or until vegetables are tender. Remove meat from bone. When vegetables are cooked, add meat. Cool to room temperature and refrigerate overnight. Remove layer of fat, heat, and serve.

By permission of American Dairy Association
Traditions

Old-Fashioned Vegetable Soup

3 pounds stew beef
4 cups water
1 cup cubed carrots
2 cups small cubes of Irish
potatoes
1½ cups corn
¾ cup very thinly sliced
okra

1 cup baby lima beans
½ cup chopped celery
1 medium onion, chopped fine
6 cups chopped tomatoes or
tomato juice
2 teaspoons salt
1 teaspoon pepper
½ teaspoon sugar

Cover beef with water and heat to boiling. Reduce heat; cover and simmer 1–2 hours, until meat on shanks is fork-tender. Let cool and pull meat from shanks into small cubes. Skim fat from cooled stock. Strain stock into large saucepan; add meat cubes and remaining ingredients. Heat to boiling, cover, and simmer 1 hour, or until vegetables are tender, adding more water or tomato juice if mixture gets too thick. Makes 20–25 (1-cup) servings.

The Foxfire Book of Appalachian Cookery

Garden Patch Vegetable Soup

1 soup bone, or prepared
  chicken stock
1 gallon water
1½ pounds tomatoes, chopped
1 quart corn
1 quart butter beans
2 cups sliced okra
2 cups chopped cabbage
4 tablespoons margarine
2 cups diced potatoes
1 cup sliced carrots

1 cup chopped bell pepper
1 cup chopped celery
1½ cups diced onions
1 tablespoon sugar
1 tablespoon salt
Black pepper to taste
¼ teaspoon dried parsley
¼ teaspoon basil
¼ teaspoon oregano
⅛ teaspoon dried tarragon
⅛ teaspoon thyme

Wash soup bone thoroughly. Place in large stockpot. Add water and simmer for several hours. Skim off fat. Add vegetables and seasonings. Bring to a boil, then simmer 2 hours. Remove soup bone. You may add additional seasonings of your choice.

Note: For a vegetarian soup, increase tomatoes to 3 pounds and substitute beef or chicken bouillon cubes for the soup bone.

Our Favorite Recipes

BabyLand General Hospital, housed in a circa 1900s medical clinic in Cleveland, is the home and adoption center of the original Cabbage Patch Kids.

Cold Remedy Soup

3 tablespoons butter
1 onion, chopped or diced
2 chicken wings, whole
3 carrots, sliced or shredded
2 baked potatoes, cut into pieces
1 teaspoon minced garlic

2½ cups water
1 teaspoon Season-All
1 dash black pepper
Chicken bouillon to taste
  (optional)

Melt butter in a medium saucepan (low heat). Add chopped onion, chicken (boneless breasts are optional, but don't contain same amount of nutrients), carrots, potatoes, garlic, and water. Increase heat and bring to a boil. Add Season-All and pepper. Cover and boil on medium heat for about 25 minutes; stir and monitor water level. Add chicken bouillon, if desired.

Culinary Classics

Split Pea Soup with Beer

1 tablespoon butter
1 cup chopped onion
1 cup sliced carrots
½ cup chopped celery
1 ham bone
1 (16-ounce) package dried
  split peas
1 (12-ounce) can beer

7½ cups water
1 bay leaf
¼ teaspoon thyme
1 tablespoon vinegar
2–3 teaspoons salt
½ teaspoon pepper
½ teaspoon Tabasco

In large Dutch oven, melt butter. Add onion, carrots and celery; cook 10 minutes. Add ham bone, peas, beer, water, bay leaf, thyme, vinegar, salt, pepper, and Tabasco. Cover and bring to a boil. Reduce heat, skim off any foam, and simmer, covered, 2 hours. Remove bone. Chop and reserve meat. Purée soup in blender. Return to pan. Add meat and adjust seasonings. Makes 8 servings.

Second Round: Tea-Time at the Masters®

Mama Tucker Soup

This is even better the next day.

1 large or 3 small ham hocks
3 (16-ounce) cans tomatoes, mashed
1–2 stalks celery, chopped
1–2 (12-ounce) packages frozen carrots
2–3 onions, chopped fine
2 (12-ounce) packages frozen peas (optional)
2 (12-ounce) packages frozen butter beans
2 (17-ounce) cans whole-kernel corn
1–2 (12-ounce) packages frozen okra
1 bell pepper, chopped
Salt and pepper

Cook ham hocks 4–5 hours in 8–9 quarts water. Add tomatoes, celery, carrots, and onions; cook 2 hours longer. Add peas and butter beans; cook 30 minutes. Add corn and okra; cook 30 more minutes. Add bell pepper 30 minutes before serving. Season with salt and pepper to taste. Serve with crackers or cornbread.

Main Street Winder

Country Sausage Soup

A very thick soup. Excellent for a wintery night supper.

1½ pounds smoked large link sausage
3 (16-ounce) cans chopped tomatoes
9 cups water, divided
4 average potatoes, peeled
2 medium onions, finely chopped
1¾ cups uncooked rice (not instant)
Salt to taste

Cut sausage into ¼-inch slices; cut slices in half. In a large heavy pan or Dutch oven, bring tomatoes and 2 cups water to a boil; add sausage, cover, and cook 30 minutes. Dip grease off top and discard.

While sausage is cooking, cut potatoes into very small cubes, about ½–¾ inches. Add remaining water to tomatoes and return to boil. Add onions and potatoes; reduce heat, cover and simmer 30 minutes. Add rice, cover, and continue to cook for 30 minutes, or until rice is tender. Add salt, if needed.

Note: Once rice is added, you must stir often to prevent sticking. This is a thick soup. You do not want it watery.

Delightfully Southern

Grilled Eggplant Soup

1 large Vidalia or Spanish
 onion, sliced
2 small firm eggplants, peeled
 and sliced
¼ cup olive oil, divided
2 tablespoons chopped garlic
2 bay leaves
¼ cup cored, seeded, and
 chopped poblano chile
2 (14-ounce) cans diced
 tomatoes in juice

3 cups Basic Chicken Broth
1 teaspoon toasted whole
 cumin seed
2 tablespoons minced fresh
 thyme
1 tablespoon red wine vinegar
Salt and pepper to taste
½ cup Red Pepper Sauce

Light a charcoal grill or the oven broiler. Brush onion and egg-plant slices with most of the olive oil. Grill until soft and golden. Chop onion slices to make about 1 cup, and the eggplant to make about 2 cups.

In a non-corrosive soup pot, combine onion, eggplant, garlic, bay leaves, poblano, tomatoes, chicken broth, and cumin seed; simmer over medium heat, uncovered, for 20 minutes to combine the flavors. Remove bay leaves; stir in the thyme, vinegar, salt, pepper, and remaining olive oil. Purée soup in batches in a food processor or blender. Divide soup among 6 soup bowls and drizzle the Red Pepper Sauce on top of the soup just before serving. Serves 6.

Note: Canned chicken broth may be substituted for the Basic Chicken Broth, but be sure to eliminate the salt from the recipe.

BASIC CHICKEN BROTH:
1 carrot, chopped
½ large onion, chopped
2 celery stalks, chopped
3 whole peppercorns
1 bay leaf

6 parsley sprigs
2 quarts chicken bones (skinless
 carcasses from 2 roasted
 chickens)
5 cups water

In a large soup pot on high heat, combine all ingredients and bring to a boil. Reduce heat to low; remove any scum that forms on top. Simmer for 30 minutes, then cool for 10 minutes; strain. Discard solids and refrigerate broth. The chicken fat can easily be removed from the surface when the broth is cold. Makes 4 cups.

Note: Two pounds of chicken backs may be used if you don't plan to roast chicken. At home I always buy bone-in chicken breasts, debone the breasts, and freeze the bones to be used for broth at a later date.

(continued)

Grilled Eggplant Soup (continued)

RED PEPPER SAUCE:

2 large red bell peppers, cored, seeded, and cut into quarters
½ cup water
½ cup diced onion (½-inch dice)
1 tablespoon peeled and minced fresh ginger
1 teaspoon hot chili sauce
½ teaspoon salt
1 tablespoon red wine vinegar

In a skillet with a lid, combine all ingredients except vinegar. Bring to a boil over high heat, then lower the heat, cover, and simmer 30 minutes, until peppers are very soft. Cool for 15 minutes only, then peel skin from the peppers and discard skin. Purée vegetables in the bowl of a food processor. Stir in the vinegar.

Variation: Replace red bell peppers with yellow bell peppers for a lovely, mild yellow pepper sauce.

Savannah Seasons

Slow-Roasted Onion Soup

4 medium-size sweet onions, Vidalia or Texas
¼ cup olive oil
2 bay leaves
4 cups chicken stock (or water)
1 cup heavy cream
1 tablespoon unsweetened butter
Salt and pepper to taste
Dollop of sour cream and chives for garnish
Truffle oil for garnish

Slice onions; put on baking sheet and sprinkle with olive oil. Bake in oven at 325° for 20 minutes. Place onions in stockpot over medium heat; caramelize for 15 minutes. Add bay leaves and chicken stock, and simmer 30–40 minutes. Mix soup in a blender; add cream and butter. Purée and strain. Add salt and pepper to taste. Garnish with a dollop of sour cream and chives and drizzle with truffle oil. Serves 6.

Editor's Extra: Truffle oil is created when truffles are soaked in olive oil. Available in most gourmet stores, a few drops of truffle oil will give the final touch of class to an unforgettable meal.

Fine Dining Georgia Style

French Onion Soup II

The very best!

4 slices French bread
3 tablespoons butter
3 large Vidalia sweet onions,
 finely sliced
1 tablespoon flour
1 teaspoon freshly ground
 pepper

3 (10¾-ounce) cans beef
 bouillon
1 (14-ounce) can beef broth
4 tablespoons grated Parmesan
 cheese
4 slices Swiss or mozzarella
 cheese

Toast French bread slices. In a large saucepan, melt butter and sauté onions until clear in color. Add flour and stir constantly for 3 minutes. Stir in pepper; add beef bouillon and beef broth. Bring to a boil, then lower heat; simmer 30 minutes (covered with lid slightly tilted). When ready to serve, warm soup bowls slightly. Spoon soup into individual bowls and float one piece of toasted French bread in each. Sprinkle with Parmesan cheese. Cover each bowl completely with Swiss or mozzarella. Place bowls under broiler until cheese is slightly browned and bubbly. Serve immediately. Serves 4.

Editor's Extra: Canned bouillon is stronger than broth, so if you cannot find canned bouillon, I suggest using broth but adding a beef bouillon cube or two.

Vidalia Sweet Onion Lovers Cookbook

Creamy Broccoli Soup

1 medium onion, chopped
1 clove garlic, crushed
1 bay leaf
1 tablespoon sunflower or
    vegetable oil
1 (16-ounce) package frozen,
    chopped broccoli
2½ cups light vegetable stock
1 small potato, coarsely
    chopped
Juice of ½ lemon
Salt and pepper to taste
¼ cup low-fat plain yogurt

Sauté onion and garlic with bay leaf in oil in saucepan 3–4 minutes. Add broccoli, stock, and potato; mix well. Simmer, covered, for 10 minutes or until broccoli is tender-crisp and still bright green, stirring occasionally. Discard bay leaf; cool slightly. Process in blender until almost smooth; return to saucepan. Stir in lemon juice. Season with salt and pepper. Cook just until heated through, stirring frequently. Ladle into soup bowls. Top with yogurt. Yields 4 servings.

Note: May sauté onion and garlic in saucepan sprayed with nonstick cooking spray. May substitute sour cream for yogurt.

Simple Decent Cooking

Cynthia's Quick and Easy Gumbo

2 (8-ounce) cans whole-kernel
    corn
2 (14-ounce) cans diced
    tomatoes
1 (8-ounce) can tomato sauce
1 (12-ounce) package beef
    sausage, sliced
1 pound okra, fresh or frozen
¼ cup sugar
Salt, pepper, and spices to taste

Combine corn, tomatoes, and tomato sauce in pot. Bring to a slow boil on medium heat. Stir; add sausage and okra. Continue to cook on medium heat about 15 minutes. Add sugar; stir and simmer another 10 minutes. Season to taste. Serve over rice, if desired.

Heart & Soul

Georgia Peanut Soup

1 shallot, chopped
2 stalks celery, chopped
2 teaspoons butter or margarine
1 tablespoon flour
1 cup chicken stock, divided
3 tablespoons smooth, salt-free
  peanut butter, made from
  freshly ground peanuts

½ cup low-fat milk
½ cup water
2 tablespoons crushed, salt-free
  Georgia peanuts

Sauté shallot and celery in melted butter in a medium skillet for 5 minutes. Add flour, tossing to coat well. Stir in half the chicken stock; simmer 5 minutes. Add remaining chicken stock; simmer 5 minutes longer. Strain, separating liquid from vegetables. Blend peanut butter into reserved liquid in a saucepan. Stir in milk.

Combine ¾ cup peanut butter and stock mixture with reserved vegetables in a blender or food processor; process until smooth; stir into saucepan. Cook until heated through, adding water as needed for desired consistency. Serve hot or cold, topped with crushed peanuts. Serves 4.

True Grits

 The official state crop of Georgia is the peanut. Georgia produces almost half of the total U.S. peanut crop. More than 50% of the crop goes to peanut butter production.

Potato Soup with Shrimp

Potato soup is an unsung hero of the soup world; there is just nothing more belly-pleasing. As the potatoes cook, the soup thickens, leaving behind some chunks of potato. Cook the shrimp separately and add them at the last minute. They add great flavor and color, but if you don't have any shrimp on hand, the soup is still terrific without them.

½ stick butter
1 small onion, diced
2 medium carrots, diced
2 tablespoons all-purpose flour
8 medium russet potatoes,
  peeled and cubed
2 chicken bouillon cubes,
  dissolved in ¼ cup hot milk

4 cups milk
1 cup half-and-half
1 teaspoon salt
¼ teaspoon pepper
1 pound medium shrimp
Crumbled bacon bits for garnish
Grated sharp Cheddar cheese
  for garnish

In a 4-quart saucepan, melt the butter and sauté the onion and carrots until both are slightly tender, about 5 minutes. Whisk in flour; cook 1 minute. Add potatoes, bouillon cubes, and milk. Cook over medium heat for 15 minutes, until potatoes are very soft and some have begun to dissolve into mush. Add half-and-half, salt, and pepper. Let cool, then refrigerate until party time.

In a small saucepan, bring 2 cups lightly salted water to a boil. Add shrimp all at once; stir well. Watch shrimp closely; as soon as they all turn pink, turn off the heat and drain. The shrimp should be slightly undercooked. When they are cool, peel, chop roughly into big chunks, and place in a plastic bag. Refrigerate until party time.

Reheat soup over very low heat (it will stick to the bottom of the pot if you heat it too quickly) about 45 minutes before the party. When the soup is hot, add the shrimp and stir well. Encourage your guests to sprinkle the soup with bacon bits and grated Cheddar cheese. They won't be sorry they did!

Paula Deen & Friends

Savannah Shrimp Bisque

A luscious, light and elegant beginning for any dinner.

1 tablespoon unsalted butter
1 tablespoon vegetable oil
½ cup finely chopped yellow
   onion
½ cup finely chopped celery
⅓ cup finely chopped carrot
2 tablespoons all-purpose flour
3 cups chicken broth
1 (14½-ounce) can whole
   tomatoes, drained and
   chopped
½ cup dry white wine or
   fish stock

1 bay leaf
1 teaspoon dried marjoram
⅛ teaspoon nutmeg
1 pound medium shrimp,
   peeled and deveined, cut
   into ½-inch pieces
1 cup whipping cream
½ teaspoon salt
2 tablespoons fresh lemon juice
Fresh marjoram sprigs for
   garnish

Heat butter and oil in a large saucepan over medium-high heat. Stir in onion, celery, and carrot; sauté 5 minutes, or until tender. Add flour and cook and stir until bubbly. Stir in broth, tomatoes, wine, bay leaf, marjoram, and nutmeg. Bring to a boil; reduce heat and simmer, covered, for 15 minutes. Discard bay leaf and let mixture cool.

Purée soup in batches in a food processor or blender until smooth. Return soup to saucepan. Add shrimp and cook, uncovered, over medium heat 1 minute. Blend in cream; cook 2 minutes longer, or until soup is heated through and shrimp are firm and pink. Remove from heat and season with salt and lemon juice. Garnish with marjoram sprigs. Makes 6 (1-cup) servings.

For a lighter version, use 1 cup low-fat milk and 2 tablespoons whipping cream instead of 1 cup whipping cream.

First Come, First Served...In Savannah

In 1864, General Sherman's infamous "March to the Sea" ended at what is now Fort McAllister State Historic Park. When Mr. Sherman visited Savannah, he spared the city from ruin because of its beauty; thus, much of Savannah's history survived. Rather than burn Savannah, Sherman gave it as a "Christmas present" to President Lincoln.

Vic's Shrimp Chowder

½ cup butter
2 ribs celery, chopped
2 large onions, chopped
2 garlic cloves, minced
Flour to thicken
4 cups milk
1 (8-ounce) package cream
　cheese, cut into pieces
4 cups half-and-half

Salt and pepper to taste
1 (14-ounce) can chicken broth
1 egg yolk
2 (11-ounce) cans white shoepeg
　corn, drained
Pinch of sugar, or to taste
2 (10-ounce) cans cream of
　potato soup
8–12 ounces shrimp, peeled

Melt butter in a large saucepan. Add celery, onions, and garlic. Sauté over low heat until onion is translucent. Stir in enough flour to absorb the butter. Add milk gradually; whisk constantly. Bring to a simmer; simmer until thickened. Add cream cheese, stirring until melted. Whisk in half-and-half, salt and pepper. Whisk in chicken broth and egg yolk. Stir in corn, sugar, and soup. Simmer 30 minutes. Whisk in additional flour and simmer until of the desired consistency. Stir in the shrimp; cook until they are pink; do not overcook. Ladle into bowls. Yields 12–14 servings.

From Black Tie to Blackeyed Peas

Chicken Corn Chowder

1 (8-ounce) carton fresh
　mushrooms, sliced
1 onion, chopped
1 tablespoon butter
2 (10-ounce) cans chicken broth
1 (10¾-ounce) can cream of
　chicken soup
1 (14-ounce) package frozen
　shoepeg corn

½ cup orzo (rice-shaped pasta),
　uncooked
½ teaspoon rosemary or thyme
½ teaspoon salt
½ teaspoon pepper
½ teaspoon basil
2 cups diced cooked chicken
1 cup milk mixed with 3
　tablespoons flour

Sauté mushrooms and onion in butter. Add remaining ingredients, except chicken and milk. Simmer until orzo is done, about 20 minutes. Add chicken and milk mixed with flour. Heat and serve.

Home Run Recipes

Yellow Tomato Gazpacho

1 pound yellow bell peppers
1½ pounds yellow tomatoes,
  peeled and seeded
1 pound cucumbers, peeled
  and seeded
½ cup chopped sweet onion,
  preferably Vidalia
2 medium cloves garlic,
  coarsely chopped
1½ slices white bread,
  crusts removed

⅓ cup mayonnaise
2 tablespoons olive oil
2 tablespoons white wine
  vinegar
1 teaspoon salt
⅓ teaspoon white pepper
3 dashes hot sauce
1 red tomato, finely chopped
  for garnish

Roast peppers over open flame until blackened; remove skin, interior ribs, and seeds. Put all the ingredients, except red tomato for garnish, in a food processor fitted with the steel blade, and process until smooth.

Store soup in the refrigerator for several hours. If too thick, thin with a few ice cubes. Garnish with the red tomato. Olive bread is a nice accompaniment.

A Traveler's Table

In 1958, Georgia had roughly eighty historic covered bridges in the state. But by 1968, before anyone realized how fast they were disappearing, there were only twenty-eight left. Time has continued to take its toll, and now there are only fourteen. The 229-foot covered bridge at Watson Mill Bridge State Park near Comer is Georgia's longest covered bridge, and is still in its original location.

Black Bean Chili

4 large onions, chopped
1 large green bell pepper,
 chopped
3 tablespoons vegetable oil
1 tablespoon minced garlic
1 (16-ounce) can Mexican
 stewed tomatoes, undrained
3 (16-ounce) cans black beans,
 undrained
1 cup water
1 (6-ounce) can tomato paste

1 tablespoon chili powder
1 teaspoon cumin seeds
½ cup chopped fresh tomato
½ cup chopped green chiles
½ cup chopped onion
½ cup chopped jalapeños
1 cup sour cream
1 cup shredded Cheddar cheese
1 (9-ounce) package tortilla
 chips

Sauté 4 onions and green bell pepper in oil in 6-quart saucepan over medium-high heat for 3 minutes, or until tender. Add garlic and mix well; sauté for 1 minute. Stir in tomatoes, beans, water, tomato paste, chili powder, and cumin. Simmer 45 minutes, stirring occasionally. Ladle into chili bowls. Top with tomato, chiles, ½ cup chopped onion, jalapeños, sour cream, and cheese. Serve with tortilla chips. Makes 6 servings.

Simple Decent Cooking

Chili con Carne and Frijoles

1 pound red kidney or pinto
 beans, or combination
4 medium onions, sliced
3 garlic cloves, chopped
5 tablespoons bacon grease
3 pounds beef chuck, cut in
 ½-inch cubes
7 cups stewed tomatoes and
 juice, or 2 (28-ounce) cans

2–3 tablespoons chili powder
½ teaspoon oregano
½ teaspoon crushed red
 pepper
2½ teaspoons cumin seed
2 tablespoons salt

Soak kidney or pinto beans overnight.

Brown onions and garlic in hot bacon grease. Add meat and brown. Add other ingredients and simmer approximately 2½ hours, uncovered. Boil beans until tender, about 1 hour. Add to chili and simmer for 1 hour; serve. Serves 12.

Note: Good with rice or saltines. Freezes well.

Cook and Love It

Chilean Harvest Stew

1 onion, chopped
1 clove garlic, chopped
1 teaspoon chili powder
1 dried red pepper, crushed
Salt and pepper to taste
Oregano to taste
3 tablespoons vegetable oil
2 (16-ounce) cans tomatoes

2 cups winter squash or
　pumpkin, peeled and cubed,
　or 1 (16-ounce) can pumpkin
1 (16-ounce) package frozen
　kernel corn
2 cups white beans, cooked
Peanut butter to taste (optional)

Sauté onion, garlic, chili powder, red pepper, salt, pepper, and oregano in oil. Add tomatoes, squash or pumpkin, and corn. Cook until tender. Add white beans (drain and rinse if using canned beans). Stir in peanut butter, if desired. Serves 6.

It's the People; It's the Food

Special Oyster Stew

1 quart oysters, with liquid
½ cup butter
1 cup light cream
4 cups milk
Salt and pepper to taste

6 slices buttered toast
1 tablespoon grated onion
　(optional)
Paprika for garnish
Celery salt for garnish

Cook oysters in butter until edges curl. Gradually add cream and milk. Heat to boiling point and season with salt and pepper. Serve topped with buttered toast triangles which have been sprinkled with onion, if desired, paprika, and celery salt. Makes 6 portions.

What's Cookin'? in Winder, Georgia

Mama's Oyster Stew

1½ pints oysters, or more to
  your taste
1 large onion, finely chopped
2 quarts whole milk

1 (12-ounce) can evaporated
  milk
Salt and pepper to taste
½–¾ stick butter

Drain oysters; reserve liquid. Look the oysters over for shells. Cut oyster if it is too large to fit in a soup spoon. Put oysters back in their liquid.

Just barely cover the bottom of the boiler with water; cook onion until soft. Add both milks; do not cook on high heat or it will scorch; do not let it boil. When milk is to the boiling point, add oysters and liquid, salt, pepper, and butter. When oysters rise to the top, it is ready to serve.

Special Treasures

The Lady & Sons Crab Stew

4 tablespoons butter
3 tablespoons all-purpose flour
1 tablespoon minced garlic
2 cups heavy cream
2 cups half-and-half
2 fish-flavor bouillon cubes
1 pound crabmeat, picked free
  of any broken shells

¼ cup sherry
½ teaspoon white pepper
1 (8-ounce) bottle clam juice
  (optional)
Grated Parmesan for garnish
Snipped chives for garnish

Heat butter in a large saucepan over medium heat. Add flour, stirring to blend in; add garlic. Gradually add cream and half-and-half, stirring constantly. Add bouillon cubes and stir well. As the mixture begins to thicken, add crabmeat, sherry, and pepper. If the stew seems too thick, thin it with clam juice, which will also add a lot of flavor. Serve in a mug, garnished with grated Parmesan and snipped chives. Serves 10–12.

The Lady & Sons, Too!

Brunswick Stew

2 pounds pork or chicken, chopped
½ teaspoon black pepper
1 teaspoon hot sauce
2 tablespoons Worcestershire
⅓ cup pork or bacon drippings
½ cup barbecue sauce
1½ cups ketchup
2 cups diced potatoes, cooked
3 (17-ounce) cans cream-style corn
Salt to taste

Place all ingredients in saucepan; cover and heat slowly. Salt and more hot sauce may be needed according to taste. Makes about 2 quarts.

Famous Recipes from Mrs. Wilkes' Boarding House

Brunswick Stew

1 (3-pound) chicken
1 pound lean beef
1 pound lean pork
Salt and pepper to taste
3 medium onions, chopped
4 (16-ounce) cans tomatoes
5 tablespoons Worcestershire
1½ (14-ounce) bottles ketchup
1 tablespoon Tabasco
2 bay leaves
½ (12-ounce) bottle chili sauce
½ teaspoon dry mustard
¼ cup butter
3 tablespoons vinegar
2 (16-ounce) cans lima or butter beans
2 (16-ounce) cans cream-style corn
1 (15-ounce) can small green peas
3 small Irish potatoes, chopped (optional)
1 (10-ounce) package frozen sliced okra (optional)

Place the chicken, beef, and pork in a large heavy pot. Season with salt and pepper. Add onions. Cover with water; simmer for several hours, or until the meat falls from the bones. Remove from heat. Drain, reserving the stock. Shred the meat, discarding the bones. Combine the shredded meat and reserved stock in the pot. Add the tomatoes, Worcestershire, ketchup, Tabasco, bay leaves, chili sauce, mustard, and butter; stir to combine. Cook for 1 hour, stirring occasionally. Add vinegar, beans, corn, peas, potatoes, and okra; stir to combine. Cook over low heat until stew thickens. Yields 20 servings.

From Black Tie to Blackeyed Peas

SALADS

PHOTO © GEORGIA DEPARTMENT OF ECONOMIC DEVELOPMENT

Atlanta was largely destroyed when General Sherman burned the city on November 15, 1864. Today, the city's symbol is the Phoenix, a legendary bird of Egyptian mythology that rose from its own ashes with renewed strength and beauty.

Marinated Pea Salad

A good salad for a picnic.

¾ cup vinegar
¾ cup sugar
1 tablespoon water
1 teaspoon salt
½ teaspoon pepper
1 (15-ounce) can English peas,
  drained

1 (11-ounce) can shoepeg corn,
  drained
1 (2-ounce) jar pimentos,
  chopped and drained
1 cup finely chopped celery
1 cup finely chopped onion

Combine vinegar, sugar, water, salt, and pepper in a small saucepan. Bring mixture to a boil and cook 1 minute. Let cool. Toss peas, corn, pimentos, celery, and onion in a bowl. Pour marinade over vegetables. Stir gently and refrigerate overnight. Serves 10–12.

Traditions

Black-Eyed Pea Salad
with Tomato and Pineapple

2 tablespoons vegetable oil
¼ teaspoon freshly grated
  nutmeg
½ teaspoon ground cinnamon
½ teaspoon freshly cracked
  black pepper
1 teaspoon hot pepper sauce
2 cups black-eyed peas, cooked
  according to package
  directions, or 1 (15-ounce)
  can black-eyed peas, rinsed
  and drained

¼ cup minced celery heart
¼ cup minced celery leaves
¼ cup minced fresh basil
½ cup chopped green onions
2 cups fresh garden tomatoes,
  cut into ½-inch dice
1 cup peeled fresh pineapple,
  cut into ¼-inch dice

In a small skillet over medium heat, warm oil and add nutmeg, cinnamon, and black pepper. Simmer for 2 minutes until oil is well flavored; stir in the hot pepper sauce. Put black-eyed peas in a large salad bowl, then pour warm oil over them; toss. Add celery heart and leaves, basil, green onions, tomatoes, and pineapple. Serve at room temperature. Serves 6.

Savannah Seasons

Summer's Bounty Salad

The best of your summer garden accented with mint.

2 large seedless cucumbers
⅓ cup red wine vinegar
1 tablespoon sugar
1 teaspoon salt
⅔ cup coarsely chopped
   Vidalia, or other sweet onion

3 large tomatoes, chopped
½ cup chopped fresh mint
3 tablespoons olive oil
8 ounces mozzarella cheese,
   cubed
Salt and pepper to taste

Slice cucumbers in half lengthwise; cut on the diagonal into ½-inch slices. Mix cucumbers, vinegar, sugar, and salt in a large bowl. Let stand for 1 hour, stirring occasionally. Add onion, tomatoes, mint, olive oil, and cheese. Season with salt and pepper. Toss to mix. Serves 10.

Par 3: Tea-Time at the Masters®

Pickled Peach Halves

1 (29-ounce) can peach halves
   in syrup
¼ cup cider vinegar
½ cup sugar

¼ teaspoon allspice
½ teaspoon whole cloves
½ stick cinnamon

Drain peaches. Reserve syrup. Add vinegar, sugar, and spices to syrup. Boil 5 minutes. Add peaches. Simmer 5 minutes. Chill fruit overnight in syrup. Keeps well left in syrup mixture and refrigerated. Serves 7–8.

Note: A nice accompaniment for meats or salad plates.

The South's Legendary Frances Virginia Tea Room Cookbook

Carrot Salad

2 cups grated raw carrots
2 cups grated unpeeled
  tart apples
1 green bell pepper, chopped

1 red bell pepper, chopped
1 tablespoon mayonnaise
1 tablespoon peanut butter

Blend together carrots, apples, and peppers. Toss with mayonnaise and peanut butter, and serve. Makes 8 servings.

The Foxfire Book of Appalachian Cookery

Marinated Carrot Salad

Great for picnics and cookouts.

1 (10¾-ounce) can tomato
  soup, undiluted
½ cup corn oil
¾ cup herb vinegar or cider
  vinegar
1 cup sugar
1½ teaspoons Worcestershire
1 teaspoon dry mustard
1 tablespoon salt
½ tablespoon pepper

⅛ teaspoon red pepper
3 (16-ounce) cans sliced carrots,
  drained
1 (8-ounce) can whole-kernel
  corn, drained
1 cup chopped celery
1 medium onion, chopped
1 medium green pepper,
  chopped

Combine and mix well. Store in refrigerator in covered bowl. Stir occasionally. Drain and serve. Make at least 2 days before. Serves 10–12. Keeps for 2 weeks in refrigerator.

Cook and Love It

Corn, Tomato, and Vidalia Sweet Onion Salad

1½ cups diced ripe tomatoes
⅓ cup chopped Vidalia sweet onion
2 medium ears fresh corn, cooked and cooled
⅛ teaspoon salt

1 tablespoon plus 1 teaspoon balsamic vinegar
1 tablespoon olive oil
15 fresh basil leaves
Salt and ground pepper to taste

Combine tomatoes and onion. Scrape corn and juice off cobs; this should equal about 1 cup. Add corn to tomatoes and onions. Whisk together salt and vinegar. Add oil and whisk. Stack basil leaves and slice into shreds. Add to tomato mixture. Combine vinegar mixture with vegetables and toss to coat. Season with salt and pepper. Cover and refrigerate 1 hour to 2 days. Serves 4.

Note: This salad is good with grilled fish.

Vidalia Sweet Onion Lovers Cookbook

Special Spinach Salad and Dressing

DRESSING:
1 cup oil
⅓ cup vinegar
1 teaspoon sugar
½ teaspoon salt
½ teaspoon celery salt

¼ teaspoon dry mustard
¼ teaspoon cayenne pepper
1 clove garlic, minced
Dash of Tabasco

Mix all ingredients together in a jar and shake.

SALAD:
Spinach
Boiled eggs
Monterey Jack cheese

Cooked bacon
Capers (optional)

Wash spinach and tear onto salad plate. Grate the boiled eggs and cheese; crumble bacon; sprinkle over spinach. Capers may be added. Add Dressing.

Main Street Winder

Indian Spinach Salad

8 cups torn fresh spinach
(approximately 10 ounces)
1½ cups chopped apples,
unpared

½–¾ cup golden raisins
½ cup crushed peanuts
2–3 tablespoons chopped
green onions

Combine all ingredients. Toss with Dressing. Makes 6–8 servings.

DRESSING:
¼ cup white wine vinegar
¼ cup vegetable oil
2 tablespoons chutney
½ teaspoon sugar

½ teaspoon salt
1½ teaspoons curry powder
1 teaspoon dry mustard

Combine all ingredients in jar. Shake well. Chill before serving.

Second Round: Tea-Time at the Masters®

New Echota was the first capital of the Cherokee Nation from 1825–1838, prior to the Cherokee's forced removal from the Southeast, which marked the beginning of the "Trail of Tears." Today New Echota is an active State Historic Site where visitors can tour original and reconstructed historic structures and learn about the dreams and lives of the Indians who tried to pattern their government and lifestyle after the white man.

Two Potato Salad with Dill Dressing

½ cup fat-free, plain yogurt
1 tablespoon light mayonnaise
  or salad dressing
1 teaspoon chopped fresh dill
  weed, or ½ teaspoon dried
  dill weed
1 teaspoon Dijon mustard
¼ teaspoon salt
1 small stalk celery, chopped

2 cups cubed, cooked white
  potatoes
2 cups cubed, cooked sweet
  potatoes
½ cup sliced radishes
1 small stalk celery, chopped
2 tablespoons chopped green
  onions

Mix yogurt, mayonnaise, dill, mustard, and salt in a large glass or plastic bowl. Add remaining ingredients; toss, cover, and refrigerate about 4 hours or until well chilled.

Cooking with Herbs Volume I

German Potato Salad

Delicious!

2 pounds potatoes
½ cup chicken or beef stock

½ onion, chopped

Wash potatoes and boil in water to cover until tender. Cool, peel, and slice into large bowl. Pour stock over potatoes. Allow time for stock to be absorbed, then add onion. Add Dressing.

DRESSING:
6 tablespoons wine vinegar
6 tablespoons vegetable oil
1 egg yolk
1 teaspoon salt

2 teaspoons freshly ground
  pepper
4–6 strips bacon, cooked and
  crumbled

Mix all ingredients except bacon; beat well. Pour over potatoes. Sprinkle crumbled bacon on top. Serve hot or cold. Makes 4 servings.

Flavors of the Gardens

Potato Salad

10 potatoes, diced
1 cup mayonnaise
4 hard-boiled eggs
1 small onion, chopped
2 celery stalks, diced

2 cups sweet pickle relish
1 (2-ounce) jar pimentos
½ teaspoon salt
½ teaspoon pepper

Place potatoes in a large pot and add enough water to cover. Bring to a boil on high heat and cook 20–25 minutes, or until fork-tender. Drain and allow to cool in a large bowl, adding mayonnaise, eggs, onion, celery, relish, pimentos, salt, and pepper. Mix well until combined. Cover and chill.

Heart & Soul

Olive Macaroni Salad

1 (8-ounce) box macaroni, boiled
2 tomatoes, peeled and diced
1 (4-ounce) can sliced black olives
2 stalks celery, cut small
Garlic salt to taste

Salt and pepper to taste
Chopped pimentos, enough for color
¼ pound sharp cheese, grated
Onion, grated
Mayonnaise

Drain macaroni and dry on a towel. Mix with all other ingredients, adding onion and mayonnaise to taste. Let it sit overnight or from morning until night. Makes a large bowl.

Sherman Didn't Burn Our Recipes, Bartow's Still Cooking

Broccoli Salad

2 heads broccoli
12 slices bacon
1 tablespoon sugar
1 tablespoon vinegar

1 cup mayonnaise
1 cup raisins
1 medium onion, diced

Wash broccoli and dry completely. Separate into very small pieces. Cook bacon in microwave so it will be very crisp; cool; break into small pieces. Mix sugar and vinegar into mayonnaise. Toss broccoli, bacon, raisins, and onion with mayonnaise mixture. Chill before serving.

Bread of Life–Salem Baptist Church

Broccoli Slaw Salad

½ cup sugar
½ cup white vinegar
½ cup canola oil
2 (3-ounce) packages beef-
  flavored ramen noodles,
  flavor packets reserved

1 (16-ounce) package broccoli
  slaw
½ cup sliced almonds
½ cup sunflower seed kernels
1 (15-ounce) can Mandarin
  oranges, drained

In large resealable plastic bag, combine sugar, vinegar, oil, and reserved beef flavor packets, shaking well to mix. Add broccoli slaw, shaking well to coat with dressing. Break ramen noodles apart by hand into bite-sized pieces over broccoli slaw. Shake well to mix noodles and slaw with dressing. Refrigerate for at least 6 hours, shaking the bag occasionally to mix the salad. Just before serving, transfer salad to a serving bowl. Add remaining ingredients; toss well to mix. Makes 8 servings.

Note: If broccoli slaw is not available, you can substitute cabbage slaw with similar results. It must be made at least 6 hours before serving, so plan accordingly.

The One-Armed Cook

Shrimp Salad

1 pound shrimp, coarsely
  chopped
½ cup chopped celery
3 tablespoons finely chopped
  onion
2 hard-cooked eggs, peeled
  and chopped

1 tablespoon lemon juice
2 tablespoons chives
Salt and pepper to taste
½ cup mayonnaise

Toss shrimp, celery, and onion together. Add eggs together to blend; fold in lemon juice and chives; add salt and pepper. Add just enough mayonnaise to bind mixture together. Chill until ready to serve, 3–4 hours or overnight. May be served on a bed of lettuce, open-face on slices of French bread, or with rye bread as sandwiches. Makes 4 servings.

The Gingerbread House Cookbook

Crunchy Chicken Salad

An unexpected combination of flavors and textures.

DRESSING:

2 (3-ounce) packages chicken-
flavored ramen noodles
¾ cup vegetable oil

⅓ cup white vinegar
¼ cup sugar

Combine contents of seasoning packets from ramen noodles, oil, vinegar, and sugar in a bowl and mix well.

SALAD:

1 (12-ounce) package broccoli
slaw
1 Red Delicious apple, cored
and sliced
1 cup sunflower kernels
1 cup sweetened dried
cranberries or raisins

1 bunch green onions, chopped
1 red bell pepper, chopped
1 cup slivered almonds
1 rotisserie chicken, boned
and chopped

Combine broccoli slaw, apple, sunflower kernels, dried cranberries, green onions, bell pepper, almonds, and chicken in a large bowl. Add dressing and toss to coat. Crumble ramen noodles and add just before serving. Toss to mix. Serves 8.

Par 3: Tea-Time at the Masters®

Curried Chicken Salad with Chutney

The perfect luncheon dish

¾ cup chutney
1¼ cups mayonnaise
1½ teaspoons curry powder
3 teaspoons grated lime peel
⅜ cup fresh lime juice
¾ teaspoon salt
6 cups cooked and diced white
chicken meat

1½ cups pineapple chunks
¾ cup chopped green onions
¾ cup slivered almonds,
toasted
⅛ cup currants
Green or red leaf lettuce

Combine first 6 ingredients, mixing well. Combine in a bowl, chicken, pineapple, onions, almonds, and currants. Pour mayonnaise mixture over chicken and toss lightly. Serve on lettuce leaves. Serves 6–8.

A Southern Collection: Then and Now

Miniature Chicken Salad Puffs

PUFF PASTRIES:

Butter for greasing baking
  sheets
1 cup water
8 tablespoons butter

¼ teaspoon salt
1 cup flour
4 eggs

Preheat oven to 400°. Lightly grease 2–3 baking sheets. Combine water, butter, and salt in saucepan. Heat to a boil; stir to combine. Remove from heat. Add flour all at once. Stir vigorously with wooden spoon until mixture leaves side of pan and sticks to spoon. Set aside and cool for 2–3 minutes. Add eggs, one at a time, beating well after each addition. Drop mixture by rounded teaspoonfuls onto prepared sheets. Leave 2-inches between puffs. Bake for 10 minutes. Reduce heat to 350° and bake an additional 12–15 minutes, until golden brown and rigid to touch. Slit puffs in the side. Pull out insides and discard. Fill with Salad and garnish.

SALAD:

4 cups cooked chopped chicken
4 tablespoons chopped green
  olives
4 tablespoons chopped ripe
  olives
1 cup chopped celery

1 cup toasted chopped almonds
4 tablespoons salad pickles
4 hard-cooked eggs, chopped
1½ cups mayonnaise
1 tablespoon cooking sherry

Combine all ingredients. Fill Puff Pastries with Salad. Garnish with slices of green and ripe olives and fresh parsley. Makes 36 servings.

Our Favorite Recipes

Gainesville has a city ordinance (just for fun) against eating their delicious local fried chicken with a knife and fork.

Dixie Cornbread Salad

1 (6-ounce) box cornbread mix
1 (12-ounce) package bacon
3 large tomatoes, diced
1 large Vidalia onion, diced
1 large bell pepper, diced
½ cup sweet pickle relish
½ cup sweet pickle juice
1 cup mayonnaise (or to taste)

Prepare cornbread according to package directions. Cool; crumble into very small pieces. Cook bacon, drain and crumble or chop. In large glass bowl, layer ½ cornbread, ½ tomatoes, ½ onion, ½ pepper, ½ bacon, ½ sweet pickles, and sweet pickle juice. Top with a thin layer of mayonnaise. Repeat layering until remaining ingredients are used. To make salad more attractive, save a little of each ingredient (except mayonnaise) to garnish the top.

Bread of Life–Salem Baptist Church

Pears and Toasted Pine Nuts on Mixed Baby Greens

3 cups mixed baby greens,
  washed and spun dry
1 ripe pear, sliced
¼ cup pine nuts, toasted
4 ounces crumbled blue cheese
3 scallions, chopped
½ red pepper, sliced very
  thinly
2 tablespoons balsamic vinegar
6 tablespoons extra virgin
  olive oil
1 tablespoon honey
1 clove garlic, chopped
1 teaspoon Dijon mustard
Salt and freshly ground black
  pepper to taste

Combine the first 6 ingredients in a large bowl; set aside. Mix together the next 7 ingredients and drizzle over the salad mixture; toss to coat evenly.

Note: To toast pine nuts, place nuts in a shallow saucepan over high heat; toss continuously for about 1 minute; nuts will become lightly browned.

Tried & True Recipes from Covington, Georgia

Buttermilk Sky Salad

1 (20-ounce) can crushed
  pineapple, drained
2 (3-ounce) boxes gelatin
  (peach is best)

2 cups buttermilk
1 (8-ounce) carton whipped
  topping

In a saucepan, bring pineapple and gelatin to a boil; cool. Add buttermilk; chill until consistency of unbeaten egg white. Fold in whipped topping. Spoon into large dish; chill until firm.

Special Treasures

Congealed Salad

A Thanksgiving tradition; good replacement for cranberry sauce.

2 (3-ounce) packages black
  cherry Jell-O
2 cups boiling water
1 (16-ounce) can dark pitted
  cherries

1 (20-ounce) can crushed
  pineapple
Nuts for topping (optional)

In a square glass dish, mix Jell-O with boiling water; stir until dissolved. Add cherries and pineapple with juices. Refrigerate till congealed.

Heritage Cookbook

Jellied Cabbage Salad

4 (¼-ounce) envelopes gelatin
3 cups cold water, divided
½ cup white wine vinegar
4 tablespoons lemon juice
1 teaspoon salt
3 dashes red pepper
2 cups finely sliced cabbage,
cut in ¾-inch lengths

½ cup finely diced onion
½ cup finely diced celery
½ cup finely diced green bell
pepper
6 ounces sliced pimentos,
slightly chopped and drained

In small bowl, stir gelatin into 1 cup cold water until soft. Set bowl in larger bowl of warm water until gelatin is well dissolved. In large bowl, mix vinegar, lemon juice, the remaining cold water, salt, pepper, and dissolved gelatin. Put mixture in refrigerator until it begins to set, 45 minutes to 1 hour. Stir in cabbage, onion, celery, green pepper, and pimentos.

Lightly wipe the inside of 2-quart mold with a little vegetable oil, or use 2 (1-quart) molds. Pour the mixture into the mold(s) and smooth top surface. Place mold(s) in the refrigerator for several hours, or overnight, until salad is firm. When ready to eat, unmold on lettuce leaves and serve with mayonnaise (preferably homemade). Serves 16–18. Can make half the recipe to serve 6–8.

Note: A ring mold with the mayonnaise in a small bowl in the center makes an attractive presentation.

A Traveler's Table

 An itinerant stonecutter traveling through the north Georgia hills in 1835 noticed an outcropping of particularly fine marble. The small quarry he founded near the present site of Jasper was the first exploitation of a vein estimated to be large enough to supply the world's building needs for 3,000 years. The town hosts the Georgia Marble Festival each year during the first full weekend of October.

Coleslaw Soufflé Aspic

Southern Foodways Alliance "Coleslaw Award" finalist.

1 (3-ounce) package lemon
   gelatin
1 cup boiling water
½ cup cold water
2 tablespoons vinegar
½ cup mayonnaise
¼ teaspoon salt

Dash of white pepper
2 cups finely chopped cabbage
½ cup finely chopped celery
2 tablespoons minced green
   pepper
1 tablespoon minced onion

Dissolve gelatin in boiling water. Add cold water, vinegar, mayonnaise, salt, and pepper. Beat well until thoroughly blended; chill. When slightly thick, whip until fluffy. Add remaining ingredients. Pour into molds; chill. Serves 6–8.

The South's Legendary Frances Virginia Tea Room Cookbook

Congealed Apricot Salad

2 (3-ounce) boxes apricot Jell-O
2 cups hot water
1 cup small marshmallows
1 (20-ounce) can crushed
   pineapple, drained, save juice

2 bananas, diced
1 cup chopped pecans

Mix Jell-O with hot water. Stir in marshmallows until melted. (Heat on stove if necessary.) Combine crushed pineapple, bananas, and pecans with Jell-O. Put in refrigerator to set.

TOPPING:
1 egg, well beaten
1 tablespoon flour
½ cup sugar

2 tablespoons butter
1 (2.6-ounce) box Dream Whip

Beat egg; add flour, ½ cup saved pineapple juice, sugar, and butter. Cook mixture until thick, stirring constantly. Let cool in refrigerator overnight if possible, or until cold. After Jell-O and topping have cooled, prepare both envelopes of Dream Whip as directed and fold into Topping mixture; beat again. Spread Topping on Jell-O mixture.

A Gift of Appreciation

Peach-y Peaches

Peaches were first grown in Georgia during the 1700s. After the Civil War, Georgia peach growers developed superior new varieties, which boosted the commercial peach industry, and led to Georgia being dubbed the Peach State. The peach became Georgia's official state fruit in 1995.

PEACH SELECTION TIPS:
- Smell the peach. The peach is a member of the rose family and should have a pleasingly sweet fragrance.
- Look for a creamy gold to yellow under-color. The red or "blush" of a peach is an indication of variety, not ripeness.
- Peaches should be soft to the touch but not mushy.
- Look for a well-defined crease that runs from stem to point.
- Don't squeeze peaches; they bruise easily.
- Place firm peaches on the counter for a day or two to ripen.
- Promptly refrigerate ripe peaches and eat them within a week.
- To peel a peach, dip it into boiling water for 30 seconds, then into cold water. The peeling should slide off easily.
- To keep sliced peaches from darkening, add lemon juice.

HOW TO PLANT A PEACH PIT:
- After you have eaten the peach, clean the pit and store it in the refrigerator until September or October.
- Place the pit about five inches beneath the soil surface.
- Your tree will begin to grow in the spring.
- Keep the tree watered and fertilized and you'll have fruit in 2–3 years.

PHOTO © GEORGIA DEPARTMENT OF ECONOMIC DEVELOPMENT

Known as the sweetest onion in the world, Vidalias can only be grown in the fields around Vidalia and Glennville. The Vidalia onion was officially designated the state vegetable of Georgia in 1990.

Blue Willow Inn's Famous Fried Green Tomatoes

The Blue Willow Inn's Fried Green Tomatoes are legendary, having put the newly opened restaurant on the map shortly after a visit from famed columnist Lewis Grizzard in 1992. Following his visit, Grizzard authored a column in which he raved about the Blue Willow Inn Restaurant and the food it served—especially the Fried Green Tomatoes. Following the national publicity the restaurant received from Grizzard's column, Fried Green Tomatoes became a delicious Blue Willow tradition, and they are always served at every meal with a side of Tomato Chutney (page 93).

3 green tomatoes	1 teaspoon black pepper, divided
1½ cups buttermilk	1 tablespoon plus 1½ cups
2 eggs, lightly beaten	self-rising flour, divided
1 teaspoon salt, divided	2 cups vegetable oil

Wash and slice tomatoes into ¼-inch slices. In medium bowl, mix buttermilk and eggs. Add ½ teaspoon salt, ½ teaspoon pepper, and 1 tablespoon flour; mix well. Place tomato slices in the buttermilk and egg mixture. Set aside to rest.

Preheat oil to 350° in heavy skillet or electric fryer. In medium bowl, mix remaining flour, salt, and pepper. Remove tomato slices from buttermilk/egg mixture and toss, one at a time, in flour mixture, coating thoroughly. Carefully place tomato slices in heated oil and fry until golden brown; turn 2–3 times. Be careful not to crowd tomatoes during frying. Do not allow them to overlap or they will stick together. Cook until crisp. Drain on paper towels. Serve immediately. Makes 6 servings.

The Blue Willow Inn Bible of Southern Cooking

Fried Green Tomatoes with Remoulade

2 medium green tomatoes
1 tablespoon salt, divided
1 tablespoon freshly cracked
  black pepper, divided
2 cups panko (Japanese
  bread crumbs)

2 tablespoons paprika
1 cup chopped fresh
  parsley
4 eggs
2 cups all-purpose flour
2 cups vegetable oil

Slice tomatoes and sprinkle with salt and pepper. Combine panko, paprika, parsley, and remaining salt and pepper. Crack eggs in separate bowl, and put flour in another. Dip tomatoes into flour, shaking off excess—this is very important; dip into egg, letting excess drip off. Press tomatoes into bread crumbs, thoroughly coating both sides. Heat oil in skillet. When oil is hot, add tomatoes, frying on medium heat. Cook until golden on both sides. Drain on paper towels. Drizzle with Remoulade and serve with a fresh lemon slice. Serves 8.

REMOULADE:
¼ cup ketchup
1 cup mayonnaise
¼ cup chopped fresh
  parsley
2 teaspoons hot pepper sauce

1 medium shallot
2 tablespoons capers
2 teaspoons vinegar
1 tablespoon paprika
2 teaspoons lemon juice

Combine all ingredients in food processor. Blend until smooth. Refrigerate for 2 hours.

Fine Dining Georgia Style

Fried Green Tomatoes

2 medium green tomatoes,
   chilled
1 teaspoon Dijon mustard
1 teaspoon sugar
½ teaspoon salt

¼ teaspoon paprika
⅛ teaspoon ground red pepper
1½ teaspoons Worcestershire
½ cup yellow cornmeal
¼ cup hot bacon drippings

Cut tomatoes into ½-inch slices. Stir together mustard and next 5 ingredients. Spread on both sides of tomato slices. Coat with cornmeal. Fry tomato in hot drippings in a skillet over medium heat 3 minutes on each side or until browned; drain. Makes 4 servings.

Cooking with Watkinsville First Christian Church

Baked Tomatoes with Fresh Herbs

Use only fresh herbs for this recipe. Great with grilled chicken!

½ cup finely chopped fresh
   parsley leaves (Italian flat-
   leaf is best)
1 cup finely chopped fresh
   basil leaves

3 cloves garlic, minced
3 large ripe tomatoes
½ cup olive oil, divided
Salt and pepper to taste
¼ cup fine bread crumbs

Combine parsley, basil, and garlic in small bowl. Set aside. Peel and core tomatoes. Slice each tomato into 3 slices. Put a little olive oil in a shallow baking dish and grease the dish thoroughly. Lay tomatoes in the dish in a single layer. Sprinkle with salt and pepper. Distribute the herb-garlic mixture over the tomato slices. Sprinkle the bread crumbs over them; drizzle with the olive oil. Bake in a 450° oven for 10–15 minutes or until tops are golden brown. Serves 4.

Cooking with Herbs Volume I

The University of Georgia's main library houses the original Constitution of the Confederate States of America. It is on display once annually on April 26th, Confederate Memorial Day.

Jessie's Stewed Tomatoes

½ stick butter
1 (28-ounce) can peeled
  tomatoes
¾ cup chopped onion
2 teaspoons sugar

1½ tablespoons cider vinegar
¼ teaspoon ground allspice
1 teaspoon vanilla extract
Salt and black pepper to taste

In an iron skillet, melt butter, then add tomatoes; simmer until slightly thickened, about 30 minutes; add onion. Continue cooking until quite thick, 15–30 minutes. Add sugar, vinegar, allspice, vanilla, salt and pepper. Simmer another 10 minutes.

A Traveler's Table

Tomato Chutney

This recipe is served with every meal at the Blue Willow Inn Restaurant. It is delicious with fried green tomatoes, green beans, and cooked greens. It can also be used as an appetizer served with cream cheese and crackers.

1 (14-ounce) can whole
  tomatoes, chopped, not
  drained
1 cup firmly packed light
  brown sugar
½ cup granulated sugar
2 green bell peppers, finely
  chopped

1 medium onion, finely
  chopped
2 tablespoons ketchup
6 drops Tabasco
1 teaspoon black pepper

In a saucepan or small stockpot on medium heat, mix tomatoes, brown sugar, granulated sugar, bell peppers, onion, ketchup, Tabasco, and pepper. Bring to a boil. Reduce heat and allow mixture to simmer 2 hours or until cooked to a thick sauce. Makes 6 cups.

The Blue Willow Inn Bible of Southern Cooking

Callaway Gardens
Historical Timeline

1952: Gardens open on May 21 under the name of Ida Cason Gardens.

1953: Robin Lake Beach opens June 23, and is the world's longest man-made, inland white-sand beach.

1955: Ida Cason Gardens is renamed Ida Cason Callaway Gardens.

1956: The Gardens welcomes its one millionth visitor. (Today, approximately one million guests visit annually.)

1959: The Masters Water-Ski Tournament on Robin Lake begins.

1961: Ida Cason Callaway Gardens is renamed Callaway Gardens; founder Cason J. Callaway dies on April 12 at the age of 66.

1962: The 7.5-acre Mr. Cason's Vegetable Garden opens; the Ida Cason Callaway Memorial Chapel is dedicated.

1965: Mountain View and Sky View golf courses open.

1967: Callaway Education Department is established.

1968: Gardens View golf course opens.

1971: The Callaway School of Needlearts is established.

1972: Virginia Callaway establishes the 3,000-acre Cason J. Callaway Memorial Forest; the Meadowlark Garden opens.

1979: The Prunifolia Society was created to provide extra funding through donors.

1981: Construction of Mountain Creek Villas begins.

1984: The John A. Sibley Horticultural Center opens.

1985: The Steeplechase at Callaway Gardens begins.

1986: The Southern Garden Symposium begins.

1988: The Cecil B. Day Butterfly Center officially opens as the first and largest butterfly center in the world.

1989: The 10-Mile Discovery Bicycle Trail opens; a permanent Beach Dome is erected at Robin Lake Beach.

1990: Fantasy in Lights begins.

1995: Virginia Hand Callaway dies on February 11, just days before turning 95 years old.

1999: The Callaway Brothers Azalea Bowl opens; the Sky High Hot Air Balloon Festival begins.

2000: The Virginia Hand Callaway Discovery Center opens; the Daily Birds of Prey shows make their debut.

2002: Callaway Gardens changes its name to Callaway. Within this name fall The Gardens at Callaway, The Resort at Callaway, and The Preserve at Callaway.

Vidalia-Tomato Pie

6 medium tomatoes, peeled
  and seeded, divided
1 (5-count) can biscuits, or
  1 (9-inch) deep-dish pie shell
1 medium Vidalia onion,
  finely chopped, divided
½–1 teaspoon garlic powder,
  or to taste

1 teaspoon basil
Salt and pepper to taste
1 (8-ounce) package shredded
  Monterey Jack cheese
1 cup mayonnaise

Squeeze juice from tomatoes; drain in strainer for 30 minutes. Tear biscuits apart and press thinly in a pie plate to make crust, or use a deep-dish pie shell. Spread ½ onion and ½ tomatoes on crust. Sprinkle with spices. Top with remaining onion and tomatoes. Mix cheese and mayonnaise; spread on top. Bake at 400°, uncovered, 45 minutes or until lightly browned.

Note: The most important "to-do" in this recipe is squeezing the juice out of the tomatoes so the pie will not be soggy. Make 2 pies so you have some cold leftovers for snacks or a light meal!

Flavors of the Gardens

Open since 1952, Callaway Gardens is a world-famous 13,000-acre resort known for its azaleas. Each spring, the Callaway Gardens landscape explodes with the world's most beautiful display of over 20,000 azaleas, plus mountain laurel, dogwoods, daffodils, and daisies.

Okra and Tomatoes

3 slices bacon
2 pounds okra, sliced
1 medium green pepper,
  chopped

1 small onion, chopped
2 pounds fresh tomatoes,
  peeled and cubed
Salt and pepper to taste

Fry bacon until crisp; cook okra in drippings. Add pepper, onion, tomatoes, and crumbled bacon. Add salt and pepper. Cover and simmer 15 minutes. Serves 8.

Montezuma Amish Mennonite Cookbook I

Vidalia Onion Tart

PASTRY:
10½ tablespoons butter or
  margarine, chilled, chopped
2 cups plus 1 tablespoon flour

Salt to taste
¼ cup ice water

In a bowl, cut chilled butter into flour and salt until crumbly. Add ice water; mix lightly to form a dough. Chill for 2 hours or longer. Roll the dough ⅛ inch thick on a floured surface. Fit into a pie plate. Prick all over with a fork and set aside.

FILLING:
3 Vidalia onions, chopped
2 tablespoons butter or
  margarine
1 cup whipping cream
1 egg

1 egg yolk
Nutmeg
Salt and pepper to taste
Cumin seeds to taste

Sauté onions in butter in a skillet until tender. Add cream; cook until thickened and reduced to the desired consistency. Stir in egg and yolk. Season with nutmeg, salt and pepper. Spoon into prepared pie plate; sprinkle with cumin seeds. Bake at 400° on lower oven rack for 25 minutes or until set. Serves 6.

Guenter Seeger, Executive Chef
The Dining Room, The Ritz-Carlton, Buckhead
True Grits

Dixie's Vidalia Casserole

3–4 Vidalia onions, sliced thin
Butter for sautéing
1 (10¾-ounce) can cream of
   chicken or cream of
   mushroom soup, undiluted
½ soup can of milk

1 tablespoon soy sauce
Pepper to taste
¼ pound grated Swiss cheese
French bread, sliced, quartered
   and buttered

Heat oven to 350°. Sauté onions in small amount of butter until yellow and soft. Blend and heat soup, soy sauce, milk, and pepper. Place onions in ungreased 1½-quart shallow baking dish. Place grated cheese on top of onions; add soup mixture. Place quartered buttered bread on top. Bake uncovered 30 minutes. Serves 6.

Vidalia Sweet Onion Lovers Cookbook

Kickin' Chicken Fajita Stuffed Vidalia Onions

3 onions, peeled and halved
1 cup cooked, diced chicken
1 cup wild rice, cooked
¼ cup diced bell pepper,
   any color
½ cup black beans

1 tablespoon fajita seasoning
½ teaspoon salt
½ teaspoon minced garlic
¾ cup Mexican blend cheese
   with jalapeños, divided
6 Roma tomato slices

Remove center of onions, leaving 2 outer rings. Place a piece of onion in center to cover hole. Microwave 3 minutes. Mix together next 7 ingredients and ½ of cheese. Spoon into onions. Top with tomato; sprinkle with remaining cheese. Microwave until heated through and cheese is melted.

Georgia National Fair Blue Ribbon Cookbook

Over sixty years ago, farmer Mose Coleman discovered in the late spring of 1931 that the onions he planted were not hot, as expected—they were sweet! In the 1940s, word began to spread about the onions from Vidalia. Consumers, then, gave the onions their famous name.

Baked Stuffed Onions
or What Else Can You Do with Vidalias?

4 large, flat Vidalia onions, peeled
Weight Watchers butter-flavored spray
1 clove garlic, minced
1 teaspoon canola oil
1 teaspoon lemon juice
1 (10-ounce) package frozen chopped spinach, defrosted and squeezed dry
¼ teaspoon black pepper
¼ cup bread crumbs
¼ cup feta cheese, crumbled

Spray onions with butter spray. Place onions in microwave casserole and cover; cook on HIGH 10–12 minutes or until onions are tender. Cool; scoop out centers, leaving a 2- to 3-layer shell. Cut a small amount off bottom, if necessary, to keep flat. Chop centers. Toss centers with garlic; cook in microwave with oil for 2 minutes on HIGH. Stir in lemon juice, spinach, and pepper. Cook, uncovered, on HIGH for 3 minutes. Fold in bread crumbs and cheese. Mound spinach mixture into onions; place on plate. Cover with wax paper and microwave on MEDIUM power for 6–8 minutes, until heated through. Turn dish at least once. Let stand, covered, for 5 minutes.

Family Collections

The world's only double-barreled cannon was built in Athens, and is displayed on the grounds of City Hall. The prototype was a spectacular failure in test firings, so it was never used in combat.

Vidalia Onion Casserole

5 jumbo Vidalia onions
Salt and pepper to taste
14 Ritz Crackers, crushed,
   divided
1 stick butter or margarine,
   melted, divided

1 cup grated Parmesan cheese,
   divided
1 cup milk

Peel and slice onions in ⅝-inch-thick rings. Cook in boiling salt-ed water until half done; drain in colander. Butter an 8-inch-square casserole dish. Place ⅓ the onions in bottom, and sprin-kle with salt and pepper. Sprinkle with ⅓ crushed crackers; drizzle with ⅓ melted butter, and ⅓ of cheese. Repeat with two more layers. Sprinkle milk on top layer. Bake at 350° for 20–25 minutes.

Tried & True Recipes from Covington, Georgia

French-Fried Onions

Large white onions

Cut onions in half crosswise, then make slices ⅛ inch thick. Separate rings. Use only large ones. Put all rings in bowl. Cover with ice-water; let stand at least one hour. Drain on cloth. Dip in Batter.

BATTER:
1 cup flour
¼ teaspoon salt
¾ cup water

2 tablespoons salad oil
1 egg white, beaten stiff

Mix and sift dry ingredients; add water and oil. Fold in stiffly beaten egg white. Fry rings in deep fat until delicate brown, about 2 minutes.

What's Cookin'? in Winder, Georgia

Southern Baked Beans

1 pound dried navy beans	3 tablespoons molasses
6 cups water	¼ cup catsup
2 minced garlic cloves	1 teaspoon dry mustard
2 large onions, sliced	½ teaspoon ground ginger
1 small, dried, hot red pepper	1½ teaspoons Worcestershire
1 bay leaf	½ teaspoon salt
¾ pound sliced salt pork, or	¼ cup firmly packed brown
4 strips bacon	sugar

Cover beans with water and bring to a boil; boil for 2 minutes. Cover and let stand 1 hour. Add next 5 ingredients; cook until beans are tender. Drain; save 2 cups liquid. Add remaining ingredients, except sugar, to liquid. Place beans in a shallow 2-quart baking dish. Arrange slices of pork on top and add liquid. Sprinkle with brown sugar. Bake at 400° for 1 hour.

Puttin' on the Peachtree...

Barbecued Beans

1 pound ground beef	2 tablespoons vinegar
½ cup chopped onion	2 tablespoons Worcestershire
½ teaspoon salt	¼ teaspoon Tabasco
¼ teaspoon pepper	1 (16-ounce) can pork and beans
½ cup ketchup	

Brown ground beef, onion, and all remaining ingredients, except pork and beans, in frying pan. Pour pork and beans in a greased 1½-quart casserole dish; add other ingredients and mix well. Bake at 350° for 30 minutes.

The Day Family Favorites

 Located in Rome, Marshall Forest is the only natural forest within a city in the United States.

Hoppin' John

A traditional New Year's Day feast; peas for good luck, "greens" for money.

1 cup dried cowpeas or black-eyed peas	1 quart cold water
1 cup raw rice	1 teaspoon salt
½ pound slab bacon, or 1 ham hock	¼ teaspoon pepper
	⅛ teaspoon cayenne pepper
	Chopped onion

Wash and soak peas according to package directions. Cook rice according to package directions. Cut bacon or ham hock into small pieces and fry. Cook peas in 1 quart cold water, adding a little bacon grease. Add salt, pepper, and cayenne. Cook until peas are tender but firm, about 45 minutes. Approximately 1 cup of liquid should remain. Add cooked rice. Heat 2–3 minutes; serve. Garnish with chopped onion and drained bacon or ham. Serves 4–6.

Atlanta Cooknotes

New South Succotash

This makes an excellent accompaniment to grilled fish or chicken. The chicken gravy gives it depth and helps to bring the flavors together.

1 teaspoon olive oil	2 cups fresh spinach, washed, stemmed, and julienned
½ cup diced red onion	1 cup creamed chicken gravy
1 teaspoon minced garlic	½ cup chicken broth
½ cup diced red bell pepper	Salt and freshly ground black pepper to taste
1½ cups cooked, fresh, yellow corn kernels	
2 cups cooked butter beans	
20 large shrimp, peeled and deveined	

Heat oil in a heavy saucepan over medium heat. Add onion, garlic, bell pepper, and corn; sauté 2–3 minutes or until onion is translucent. Mix in beans. Add shrimp, spinach, gravy, and broth. Simmer and stir until shrimp are pink and begin to curl. Season with salt and pepper. Serve immediately. Serves 4.

First Come, First Served...In Savannah

Asparagus Soufflé

4 eggs, beaten
1 cup mayonnaise
1 teaspoon salt
1 (15½-ounce) can asparagus,
chopped

1 (10¾-ounce) can cream of
mushroom soup, undiluted
1 cup grated sharp Cheddar
cheese

Blend eggs in a large mixing bowl; add other ingredients, mixing well. Pour into a buttered casserole set in a pan of water. Cook in a 350° oven for 1 hour or until a knife inserted in the center comes out clean.

Glorious Grass

Asparagus in Mousseline Sauce

3 egg yolks
6 tablespoons water
¼ pound cold butter

1 teaspoon salt
1 (16-ounce) can asparagus tips

Whisk egg yolks, one by one, into water. Continue whisking until the whole thing is frothy. Bring to a heat just below boiling point. Whisk; lower heat, and whisk in butter and salt until sauce is thickened. Pour over the heated drained asparagus tips and serve in a silver dish.

Glorious Grass

Robert Tyre "Bobby" Jones, Jr. (born March 17, 1902, in Atlanta; died December 18, 1971) was arguably the greatest golfer who ever competed on a national and international level. He was a child prodigy who won his first children's tournament at the age of six, and made the third round of the U.S. Amateur Championship at fourteen. He hit his stride in 1923, when he won his first U.S. Open. He won thirteen major championships (as they were counted at that time) out of twenty attempts, ranking him only behind Jack Nicklaus. Jones was the first player to win "The Double," both the U.S. Open and the British Open in the same year. He is still the only player ever to have won the Grand Slam, or all four major championships in the same year. Jones is considered one of the five giants of the 1920s American sports scene, along with baseball's Babe Ruth, boxing's Jack Dempsey, football's Red Grange, and tennis' Bill Tilden. After his retirement from golf, Jones worked with A.G. Spalding & Co. to develop the first set of matched clubs, co-designed the Augusta National course with Alister MacKenzie, and was one of the founders of the Masters® Tournament, first played in Augusta in 1934.

Bacon-Wrapped Grilled Corn on the Cob

8 ears fresh corn with husks   **Butter**
8 slices bacon

Gently pull back husks, completely exposing attached kernels; do not remove the husks. Remove the corn silk, using a brush to make sure all the silk is removed. In a large pot filled with water, soak the corn for 30 minutes.

Preheat the grill to medium. Remove the corn from the water and pat dry. Take a slice of bacon and wrap it spiral-fashion around an ear of corn. Fold the husk back over the corn and bacon. Tie the husk with butcher string. Repeat the process for each ear of corn. Place the corn on the hot grill and cook, turning occasionally, until the bacon is cooked and the corn is tender, 15–20 minutes. The bacon will not be brown, which doesn't bother me one bit, but if it bothers you, gently pull the husks back and run the corn under the broiler for a few minutes until the bacon is brown. Serve with butter! Serves 8.

Paula Deen & Friends

LIBRARY OF CONGRESS, PRINTS & PHOTOGRAPHS DIVISION

Bobby Jones

Corny Fiesta Bake

1 (16-ounce) package frozen
　white cream-style corn
1 (16-ounce) package frozen
　yellow cream-style corn
1 (4-ounce) can chopped green
　chiles
1 cup sour cream
2 tablespoons taco seasoning
1 (8-ounce) package shredded
　Mexican blend cheese, divided

1 egg
½–1 teaspoon salt (optional)
1 teaspoon pepper
5 (6-inch) soft corn tortillas
3 tablespoons diced Italian
　plum tomatoes
3 tablespoons chopped green
　onions

Cook frozen corn as directed on package. Spray 2-quart soufflé or casserole dish with nonstick cooking spray. In large bowl, combine corn, chiles, sour cream, taco seasoning, 1 cup cheese, egg, salt, and pepper; mix well. Spoon ¼ of corn mixture into sprayed dish.

Heat oven to 350°. Stack 5 tortillas uniformly. Cut through stack in 3 wedges, making 15 wedges. Place 5 tortilla wedges evenly over corn mixture. Repeat layering with corn mixture and tortilla wedges, ending with corn mixture. Bake at 350° for 15 minutes. Top with remaining cheese. Bake an additional 10–15 minutes, or until cheese is melted and edges are bubbly. Sprinkle tomatoes and green onions around outer edge.

Georgia National Fair Blue Ribbon Cookbook

Impossible Garden Pie

Easy, light meal.

2 cups quartered and sliced
　zucchini
1½ cups diced tomatoes
½ cup chopped onion
½ cup grated Parmesan
　cheese

¼ teaspoon pepper
1½ cups skim milk
¾ cup Bisquick
3 eggs

Place layer of zucchini, tomatoes, and onion in a lightly greased 7x11-inch casserole. Sprinkle with Parmesan and pepper. Combine milk, Bisquick, and eggs. Beat until smooth, about 1 minute, and pour over vegetables. Bake at 400° for 30 minutes. Allow to sit 5 minutes before cutting. Makes 6 servings.

A Taste of Georgia, Another Serving

Squash Dressing

3 medium squash, cooked
 and drained
1 (6-ounce) package Mexican
 cornbread mix
1 medium onion, finely
 chopped
1 stick butter, softened
2 eggs
1 (10¾-ounce) can cream of
 chicken soup
Salt and pepper to taste

Mix all ingredients; bake in greased casserole at 350° until golden brown.

Tastes for All Seasons

Cajun Squash

3 pounds yellow squash,
 washed, unpeeled, thinly
 sliced
1 teaspoon salt
1 tablespoon dried onion
5 tablespoons butter or
 margarine, divided
¾ cup coarsely chopped
 onion
¾ cup chopped celery
½ cup chopped bell pepper
1 (10¾-ounce) can cream
 of celery soup
2 tablespoons chili sauce
1 tablespoon Worcestershire
½ teaspoon Tabasco
¼ teaspoon black pepper
¼ teaspoon seasoned salt
¼ teaspoon baking powder
½ cup grated Parmesan cheese
Seasoned or buttered bread
 crumbs

Combine squash, salt, onion, and 2 tablespoons butter in saucepan. Cook 15 minutes. Do not add water. Let cook in butter and its own juice. Makes about 3½ cups.

In heavy skillet, sauté onion in remaining butter until clear. Add celery and bell pepper. Cook until barely tender; mixture should be crunchy. Add cooked squash and remaining ingredients, except cheese and bread crumbs. Simmer mixture 3 minutes. Pour into buttered casserole dish. Sprinkle top with bread crumbs and cheese. Bake at 350° for 20–30 minutes. Freezes well. Makes 8–10 servings.

Our Favorite Recipes

Summer Squash Casserole

2 pounds (6 cups) sliced
  summer squash
¼ cup chopped onion
1 (10¾-ounce) can cream of
  chicken soup
1 cup sour cream
1 cup shredded carrots

1 (8-ounce) package herb
  seasoned stuffing mix
½ cup butter, melted
1 (2-ounce) jar chopped
  pimentos, drained (optional)
1 (5-ounce) can sliced water
  chestnuts, drained (optional)

In saucepan, cook squash and onion in boiling salted water for 5 minutes; drain. Combine chicken soup and sour cream with squash and onion; stir in shredded carrots. Combine stuffing mix and butter. Spread ½ of stuffing mixture in bottom of greased 9x13-inch casserole dish. Spoon vegetable mixture on top. Spread pimentos, then water chestnuts on top. Sprinkle remaining stuffing mixture over vegetables. Bake at 350° for 45 minutes until browned on top. Makes 6 servings.

Sherman Didn't Burn Our Recipes, Bartow's Still Cooking

Squash Pudding

1 medium white onion,
  chopped
6 yellow crookneck squash,
  washed and sliced
Boiling water
1 egg
1 cup evaporated milk

1 teaspoon dry mustard
Dash of Tabasco
1½ cups shredded extra sharp
  Cheddar cheese
Bread crumbs for topping
Butter for topping

Cook onion and squash in scant amount of boiling water until tender. Drain well. Beat egg and milk together. Add mustard and Tabasco to milk mixture. Combine squash and onion with milk mixture. Stir in cheese. Pour into a greased baking dish. Cover with a layer of bread crumbs and dot with butter. Bake at 325° until set.

Mountain Folk, Mountain Food

Spinach Balls

3 (16-ounce) packages frozen
   chopped spinach
¾ teaspoon thyme
2 onions, chopped
1½ tablespoons Ac'cent
3 cups Pepperidge Farm
   stuffing

8 eggs, beaten
¾ cup grated Parmesan cheese
1¼ cups margarine, melted
¾ tablespoon pepper
1¼ tablespoons garlic powder

Cook spinach according to directions; drain. Combine spinach with remaining ingredients. Refrigerate 30 minutes. Shape into bite-size balls. Bake 20 minutes at 350°. Serve warm. Makes 70 balls.

Note: These may be frozen on a cookie sheet then bagged. If frozen, thaw 1 hour before cooking.

At the End of the Fork

Carrot Soufflé

As served at Piccadilly Cafeteria.

1½ pounds carrots, sliced
½ cup butter, softened
1 large egg
¼ cup all-purpose flour
1½ teaspoons baking powder

¾ cup white sugar
¼ cup brown sugar
¼ cup ground cinnamon
⅛ cup half-and-half

Lightly grease a 1½-quart soufflé dish and set aside. Cook carrots in boiling water to cover for 15 minutes or until tender; drain.

Preheat oven to 350°. Combine carrots, butter, egg, flour, baking powder, sugars, cinnamon, and half-and-half in a mixing bowl and mix until smooth, scraping down the sides as needed. Spoon into the prepared dish. Bake 1 hour, or until set and lightly browned. Serve immediately.

Our Best Home Cooking

Broccoli with Almonds

2 (10-ounce) packages frozen
  broccoli, cooked and drained
½ cup mayonnaise
1 tablespoon lemon juice
½ cup shredded sharp
  Cheddar cheese

1 cup cream of mushroom soup
1 cup crushed cheese crackers
1 (2-ounce) jar chopped
  pimentos, drained
¼ cup slivered almonds

Place broccoli in buttered baking dish. Combine mayonnaise, lemon juice, cheese, and soup in bowl; mix well. Pour over broccoli. Top with cracker crumbs, pimentos, and almonds. Bake at 350° for 20 minutes or until heated through and bubbly. Serves 6.

From Our House to Yours

Broccoli Rice Casserole

2 cups cooked white rice
2–3 (10-ounce) packages frozen
  chopped broccoli, cooked
  and drained
1 (10¾-ounce) can cream of
  mushroom soup
1 (8-ounce) can sliced water
  chestnuts, drained

1 (8-ounce) can bamboo shoots,
  drained
1 (8-ounce) jar Cheez Whiz
½ cup butter, melted
1 (8-ounce) package grated
  Cheddar cheese
1 (2-ounce) jar pimientos,
  drained

Preheat oven to 325°. Combine all ingredients except Cheddar cheese and pimientos. Pour into a greased 3-quart casserole. Sprinkle cheese and pimientos over the top. Bake 30–40 minutes. Serves 8–10.

Atlanta Cooknotes

Okra Fritters

1 cup sliced okra
½ cup chopped onion
¼ cup flour
½ cup chopped tomatoes
¼ cup cornmeal
1 egg
Salt and pepper to taste

Mix all ingredients together. Salt and pepper to taste. Drop by spoonful into hot oil to fry.

Cooking with Watkinsville First Christian Church

Crustless Quiche - Broccoli or Spinach

1 (10-ounce) package frozen
  chopped spinach, or chopped
  broccoli
1 cup water
4 eggs
½ cup milk
Salt to taste
½ teaspoon pepper
¼–½ cup chopped onion
½ cup grated Parmesan
  cheese, divided
1 cup pitted ripe olives, halved
1 tablespoon margarine

Cook spinach or broccoli in water for about 6 minutes. Drain well. (We squeeze the spinach in our fist to get the water out.) Beat eggs in a medium mixing bowl; stir in milk, salt, and pepper; mix. Stir in main vegetable (broccoli or spinach), onion, ¼ cup Parmesan, and olives. Melt margarine in 8-inch frying pan, making sure it coats the bottom and sides so eggs will not stick. Pour in mixture and sprinkle top with remaining cheese. Cover and cook on low heat 15 minutes. Cut into wedges. Makes 3–4 servings.

Out On Our Own

Eli Whitney invented the cotton gin near Savannah in 1793. As a result, Georgia was the first state to grow cotton commercially, and the first to run a successful cotton mill.

Italian Potatoes

14–15 large red potatoes
  (about 5 pounds)
½ cup chopped fresh parsley
½ cup chopped green onions
3 large cloves garlic, thinly
  sliced

1 heaping teaspoon salt
½ teaspoon dry mustard
1 scant tablespoon sugar
1 tablespoon Worcestershire
1 cup olive oil
½ cup tarragon vinegar

Boil the potatoes until tender. When done, peel and cut in 1-inch chunks. Sprinkle parsley and green onions over the potatoes. Make the sauce by mixing the rest of the ingredients; pour over potatoes. Stir well. Let stand all day, or at least 4 hours. Stir every hour. Do not refrigerate. Serves 16.

The Lady & Sons, Too!

Crunch Top Potatoes

3–4 large potatoes, sliced thin
6 tablespoons butter
1 teaspoon salt
1 teaspoon pepper

1 teaspoon paprika
¾ cup crushed cornflakes
1 cup grated sharp Cheddar
  cheese

Place 1 layer only of potatoes in a 2-quart casserole. Pour melted butter over top, coating potatoes well. Add salt, pepper, and paprika. Top with cornflakes and cheese. Bake at 375° for about 30 minutes until done. Serves 4–6.

Traditions

Mander's Reunion Hash Browns

1 (32-ounce) package frozen
  hash browns
1 (10¾-ounce) can cream of
  chicken soup
Lots of grated Cheddar
  cheese

1 cup diced onion
½ cup sour cream
1 cup milk
½ stick margarine, melted,
  divided
Cornflakes

Mix everything together, except ½ the melted margarine and the cornflakes. Put into greased casserole dish. Top with cornflakes and remaining margarine. Bake at 350° for 45 minutes.

My Best to You

Jean's Garlic Mashed Potato Casserole

Tastes like twice-baked potatoes for a group. You can start with fresh or leftover mashed potatoes.

6–8 potatoes, peeled and cubed
Lite salt
¼ onion, roughly chopped
4–6 cloves garlic, peeled
½ cup light butter
Pepper, freshly ground

½ cup light sour cream
⅓ cup Southwestern Egg
  Beaters
2 teaspoons freshly chopped
  parsley, chives, and/or dill
1 cup shredded 3-cheese blend

Cut up potatoes and place in just enough water to cover; add 1 teaspoon salt, onion, and garlic; bring to a boil and simmer 20–30 minutes. Drain; add butter, more salt, and pepper to taste. Add sour cream, Southwestern Egg Beaters, and herbs; mix well. Pour into greased rectangular baking dish. Top with cheese; bake at 350° for 15–20 minutes or until cheese bubbles.

Tried & True Recipes from Covington, Georgia

Sweet Potato Snowballs

This is GREAT for the holiday season!

2 cups mashed sweet potatoes	**Dash of cinnamon**
¼ cup margarine, melted	**Dash of nutmeg**
2 eggs	**Dash of allspice**
½ cup evaporated milk	**1 (10-ounce) bag marshmallows**
¾ cup sugar	**1 (3½-ounce) can coconut**

Combine sweet potatoes, margarine, eggs, milk, sugar, and spices. Beat until smooth. Halve marshmallows and cover each half with potato mixture. Roll potato balls in coconut. Place on greased baking dish; bake at 350° until marshmallow is melted. Remove from baking dish with spatula.

Southern Manna

Sweet Potato Gratin

This is a delicious, elusive recipe from the caterer of our garden club's Christmas banquet some years ago. The manager finally agreed to give me their highly coveted recipe. Now that it is in my hands, I never intend to let it go. Of course, I have had to adapt the recipe from the chef's rendition.

1 large sweet potato, peeled	**½ teaspoon granulated garlic**
4 ounces brown sugar	**2 eggs**
4 ounces honey	**½–1 pint heavy cream**

Slice potato very thin; place some slices in bottom of buttered casserole dish. Sprinkle brown sugar and drizzle honey sparingly over potatoes. Sprinkle on some of the granulated garlic (or garlic salt). Layer again and again until all potatoes are used. Beat eggs lightly, combine with cream, and pour all over the potatoes. Put casserole dish in a pan of water and bake at 325° for about 1 hour or until potatoes test tender. Serves 6.

Eating from the White House to the Jailhouse

Sweet Potato Soufflé Crunch

3 cups cooked, mashed sweet
   potatoes
1 cup sugar
½ teaspoon salt

2 eggs, slightly beaten
2½ tablespoons butter, melted
½ cup milk
1 teaspoon vanilla

Mix all together and pour into a greased 9x13-inch baking dish.

CRUNCH:
2½ tablespoons butter, melted
1 cup brown sugar

⅓ cup flour
1 cup chopped pecans

Combine ingredients; cover soufflé with Crunch and bake at 350° for 45 minutes. Serves 6–8.

Montezuma Amish Mennonite Cookbook I

Miniature Mushroom Pies

A prepare-ahead dish.

PASTRY:
1 (8-ounce) package cream
   cheese, softened

1 cup margarine, melted
2½ cups flour

Combine cheese, margarine, and flour. Mix well, roll in plastic wrap, and chill.

FILLING:
3 tablespoons margarine
1 cup finely chopped onions
½ pound mushrooms, finely
   chopped
¼ teaspoon thyme

½ teaspoon salt
½ teaspoon pepper
2 tablespoons flour
¼ cup sour cream

Melt margarine in a frying pan and sauté onions. Add mushrooms; cook about 3 minutes; continue stirring. Add thyme, salt, and pepper. Sprinkle flour over mushrooms. Stir in sour cream; cook until thickened.

Roll chilled Pastry until ¼ inch thick. Cut in 2½- to 3-inch circles. Place ½ teaspoon Filling on each circle. Fold Pastry in half over Filling and press edges together with a fork. Make small slit in top for steam to escape or pierce with fork. Place in freezer. When ready to serve, place frozen pies on cookie sheet. Bake at 350° for 25–30 minutes.

Best of the Holidays

Cheesy Apples

1 stick butter
¼ pound Velveeta cheese,
  cut in chunks
1 cup sugar

¾ cup flour
2 (20-ounce) cans sliced apples,
  drained (not apple pie filling)

Melt butter, cheese, and sugar; stir well with whisk until smooth. Blend in flour until smooth. Pour apples into greased 2-quart baking dish. Pour cheese mixture on top. Bake 30–40 minutes at 350°.

Tried & True Recipes–Residents of Wild Timber

Honey-Lime Fruit Toss

1 (20-ounce) can pineapple
  chunks, drained, reserve
  ¼ cup juice
1 (11-ounce) can Mandarin
  oranges, drained
1 banana, sliced

Sliced strawberries
Sliced kiwi fruit
¼ teaspoon grated lime peel
2 tablespoons lime juice
1 tablespoon honey

Combine fruits and toss with reserved juice, lime peel, lime juice, and honey. Chill before serving.

At the End of the Fork

Mama Livia's Chow-Chow

1 peck (8 quarts) green tomatoes
  (2–3 ripe for color)
12 green bell peppers (2–3 red
  for color)
1 head cabbage

6 large onions
10 cups vinegar
Hot pepper to taste
Salt to taste
15 cups sugar

Grind vegetables and mix with all ingredients. In large stock-pot, cook on medium heat to dull green, 20–30 minutes. Put in pint jars and seal.

Cooking with Watkinsville First Christian Church

Golden Glow Ambrosia

1 (16-ounce) can peaches (halves or slices), drained
1 (16-ounce) can pears (halves or slices), drained
1 (20-ounce) can pineapple chunks, drained (reserve ¼ cup juice)
1 teaspoon lemon juice
1 apple, peeled and sliced
1 (6-ounce) jar maraschino cherries, drained
½ cup pecan halves
⅓ cup butter
¾ cup light brown sugar
2 teaspoons curry powder

Preheat oven to 325°. Arrange peaches and pears in bottom of baking dish sprayed with nonstick spray. Scatter pineapple chunks over peaches and pears. Arrange lemon juice-coated apples in dish. Blot cherries and scatter over other fruit along with pecans. Melt butter; stir in sugar, curry, and reserved pineapple juice. Heat and stir until sugar is dissolved. Pour over fruit and bake, uncovered, basting occasionally, for 45–60 minutes. Makes 12 servings.

Grandma Mamie Jones' Family Favorites

Thar's gold in them thar hills! Twenty years before the 1849 gold rush to California, thousands of gold seekers flocked into the Dahlonega area of northeast Georgia, beginning the nation's first major gold rush. Dahlonega is located on top of the largest gold deposits found east of the Mississippi River. Since 1828 when gold was first discovered, most of the gold that could be mined economically has been removed. In 1958, the citizens of Dahlonega presented the state with a gift of gold: the metal was pounded into thin sheets and attached to the Capitol dome in Atlanta. The gold dome remains as a lasting symbol to the first of our nation's gold rushes.

Lily Poole's Green Tomato Pickles

If you like it hot, add hot peppers.

1 gallon green tomatoes
6 onions
½ cup salt
1½ cups sugar
1 tablespoon celery seed

1 tablespoon horseradish
4 cups vinegar
1 tablespoon whole allspice
2 tablespoons peppercorns

Wash, drain, and slice tomatoes. Slice onions. Mix tomatoes and onions with salt. Let stand about 12 hours. Drain well. Add sugar, celery seed, and horseradish to vinegar in large stockpot. Put spices in cloth bag and add to vinegar mixture; boil 5 minutes. Cool slightly; add tomatoes and onions. Simmer 20 minutes; bring to a boil. Pack in hot jars and seal at once.

Give Us This Day Our Daily Bread

Lazy Woman Pickles

2 bell peppers, chopped
8 small white onions, chopped
1 gallon sliced cucumbers
½ cup plain salt (not iodized)
5 cups white sugar

5 cups cider vinegar
1½ teaspoons turmeric
½ teaspoon cloves
1 teaspoon celery seed

Mix vegetables with salt. Cover with ice; stir occasionally until ice melts; drain. Combine remaining ingredients in a kettle large enough to hold the vegetables and bring to a boil. Add vegetable mixture and mix well. Have ready plenty of clean, sterilized glass jars with lids. Fill jars with cucumbers and distribute pickling liquid among the jars. Seal while hot.

Mountain Folk, Mountain Food

PASTA, RICE, ETC.

PHOTO © GEORGIA DEPARTMENT OF ECONOMIC DEVELOPMENT

Martin Luther King, Jr. was born in 1929 on Auburn Avenue in Atlanta. This nine-room home that was owned by his grandfather, A. D. Williams, has been restored and is now one of the cornerstones of the Martin Luther King, Jr. National Historic Site.

Grandma Jo's Famous
Mac and Cheese

1 (8-ounce) box macaroni
1 stick butter
1 large egg
2 cups small curd cottage
   cheese (4% butterfat)

1 cup sour cream
½ cup half-and-half
1 teaspoon salt
2 cups shredded sharp Cheddar
   cheese

Cook macaroni according to directions, then drain and add butter; set aside. Mix egg, cottage cheese, sour cream, half-and-half, and salt. Add macaroni and cheese; mix well and place in buttered pan.

TOPPING:
½ stick butter, softened
1 sleeve Ritz Crackers, crushed

1 cup shredded sharp Cheddar
   cheese

Mix all ingredients; spread evenly over top of macaroni and cheese mixture. Bake at 350° for 45 minutes.

Culinary Classics

Mac and Cheese

Macaroni and cheese is another Blue Willow tradition and is found on the menu every day. It is one of our customers' favorite dishes.

1 (8-ounce) package macaroni
1 teaspoon vegetable oil or
   shortening
1 cup grated Cheddar cheese,
   divided
½ cup Cheez Whiz

¾ cup milk
2 eggs, beaten
1 tablespoon mayonnaise
½ teaspoon prepared mustard
Salt and pepper to taste

Preheat oven to 350°. In saucepan on medium heat, cook macaroni according to package instructions, adding oil or shortening to water. Do not overcook; drain.

In large bowl, combine macaroni, ¾ cup cheese, Cheez Whiz, milk, eggs, mayonnaise, prepared mustard, salt and pepper to taste. Bake in an ungreased, 9x12-inch casserole dish for 25–30 minutes. Remove from oven and top with remaining cheese. Return casserole to oven to melt cheese. Makes 8–10 servings.

The Blue Willow Inn Bible of Southern Cooking

Pimiento-Cheese Bake

2 cups grated Cheddar cheese
1 (4-ounce) jar chopped
    pimientos
1 tablespoon chopped onion

½ cup mayonnaise
12 slices white bread, trimmed
1 teaspoon oregano

Preheat oven to 350°. Mix cheese, pimientos, onion, and mayonnaise. Spread ¾ mixture on slices of bread, and roll up jelly-roll fashion. Place each roll in a 9x13-inch casserole. Spread remaining mixture over all and sprinkle with oregano. Bake 30 minutes or until melted and browned. Serves 6.

Atlanta Cooknotes

Cheesy Baked Ziti

1 (1-pound) box ziti pasta
1 cup chopped onion
2 garlic cloves, minced
1 (14½-ounce) can low-sodium
    diced tomatoes, drained
1 (15-ounce) container low-fat
    ricotta cheese
2 cups low-fat shredded
    mozzarella cheese, divided

¼ cup grated Parmesan
    cheese, divided
½ cup skim milk
⅓ cup chopped parsley
⅓ cup chopped fresh basil
    (optional)
¼ teaspoon salt
½ teaspoon black pepper

Prepare pasta according to package directions. Drain and set aside in large bowl. Spray a nonstick skillet with cooking spray; heat over medium heat. Add onion and sauté until tender, about 5 minutes. Add garlic and sauté 1 more minute. Remove from heat. Stir in tomatoes.

Place ricotta cheese, 1½ cups mozzarella cheese, 2 tablespoons Parmesan cheese, and milk in a food processor or blender. Process until smooth. Add tomato and cheese mixtures, parsley, basil, salt, and pepper to the cooked pasta. Toss well to combine. Spray a 2½- to 3-quart oblong baking dish with vegetable spray. Spoon the pasta mixture into the dish. Sprinkle with remaining mozzarella and Parmesan cheeses. Bake at 400° for 20 minutes, or until lightly browned.

A Gift of Appreciation

Louie's Chicken Spaghetti

This is from a Greek immigrant who made this delicious dish every week. It was a big favorite.

1 medium chicken, cut up
Flour
3 tablespoons olive oil
1 large onion, chopped
1 green bell pepper, chopped
1 tablespoon minced garlic
Garlic salt to taste
Pepper to taste

Oregano to taste
2 (14-ounce) cans stewed
  tomatoes, chopped
2 (17-ounce) jars spaghetti sauce
1 (6-ounce) can tomato paste
1 cup water
Hot cooked spaghetti noodles
Grated Parmesan cheese to taste

Coat chicken lightly with flour. Brown chicken in hot olive oil in a skillet on all sides. Remove chicken and place in a Dutch oven. Drain oil from skillet, reserving 1 tablespoon. Sauté onion, green pepper, and garlic in reserved oil until tender; spoon over chicken. Sprinkle with garlic salt, pepper, and oregano. Add stewed tomatoes, spaghetti sauce, tomato paste, and water; mix well. Simmer, covered, for 30 minutes, stirring frequently. Serve over noodles; sprinkle with Parmesan cheese. Yields 6–8 servings.

From Black Tie to Blackeyed Peas

Baked "White" Spaghetti

1 (12-ounce) box spaghetti
1 cup finely chopped onion
¼ cup finely diced green
  bell pepper
3 tablespoons canola oil
2 cloves garlic, minced
1 pound ground turkey
1 (16-ounce) can diced tomatoes,
  with liquid

1 teaspoon dried oregano
1 teaspoon salt
2 cups shredded mozzarella
  cheese, divided
4 tablespoons grated Parmesan
  cheese, divided
1 (10¾-ounce) can cream of
  mushroom soup
1 soup can of water

Cook spaghetti according to package directions. Drain well; set aside. In a large skillet, sauté onion and bell pepper in canola oil until onions are slightly translucent. Add garlic; stir-fry for 1 minute. Add ground turkey, stirring to crumble. Cook until meat is browned. Add tomatoes with liquid, oregano, and salt. Simmer uncovered over medium heat about 20 minutes, stirring occasionally.

Preheat oven to 350°. Place half of the cooked, drained spaghetti into a lightly greased 9x13-inch baking dish. Top with half the ground turkey mixture, spreading evenly. Sprinkle 1 cup mozzarella cheese over meat mixture, then sprinkle on 2 tablespoons Parmesan cheese. Repeat this layering process once more, ending with the remaining Parmesan cheese. Mix cream of mushroom soup and water in a separate bowl until smooth. Pour evenly over casserole. Bake uncovered for 30 minutes.

Collard Greens and Sushi

What is supposedly the world's largest peanut is in Turner County. This 20-foot tall peanut monument symbolizes the importance of the peanut in Georgia history. Another peanut statue is located in Plains; this one honors Jimmy Carter, and even boasts his grin.

Spicy Shrimp and Pasta Casserole

2 eggs
1½ cups half-and-half
1 cup plain yogurt
½ cup grated Swiss cheese
⅓ cup crumbled feta cheese
⅓ cup chopped fresh parsley
1 teaspoon crushed dried basil
1 teaspoon crushed dried
   oregano

1 (9-ounce) package angel hair
   pasta, cooked
1 (16-ounce) jar mild salsa, thick
   and chunky
2 pounds shrimp, cleaned,
   peeled, and deveined
¼ cup grated Monterey
   Jack cheese

Preheat oven to 350°. Grease an 8x12-inch pan or glass dish with butter. Combine eggs, half-and-half, yogurt, Swiss and feta cheeses, parsley, basil, and oregano in medium bowl; mix well. Spread half the pasta on bottom of prepared pan. Cover with salsa. Add half of the shrimp. Cover with Monterey Jack cheese. Cover with remaining pasta and shrimp. Spread egg mixture over top. Bake 30 minutes or until bubbly. Let stand 10 minutes. Serves 8.

The Lady and Sons Savannah Country Cookbook

Famous Georgians

A Sampling of Famous People Born in Georgia

(City, town, or county of birth noted in parentheses)

ENTERTAINMENT

Kim Basinger (Athens)
Ray Charles (Albany)
Charles Coburn (Macon)
Ossie Davis (Cogdell)
Melvyn Douglas (Macon)
Lawrence Fishburne III
  (Augusta)
Amy Grant (Augusta)
Oliver Hardy (Harlem)
Hulk Hogan (Augusta)
Doc Holliday (Griffin)
Miriam Hopkins (Bainbridge)
Holly Hunter (Conyers)
Harry James (Albany)
Stacy Keach (Savannah)
DeForest Kelley (Atlanta)

Gladys Knight (Atlanta)
Brenda Lee (Lithonia)
Blind Willie McTell (Thomson)
Johnny Mercer (Savannah)
Bert Parks (Atlanta)
Otis Redding (Dawson)
Jerry Reed (Atlanta)
Burt Reynolds (Waycross)
Little Richard (Macon)
Julia Roberts (Smyrna)
Billy Joe Royal (Valdosta)
Ray Stevens (Clarksdale)
Travis Tritt (Marietta)
Joanne Woodward
  (Thomasville)
Trisha Yearwood (Monticello)

SPORTS

Jim Brown (St. Simons Island)
Ty Cobb (Narrows)
Bill Elliott (Dawsonville)
Larry Holmes (Cuthert)

Bobby Jones (Atlanta)
Johnny Mize (Demorest)
Jackie Robinson (Cairo)
Herschel Walker (Wrightsville)

POLITICAL / LITERARY

Conrad Aiken (Savannah)
Erskine Caldwell (Moreland)
Jimmy Carter (Plains)
James Dickey (Atlanta)
Henry W. Grady (Athens)
Cora Harris (Elbert County)
Joel Chandler Harris (Eatonton)

Martin Luther King, Jr. (Atlanta)
Carson McCullers (Columbus)
Margaret Mitchell (Atlanta)
Flannery O'Connor (Savannah)
Dean Rusk (Cherokee County)
Clarence Thomas (Savannah)
Alice Walker (Eatonton)

Buckhead Rice

3 cups warm cooked rice
¼ cup butter or margarine,
  melted
4 eggs, beaten
1 cup milk
1 (16-ounce) package shredded
  sharp Cheddar cheese
1 (10-ounce) package frozen
  chopped spinach, cooked,
  drained

1 tablespoon chopped onion
1 tablespoon Worcestershire
½ teaspoon dried marjoram
½ teaspoon dried thyme
½ teaspoon dried rosemary
½ teaspoon salt

Combine rice and butter in a large bowl. Combine eggs, milk, and cheese in a medium bowl. Add spinach to egg mixture. Stir egg mixture into rice mixture; mix well. Add onion, Worcestershire, herbs, and salt; mix well. Spoon into a greased 2½-quart baking dish. Set inside a large pan with 2 inches warm water. Bake at 350° for 45 minutes or until set.

True Grits

May's Fried Rice

3 cups chopped ham or cooked
  chicken
¼ cup cooking oil
2–3 bunches green onions,
  chopped
Garlic powder to taste
½ cabbage, chopped

2 carrots, shredded
2 stalks celery, chopped
½ bell pepper, chopped
3 tablespoons soy sauce
  (enough to darken rice)
2 eggs, scrambled
4 cups rice, cooked and cooled

Sauté ham or chicken in oil in wok or large fry pan; add green onions and garlic powder; sauté as you add. Add all other vegetables. Sauté. Stir in rice until mixed in with vegetables; add soy sauce to mixture. Let fry for a few minutes; add scrambled eggs; serve.

Tastes for All Seasons

Pork Fried Rice

4 eggs, well beaten
1 teaspoon plus 2 tablespoons
vegetable or canola oil,
divided
½ cup diced onion
½ cup julienned carrots
¼ cup diced green bell pepper
1 cup diced lean pork (use
boneless pork chops)

2 cloves garlic, minced
2 teaspoons chicken bouillon
4 cups cooked, chilled, Japanese
short-grain rice (leftover rice
is best)
4 tablespoons soy sauce,
divided

In a wok over high heat, quickly scramble eggs in 1 teaspoon oil. Remove cooked eggs and set aside. Heat remaining oil in wok over high heat, and stir-fry onion, carrots, and bell pepper until onions are slightly translucent. Add pork and continue stir-frying until pork is cooked through, about 5 minutes. Add garlic and chicken bouillon and stir-fry for 1 minute. Add rice and incorporate all ingredients well. Add reserved scrambled eggs and mix well. Turn heat to low and sprinkle about 2 tablespoons soy sauce evenly over mixture; mix in quickly. Sprinkle with remaining soy sauce and mix once more. Remove from heat immediately and serve.

Note: You can use any meat or tofu in this dish. Feel free to add more soy sauce to your taste. When preparing the cooked rice for this dish, be sure not to overcook the Japanese rice or cook it with too much water, or it will get mushy when stir-fried. Japanese rice is a little stickier in consistency than regular long-grain rice.

Collard Greens and Sushi

Rice and Mushrooms

2 small onions, chopped
¼ cup chopped bell pepper
1 stick butter⁼
1 pound (2 cups) rice,
uncooked

1 (4-ounce) can sliced
mushrooms
1 (10-ounce) can beef consommé
2 soup cans water
1 cube beef bouillon

Sauté onions and pepper in butter. Mix all ingredients together and put in a greased 3-quart baking pan. Bake at 350° for 1 hour and 15 minutes. Makes 15 servings.

Montezuma Amish Mennonite Cookbook II

Cashew Rice Pilaf
with Baby Green Peas

1/3 cup chopped onion
1/4 cup butter
1 cup uncooked rice
2 cups chicken broth
1 teaspoon salt

1/3 cup frozen baby green
   peas, thawed
1/2 cup chopped cashews
1/4 cup chopped parsley

Sauté onion in butter until soft. Stir in rice until coated; add broth and salt. Cover and simmer 25–30 minutes until rice is tender and liquid is absorbed. Stir in peas, cashews, and parsley. Serve immediately. Makes 6 servings.

The Gingerbread House Cookbook

Savannah River Red Rice

1 cup tomato juice
1 1/2 cups chicken broth
2 tablespoons tomato paste
1/8 teaspoon cayenne
1/2 teaspoon salt
1/4 teaspoon white pepper

1/2 cup chopped onion
1/2 cup finely chopped celery
1/4 cup chopped green bell
   pepper
6 tablespoons olive oil
2 cups parboiled rice

Combine juice, broth, tomato paste, cayenne, salt, and pepper in a large oven-proof saucepan. Bring to a simmer. Sauté onion, celery, and green pepper in oil in a skillet until tender. Stir in rice, coating with oil. Add rice mixture to tomato mixture; mix well. Bring to a boil. Bake, covered, at 350°, or simmer, covered, for 20–25 minutes. Yields 6 servings.

Variation: May add 4 ounces hot, cooked sausage before baking.

From Black Tie to Blackeyed Peas

The S.S. *Savannah* was the first steamship to cross the Atlantic Ocean. The *Savannah* left the port of Savannah on May 22, 1819, and arrived in Liverpool, England, on June 20, 1819.

Spring Rolls

1 cup fine rice noodles or
   bean thread noodles
1 package spring roll
   wrappers (25 large)
1 cup julienned carrots
1 teaspoon salt
2 tablespoons canola oil

1 pound ground turkey, round,
   chicken, or pork
1 egg
3 tablespoons soy sauce
1 tablespoon coarsely ground
   sesame seeds

To soften rice noodles or bean thread noodles, soak in warm water for approximately 30 minutes; drain well; cut into small pieces with kitchen shears.

Carefully separate each spring roll wrapper, covering the stack with a damp paper towel to keep them from drying out. Sauté carrots and salt in oil until just wilted; set aside to cool.

Mix ground meat, noodles, egg, soy sauce, sesame seeds, and carrots in a large bowl. Take a spring roll wrapper and place one corner of the wrapper toward you. Spoon approximately 2 tablespoons of meat mixture onto each wrapper, evenly spreading across the length of the wrapper. Bring corner closest to you over the meat mixture, and roll about midway; bring the middle corners up over the meat mixture and roll to the end. Seal the end with water. Continue until all wrappers are used, keeping finished rolls covered with a damp paper towel.

Deep-fry about 5 spring rolls per batch over medium-high heat in about 1 inch of oil until lightly browned and crispy, about 3 minutes per side. Drain on paper towels. Serve with Spring Roll Dipping Sauce.

SPRING ROLL DIPPING SAUCE:

½ cup ketchup
¼ cup prepared yellow mustard
¼ cup rice wine or seasoned
   rice vinegar

1 tablespoon coarsely ground
   sesame seeds
¼ teaspoon sesame oil
¼ cup soy sauce

Mix all ingredients together and serve as dipping sauce for springrolls.

Note: There is no need to cook the meat before filling the wrappers. The spring roll wrappers are so thin that the oil goes right through them to cook the meat. You can find spring roll wrappers in the frozen section of your local Asian market. Bean thread noodles are thin, transparent noodles made from ground mung beans. Rice wine is also known as the Japanese beverage "sake."

Collard Greens and Sushi

Lazyman's Pierogi

½ pound bacon, or bacon bits
2 onions, chopped
½ pound chopped mushrooms,
   or 1 (4-ounce) can, drained
1 jar sauerkraut, drained

1 (10¾-ounce) can cream of
   mushroom soup
1 pound spiral noodles, cooked
   and drained well

Fry bacon and crumble. Fry onions and mushrooms; set aside. Rinse sauerkraut. Combine all together with mushroom soup and noodles in a large casserole dish. Bake at 350° for 45–60 minutes.

Family Collections

Pineapple Casserole

2 (20-ounce) cans pineapple
   chunks, drained
2 cups grated cheese
1 cup sugar

6 tablespoons flour
1 stick margarine, melted
1½ cups crumbled Ritz Crackers

Combine all ingredients except crackers. Pour into buttered casserole dish. Top with cracker crumbs. Bake at 350° for 30 minutes. Great to serve with baked ham.

Grandma Mamie Jones' Family Favorites

PHOTO © GEORGIA DEPARTMENT OF ECONOMIC DEVELOPMENT

At fifty miles long, the Chattooga River is one of the longest and largest free-flowing rivers in the Southeast. Its unspoiled wilderness is protected by its designation as a National Wild and Scenic River. The movie Deliverance *was filmed on the river in Rabun County.*

Rib Roast Supreme

1 tablespoon coarsely cracked
  black pepper
1 (2¼-pound) boneless rib
  roast or beef tenderloin
¼ cup chopped fresh flat-leaf
  parsley

1 tablespoon chopped fresh
  chives
1 tablespoon chopped fresh
  tarragon leaves
1 teaspoon dried thyme

Preheat oven to 425°. Rub pepper evenly over beef, pressing gently so pepper adheres. Chop fresh herbs using kitchen shears or herb grinder. On sheet of wax paper, combine fresh and dried herbs. Roll beef in herb mixture to completely coat. Loosely tie the beef at 2-inch intervals with kitchen twine. Place beef on roasting rack. Roast until thermometer registers 155° for medium, approximately 30 minutes; rare, thermometer should read 130°, well-done, 170°. Serves 6.

Cooking with Herbs Volume II

Brisket

1 tablespoon vegetable oil
1 (4- to 5-pound) brisket (not
  corned beef)
1 teaspoon salt, divided
1 teaspoon pepper, divided
2 teaspoons Hungarian paprika,
  divided

1 (10-ounce) package frozen,
  chopped onions
1 (28-ounce) can diced tomatoes
1 cup water
1 cup red wine

Preheat oven to 325°. In large Dutch oven over high heat, heat oil; brown brisket on the first side for 4 minutes. Sprinkle brisket with half the salt, pepper, and paprika. Turn brisket over and sprinkle with remaining salt, pepper, and paprika. Cook 4 minutes. Add remaining ingredients to pot. Cover, put in oven, and bake for 2½ hours. When serving, slice the brisket against the grain and pass the sauce. Serves 4.

The One-Armed Cook

Sally's Roast Tenderloin

A favorite at Augusta cocktail parties.

1 (5- to 8-pound) tenderloin roast
  (may use rib eye or any tender
  cut of roast)
Garlic powder to taste
Coarsely ground black pepper
  or lemon-pepper to taste
1½–2 cups soy sauce

½–¾ cup bourbon
Powdered horseradish
  (if available)
Bacon or salt pork (optional)
1 onion, sliced (optional)
1 bell pepper, halved (optional)

Wipe surface of meat with paper towel. Sprinkle entire surface with generous amounts of garlic powder and pepper. Place roast in 2 large plastic bags (double thickness). If large garbage-size plastic bags are used, roast can be turned easily by rotating bag. Add soy sauce, bourbon, and horseradish. Marinate at least 2 hours at room temperature or overnight in refrigerator.

Allow roast to come to room temperature before roasting. If roast is very lean, have butcher lard it or add strips of bacon or salt pork on top. Preheat oven to 450°. Put meat in open roasting pan with a rack. Pour marinade over roast and put onion and bell pepper in pan. Reduce heat to 400° and roast 35–50 minutes or until internal temperature reaches 135° on meat thermometer for a rare roast. Fresh mushrooms that have been sliced and sautéed may be added to liquid in pan and thickened slightly for gravy.

Tea-Time at the Masters®

Swiss Steak

½ cup flour
1 teaspoon salt
⅛ teaspoon pepper
3 pounds round steak
   (1½ inches thick)
1 tablespoon oil

6 potatoes, peeled
6 carrots, scraped
1 small onion, chopped
1 (14½-ounce) can tomatoes,
   drained

Mix flour and seasonings; pound well into meat. Heat oil in large pan with lid. Brown meat well in oil on both sides. Place potatoes, carrots, and onion around meat. Add tomatoes. Cover and cook over low heat 1½ hours.

Past & Present

Aunt Tency's Spanish Steak

1 large full-cut, round beefsteak
   (1–1½ inches thick)
Flour to dredge
Salt and pepper to taste
3 tablespoons bacon drippings

1 large onion, sliced in rounds
1 (14½-ounce) can diced
   tomatoes
Flour to thicken

Wipe meat with a damp cloth and slash fat to keep edges from curling up. Dredge steak in flour mixed with salt and pepper. In a large lidded iron skillet or Dutch oven, heat drippings; brown meat well on both sides. Pour off excess fat, leaving meat and browned bits in the pan.

Place onion rounds on top of meat. Pour tomatoes over all. Cover; cook in a 350° oven for an hour. If too soupy, remove meat to a warm platter and boil down the sauce, or thicken with 1–2 tablespoons flour stirred into a paste with cold water.

Mountain Folk, Mountain Food

Rachel and Rilla Porter were the daughters of the owner of the Porter House Restaurant in Flowery Branch, a settlement outside of Gainesville at the turn of the century. They handled the cooking, and their steaks made them famous with railroad men and salesmen from across the region who dropped by for a good meal. It was here that a new term, "porterhouse steak," became part of the English language.

Tex-Mex Steak and Onions

1/3 cup Worcestershire
1/4 cup white wine vinegar
1 tablespoon oil
3–4 garlic cloves, crushed
Salt and pepper to taste
Juice and rinds of 2 limes
2 pounds round steak
2 large Vidalia sweet onions,
 sliced in long thin strips

Flour tortillas
Extra Worcestershire
Extra lime juice
Guacamole for topping
Salsa for topping
Sour cream for topping
Shredded cheese for topping

In a small bowl, mix first 6 ingredients for marinade; soak meat and onions in marinade 1 hour or more, turning occasionally. Drain off marinade and throw away rinds. Put onions in foil or in a tin pie plate. Cook meat and onions on hot grill. While meat is cooking, sprinkle with extra Worcestershire and lime juice. Keep onions stirred so they won't burn. Cook until meat is done and the onions are fairly dry. If cooked in oven, use a pan with a rack; set the oven to 350°; cook for 30–45 minutes.

Slice meat into long thin strips, depending on size of flour tortillas used. Heat tortillas right before serving. Fill tortillas with meat and onions, then top with any of the following: guacamole, salsa, sour cream, and/or shredded cheese.

Note: To make small party-size tortillas, cut out small circles from large flour tortillas.

Vidalia Sweet Onion Lovers Cookbook

Baked Steak

1 round steak (venison or cube
 steak may be used)
Flour for coating
1/2 teaspoon salt

1 teaspoon lemon pepper
1 tablespoon Worcestershire
1 (4-ounce) can mushrooms
1/2 cup water

Cut steak in pieces, shake in flour to coat, arrange in 9x11-inch glass baking dish. Sprinkle with salt, lemon pepper, and Worcestershire. Pour mushrooms and liquid on top; add water. Cover with foil. Bake at 325° for 1 hour.

Main Street Winder

Easiest-Ever Pot Roast

4 cups water
1 (1-ounce) envelope onion
soup mix

1 (4-pound) 2-inch blade-cut
chuck pot roast

Combine water and onion soup mix in the bottom of a 9x12-inch roasting pan. Place roast in pan. Bake roast at 300° for 2½ hours; at 250° for 3¼ hours; or at 475° for 30 minutes and then 200° for 4½ hours. Serves 8–12.

Some Assembly Required

No-Peek Beef Tips

1 (1-ounce) package onion soup
mix
2 pounds lean stew meat

1 (10¾-ounce) can cream
mushroom soup
1 cup ginger ale

In a greased casserole dish, sprinkle onion soup mix over beef. Spoon mushroom soup over meat; add ginger ale. Do not stir. Bake covered at 350° for 2 hours. Don't peek. Serve over rice or noodles.

At the End of the Fork

The original Varsity restaurant was opened by Frank Gordy in 1928. The Varsity has become an Atlanta institution and there are now six sister locations. The downtown location, the world's largest drive-in, can accommodate 600 cars and over 800 people inside. On days when the Georgia Tech Yellowjackets are playing a home game, over 30,000 people are served. The Varsity has earned the distinction of serving the highest volume of Coca-Cola anywhere—it dispenses nearly three million servings of Coca-Cola annually.

Muffin Tin Meatloaf

1 pound ground beef
1 medium onion, chopped
1 bell pepper, chopped
1 egg
1 cup tomato paste

½ cup oatmeal or toast
   crumbs
Salt and pepper to taste
Ketchup for garnish

Mix all ingredients except ketchup and bake in muffin tins. Put a small amount of ketchup on top of each muffin. Bake at 350° for 20 minutes.

My Best to You

Meatloaf

2 pounds ground sirloin
1 onion, minced
1 green pepper, diced
¾ cup firmly packed brown
   sugar
½ cup crushed saltines
   (10–12)

2 eggs, lightly beaten
¼ cup steak sauce
3 tablespoons ketchup
1 teaspoon salt
½ teaspoon garlic salt

Mix all ingredients together. Shape into a loaf and place into loaf pan. Brush top with Mustard Sauce, then pour Tomato Sauce on top. Bake at 375° for 1 hour; let stand 15 minutes. Drain before serving.

MUSTARD SAUCE:
½ cup packed brown sugar   ¼ cup mustard

Stir together until smooth.

TOMATO SAUCE:
1 cup canned crushed
   tomatoes
1 (8-ounce) can tomato sauce

¼ teaspoon salt
¼ teaspoon garlic salt

Stir together until blended.

Red Oak Recipes

Barbecue Meatloaf

My husband asks for this meatloaf at least once a week! It is his very favorite meal.

1 pound extra lean ground sirloin	1 cup sweet, thick barbecue sauce (or ketchup), divided
½ cup dry bread crumbs	⅛ teaspoon garlic powder
¼ cup grated Parmesan cheese	1 teaspoon Worcestershire
1 large egg, slightly beaten	1 teaspoon parsley flakes
½ teaspoon salt	(optional)
¼ teaspoon pepper	

Preheat oven to 350°. Measure all ingredients (except ½ cup barbecue sauce for topping) into a mixing bowl. Mix together with your hands or a large spoon. Line a small, shallow baking pan with aluminum foil; lightly grease or coat with nonstick cooking spray. Make a free form loaf (9x4x2-inches) of the meat mixture in pan. Spread remaining barbecue sauce evenly over top of loaf. Bake 45–60 minutes or until done (meat thermometer should read 165°–170°). Remove from oven and cool slightly before slicing. Serves 4.

Confessions of a Kitchen Diva

Meat Roll Delight

Also excellent using venison.

2 eggs, beaten
1 cup soft bread crumbs
¾ cup tomato sauce
2 tablespoons chopped parsley
½ teaspoon oregano
¼ teaspoon salt
¼ teaspoon pepper

¼ teaspoon garlic powder
2 pounds ground beef
8 thin slices deli ham
1½ cups shredded
   mozzarella cheese
3 slices mozzarella cheese

Combine eggs, bread crumbs, tomato sauce, parsley, oregano, salt, pepper, and garlic powder. Stir in ground meat, mixing well. On wax paper, pat meat into 1 (12x10-inch) rectangle. Arrange ham slices on top of meat, leaving a small margin around edges. Sprinkle shredded cheese over ham. Starting from short end, carefully roll up meat, using paper to lift as you roll. Seal edges and ends. Place roll, seam side down, in a 9x13x2-inch pan. Bake in a 350° oven 55–60 minutes, or until done. Remove from oven and place cheese slices over top of roll; return to oven 3–5 minutes or until cheese melts. Serves 8–10 slices.

Delightfully Southern

Quick Ground Beef Casserole

1½ pounds ground beef
½ medium onion, chopped
2 (10¾-ounce) cans cream of
   chicken soup
1½ cans water

1 (16-ounce) package tater tots
1 teaspoon salt
¼ teaspoon pepper
1 cup grated cheese

Brown ground beef and onion; drain. Put in baking dish. Mix soup and water. Pour over ground beef; add salt and pepper. Add tater tots. Add grated cheese during last 10 minutes of cook time. Bake at 350° for 30–40 minutes.

Give Us This Day Our Daily Bread

Meat and Tater Pie

Pie pastry for 2-crust pie
1 pound ground beef
½ cup milk
½ envelope (3 tablespoons)
dry onion soup mix

Dash of pepper
Dash of allspice
1 (12-ounce) package loose
pack, frozen hash brown
potatoes, thawed

Line 9-inch pie plate with pastry. Brown ground beef; drain. Combine meat, milk, soup mix, pepper, and allspice; mix gently. Lightly pat into pastry-lined pie plate. Top with potatoes. Top off with second pastry crust; cut design in top. Bake at 350° for 1 hour or until browned.

Heritage Cookbook

Tamale Cornbread Pie

8 ounces extra lean ground
chuck
3 cups whole-kernel corn
2 cups canned tomatoes
1 cup finely chopped green
bell pepper
1 onion, finely chopped
1 tablespoon chili powder
1 teaspoon cumin

¼ teaspoon ground red
pepper
2 cups tomato juice
¼ cup unbleached flour
1½ cups cornmeal
1 tablespoon baking powder
¾ cup skim milk
2 eggs
2 tablespoons olive oil

Brown ground chuck in skillet, stirring until crumbly; drain. Stir in corn, tomatoes, green pepper, onion, chili powder, cumin, and ground red pepper. Add mixture of tomato juice and flour; mix well. Simmer, covered, over low heat for 5 minutes, stirring occasionally. Spoon into 9x13-inch baking dish.

Combine cornmeal and baking powder in bowl; mix well. Whisk milk, eggs, and olive oil in another bowl until blended. Stir into cornmeal mixture until mixed. Spread evenly over prepared layer. Bake at 425° for 20–25 minutes or until cornbread topping is cooked through. Makes 6 servings.

Simple Decent Cooking

Shepherd's Pie

1 pound lean ground beef
1 large onion, peeled and
   chopped
2 carrots, peeled and chopped
1 tablespoon flour
1 cup beef stock

1 tablespoon tomato purée
Worcestershire to taste
Salt and pepper to taste
1 pound potatoes, boiled and
   mashed (hot, with butter)

Brown ground beef and drain well. Add onion and carrots; cook until onion is translucent. Stir in flour; cook 1 minute. Gradually stir in stock and bring to boil, stirring constantly. Add tomato purée, Worcestershire, and seasoning. Cover pan, reduce heat, and simmer for 15 minutes. Remove from heat and put meat mixture into an oven-proof dish. Allow to cool a little before topping with mashed potatoes. Fluff potatoes with a fork to make an attractive finish. Bake at 425° for 20 minutes until the potatoes are browned. Serves 4.

It's the People; It's the Food

Tigereeny

This dish freezes well.

1 large onion, chopped
1 large green bell pepper,
   chopped
3 cloves garlic, chopped
2 pounds lean ground beef
2 teaspoons chili powder
Dash of Worcestershire
Salt and pepper to taste
1 (16-ounce) can tomatoes,
   or home canned

1 (16-ounce) can cream-style
   corn
1 (3½-ounce) can ripe olives
   with juice
1 (8-ounce) can tomato sauce
6–8 ounces shell macaroni,
   cooked
Cheddar cheese, grated

Sauté onion, pepper, and garlic in small amount of oil until clear; remove from pan. Brown ground beef, then drain, if necessary; add chili powder, Worcestershire, salt and pepper. Add sautéed seasonings, tomatoes, corn, olives, and tomato sauce. Add macaroni. Mix well and pour into casserole dish. Refrigerate overnight for flavors to marinate.

Bake at 350° for about 1 hour (if dish is cold). About 15 minutes before done, top with cheese and return to oven until cheese melts.

Red Oak Recipes

Bran and Beef Stroganoff

1 egg
½ cup milk
1¼ cups bran flakes cereal
½ teaspoon garlic salt
¼ teaspoon pepper
¼ teaspoon paprika
¾ pound hamburger
1 medium onion, chopped
1 tablespoon margarine

½ cup hot water
1 (4-ounce) can mushrooms, drained
1 beef bouillon cube
1 (10¾-ounce) can cream of mushroom soup
1 (8-ounce) carton sour cream
Cooked, buttered noodles

Beat egg, milk, bran flakes, garlic salt, pepper, and paprika. Let sit for 5 minutes. Add hamburger and shape into meatballs. Bake in oven on baking pan at 400° for 12 minutes or until browned. Meanwhile, in large frying pan, cook onion in margarine until tender. Stir in water, mushrooms, and bouillon cube; simmer several minutes. Add meatballs; continue simmering 15 minutes. Combine soup and sour cream; pour over meatballs. Just before serving, pour over noodles.

Montezuma Amish Mennonite Cookbook II

Six Layer Dinner

2 medium potatoes, thinly sliced
1 cup chopped celery
1 pound lean ground beef, browned

2 medium onions, sliced
1 green pepper, sliced
1 cup drained, canned tomatoes
Salt and pepper to taste

In order given, layer ingredients in greased, 2-quart baking dish. Season each layer with salt and pepper. Bake, covered, at 350° for 1 hour. Makes 6 servings.

Main Street Winder

Sausage and Rice Casserole

1 pound mild ground sausage
2 cups uncooked rice
1 (10¾-ounce) can cream of
   chicken soup
2½ soup cans water
1 (1-ounce) envelope dried
   onion soup mix

Brown sausage and drain. Add other ingredients and bake in greased casserole dish 1 hour at 425°.

Grandma Mamie Jones' Family Favorites

Sausage and Vegetable Medley

1½ pounds smoked sausage
   links
1 cup uncooked rice
1 (14½-ounce) can chicken
   broth
1 (16-ounce) package frozen
   mixed vegetables (broccoli,
   red peppers, corn)
1 (4-ounce) can mushrooms,
   undrained
1½ tablespoons onion soup
   mix
Salt and pepper to taste
½ cup grated Cheddar cheese

Precook sausage and cut in 1½-inch pieces. Combine sausage with rice, chicken broth, mixed vegetables, and mushrooms. Add onion soup mix, salt and pepper; mix to season. Cover with foil and bake at 350° for 45 minutes or until rice is done. Remove foil, top with grated cheese, and bake until cheese melts.

Southern Manna

 On April 18, 1998, Athens hosted the largest CD release party in history: local band Widespread Panic gave a free concert that attracted almost 100,000 music fans. Athens is world-renowned for its music scene, and nurtured such bands as REM, the B-52s, Widespread Panic, Drivin' and Cryin', and Pylon, just to name a few.

Southern Pork Barbecue

1 (5- to 6-pound) pork roast,
shoulder or Boston butt

Season pork with Barbecue Dry Rub, if desired. Light fire in smoker. When coals are ashen, add hickory or oak chips that have been soaked in water for an hour and then drained. Add wood chips onto the mound of coals every hour for first 4 hours of grilling. Add more charcoal as needed. Keep temperature at 325°–350°. Place pork, fat side up, on grill over a drip pan, away from fire, or place pork on a rack in an aluminum pan on grill. Lower cover on grill to seal in smoke flavor. Barbecue until nicely browned and cooked through, 4–6 hours, or longer, until internal temperature reaches 195° and meat is tender. You can shorten the cooking time by wrapping roast in foil the last few hours.

Move cooked pork to a clean cutting board and cover meat with foil until cool enough to handle. Pull pork into pieces; discard skin, fat, and bones. With fingers or fork, pull into shreds about 2 inches long and ¼-inch wide (or you can also finely chop pork with a cleaver). Put pulled pork into a metal or foil pan and stir in some of the Vinegar Barbecue Sauce, enough to keep meat moist and flavorful. Cover with foil, and place on grill to keep warm until time to serve. Serve with additional Vinegar Barbecue Sauce.

BARBECUE DRY RUB:

2 tablespoons salt	2 tablespoons chili powder
2 tablespoons sugar	4 tablespoons paprika
2 tablespoons ground cumin	1 tablespoon garlic powder
2 tablespoons ground black pepper	1 teaspoon cayenne pepper
	½ teaspoon dry mustard

Combine and rub on the pork roast before placing on the grill.

VINEGAR BARBECUE SAUCE:

1 cup vinegar	½ teaspoon crushed red pepper
½ cup water	
¼ cup ketchup	2 tablespoons brown sugar
1 onion, sliced thin	½ teaspoon pepper
1 large garlic clove, minced	½ teaspoon salt

Bring all ingredients to a boil over high heat. Reduce heat to low, and simmer 10 minutes or until reduced to 1 cup. Serve over barbecue pork.

Our Best Home Cooking

Chef's Glazed Spareribs

BASIC RUB FOR BARBECUE:

½ cup kosher salt
½ cup granulated sugar

½ cup ground black pepper
½ cup paprika

Mix the rub in a bowl.

3 slabs spareribs
Basic Rub for Barbecue

Bourbon Mop
Bourbecue Sauce

The night before you barbecue, apply the rub evenly to ribs, saving about half of the spice mixture. Place ribs in plastic bag or wrap in plastic and place in refrigerator overnight.

Before beginning to barbecue, take ribs from refrigerator and pat them down with remaining rub. Let sit at room temperature for 30–40 minutes. If using oven, preheat to 200°. Place each slab of ribs in separate piece of heavy-duty foil. Wrap 2 sides together and wrap one end tightly so no juices escape. Open up the other end so as to pour in the Bourbon Mop, making sure that there is enough for each slab. Then roll end up so that none spills. Put in baking pan and cook for 3–4 hours until meat can easily be pulled from bones. Reserve juices and pour into saucepan. Add Bourbecue Sauce, baste ribs, and place in oven for 10–15 more minutes. Serve with remaining sauce. Serves 6.

BOURBON MOP:

¾ cup bourbon
¾ cup cider vinegar

½ cup water

Mix thoroughly and use to mop your favorite meat.

BOURBECUE SAUCE:

1 (16-ounce) bottle barbecue
 sauce (your favorite)

½ cup bourbon

Mix together and use with Chef's Glazed Spareribs.

Bread of Life–Chef Curtis Watkins

Cranberry Pork Roast

1 (2½- to 3-pound) boneless,
  rolled pork loin roast
1 (16-ounce) can whole
  cranberry sauce, mashed
½ cup sugar
½ cup cranberry juice cocktail

1 teaspoon dry mustard
¼ teaspoon ground cloves
2 tablespoons cornstarch
2 tablespoons cold water
Salt to taste

Place roast in a slow cooker. Combine cranberry sauce, sugar, cranberry juice, dry mustard, and cloves in a medium bowl; mix well. Pour over roast. Cook, covered, on LOW for 6–8 hours or until roast is tender. Remove roast; keep warm. Skim the fat from the liquid. Add enough water to liquid to measure 2 cups. Pour into a saucepan. Bring to a boil over medium-high heat. Mix the cornstarch and cold water in a small bowl to make a paste. Stir into the mixture in the saucepan to make a gravy. Cook until thickened, stirring constantly. Add salt to taste. Slice roast and serve with gravy.

Mother's Finest: Southern Cooking Made Easy

Pork Chop Casserole

1 (15-ounce) can fancy mixed
  Chinese vegetables
1 (10¾-ounce) can cream of
  mushroom soup
1 (6-ounce) box Uncle Ben's
  Wild and Long Grain Rice

1¼ cups water (or more)
8 pork chops (more or less
  as desired)
Black pepper to taste

Mix Chinese vegetables, soup, rice (both packages in box), and water together in greased casserole dish. Place pork chops on top; sprinkle with pepper. Bake uncovered at 350° for 1 hour and 20 minutes. (Add more water, if necessary.)

Note: Can use chicken instead of pork chops, if desired.

Down Through the Years

Quick Draw's
Ham and Sweet Potatoes

6 medium sweet potatoes
½ teaspoon salt
3 tablespoons butter or
    margarine
⅛ teaspoon pepper
⅛ teaspoon nutmeg
Milk
2 cups diced, cooked ham

1 (8-ounce) can pineapple
    chunks, drained, reserve juice
½ cup green pepper strips
2 tablespoons brown sugar
1 tablespoon cornstarch
2 tablespoons vinegar

Cook and mash sweet potatoes; add salt, butter, pepper, nutmeg, and enough milk to whip potatoes. Pan-fry ham in butter until golden brown. Add pineapple and green peppers. Cook 3 minutes. Combine sugar and cornstarch; blend in reserved pineapple juice and vinegar. Cook, stirring constantly, until clear and thickened. Pour mixture in shallow casserole dish. Drop spoonfuls of whipped sweet potatoes on top. Bake at 400° for 20 minutes, or until thoroughly heated. Serves 4–5.

Wanted: Quick Draw's Favorite Recipes

Atlanta's cyclorama, *The Battle of Atlanta,* is a large cylindrical painting measuring 42 feet high and 358 feet long. It vividly depicts the Civil War battle atop Leggett's Hill in Atlanta, which took place on July 22, 1864. The painting is now displayed in Grant Park.

Flavored Butter for Meats

GREEN PEPPERCORN BUTTER:

1½ tablespoons green
  peppercorns, drained
1 stick butter, softened
⅛ cup dry white wine

½ tablespoon tarragon
Juice of ¼ lemon, or to taste
⅛ teaspoon salt, or to taste

Blend all ingredients by hand. Store covered in refrigerator.
Serve with chicken, duck, or broiled meats.

MUSTARD BUTTER:

1 stick butter, softened
1–2 tablespoons Dijon mustard

2 tablespoons minced fresh
  parsley, or mixed herbs

Blend all ingredients by hand, blender, or food processor. Store
in refrigerator. Serve with kidneys, liver, steaks, or broiled fish,
or use to enrich sauces or soups.

TARRAGON BUTTER:

1 stick butter, softened
1 tablespoon lemon juice

2–3 tablespoons fresh tarragon
  (dry, if fresh is not available)

Blend all ingredients by hand, blender, or food processor. Store
in refrigerator. Serve with broiled meats and fish, or use to
enrich sauces or soups.

Puttin' on the Peachtree...

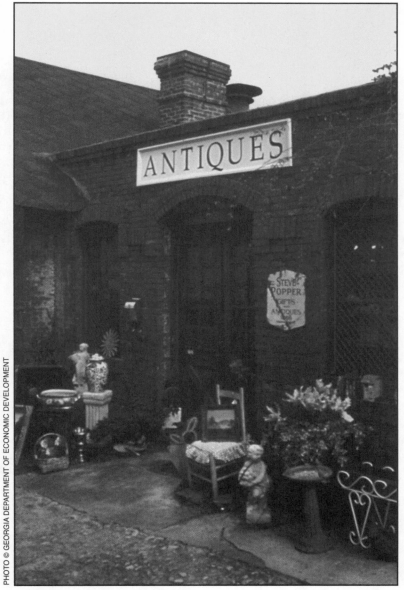

PHOTO © GEORGIA DEPARTMENT OF ECONOMIC DEVELOPMENT

Georgia's Antiques Trail includes shopping in twenty beautiful communities in Georgia's Historic Heartland travel region, where you'll find delightful shopping venues offering a wide range of goods from unique collectibles to the finest in period antiques.

Annabell's Batter-Fried Chicken

1 egg, beaten
1 cup water
1 cup all-purpose flour
1 teaspoon garlic salt
1 teaspoon savory salt
¼ teaspoon pepper

1 heaping tablespoon baking
  powder
Vegetable oil for deep-frying
1 fryer chicken, cut up and
  patted dry

In a bowl, combine egg and water; beat well. Add flour; stir until smooth. Add salts, pepper, and baking powder; blend well. Mixture should foam when baking powder is added. Place oil in a deep pot or deep-fat fryer; heat to 375°. Dip chicken pieces in batter. Deep-fry a few pieces at a time approximately 20–25 minutes until browned. Drain on paper towels on wire racks. Keep chicken warm. If chicken is not completely cooked, bake in a preheated 325° oven about 20 minutes. Chicken can be deep-fried in the morning and crisped in the oven for 30 minutes before serving. It can also be frozen, thawed, and crisped. Decant oil after frying and store for future use. Serves 4.

Atlanta Cooknotes

Buttermilk Fried Chicken

1 (2- to 3-pound) broiler or
  fryer chicken, cut up
1 cup buttermilk
1 cup all-purpose flour

1½ teaspoons salt
½ teaspoon pepper
Cooking oil for frying

Place chicken in large flat dish. Pour buttermilk over chicken; cover and refrigerate for one hour. Combine flour, salt, and pepper in a double-strength paper bag. Drain chicken pieces; toss, one at a time, in flour mixture. Shake off excess; dry on wax paper. Heat ¼ inch of oil in large skillet. Fry chicken until browned on all sides. Cover and simmer, turning occasionally, for 40–45 minutes or until juices run clear and chicken is tender. Uncover and cook 5 minutes longer.

Special Treasures

Simply Delicious
Southern Fried Chicken

The southern specialty! Mrs. Smith, wife of a past chairman of the National Broiler Council Board, has perfected this recipe after many years of close association with poultry and the poultry industry.

Salt
6 chicken breast halves, or
   3½ pounds assorted chicken
   pieces, or 1 pound chicken
   livers, halved

1 cup buttermilk
2 cups self-rising flour
1 teaspoon lemon-pepper
   seasoning
Oil for frying

Lightly salt chicken to taste. Place buttermilk in shallow dish, and place flour on wax paper. Dip each piece of chicken into buttermilk, sprinkle with lemon-pepper, and roll in flour, coating well; shake off excess flour. Heat 2-inch depth of oil in large skillet to 350°. Place chicken, a few pieces at a time, in oil. (Take care to add extra chicken pieces slowly enough that oil temperature does not drop below 325°.) Cook until chicken is crisp and richly browned, turning once. Drain well on absorbent toweling. To keep hot, hold in warm oven. Serves 6.

Perennials

The Ivan Allen, Jr. Braves Museum and Hall of Fame features more than 500 Braves artifacts and photographs that trace the team's more than 130 years of history from Boston (1871–1952) to Milwaukee (1953–1965) to Atlanta (1966–present). Some of the museum's most popular items on display include the bat and ball Hank Aaron used to hit his record-breaking 715th home run; the dugout bench from Atlanta-Fulton County Stadium; the 1995 World Series trophy; and an actual railroad car like the team traveled in for road trips through the 1950s.

Honey Pecan Fried Chicken

6 cups buttermilk
10 boneless, skinless chicken
   breasts, pounded ½ inch
   thick
2½ cups self-rising flour
1½ teaspoons salt

¾ teaspoon garlic powder
½ teaspoon cayenne pepper
2 cups butter
1 cup honey
1 cup chopped pecans
Vegetable oil

Pour buttermilk into a large bowl. Add chicken, cover, and refrigerate 1–2 hours. Combine flour, salt, garlic powder, and cayenne pepper in shallow dish. Drain chicken and dredge in flour mixture, shaking off excess. Let chicken stand 20 minutes at room temperature. Melt butter in a small heavy saucepan over low heat. Stir in honey, and bring to a boil. Add pecans and simmer 15 minutes. Add oil to a large heavy skillet, ½–¾ inch in depth. Heat oil to 375°. Add chicken; fry, in batches, about 7 minutes on each side or until golden brown and cooked through. Drain on paper towels. Arrange chicken on a serving platter. Pour honey glaze on top and serve immediately. Serves 6–8.

First Come, First Served...In Savannah

Chicken Rolls

4 boneless chicken breasts
3 ounces cream cheese, sliced
   thin
4 pieces ham, sliced thin

4 pieces Swiss cheese, sliced
   thin
4 pieces bacon

Flatten chicken between pieces of wax paper. Layer with cream cheese topped with ham and Swiss cheese, then roll. Wrap piece of bacon around roll. Place in greased baking dish and bake at 350° for 1 hour.

CHEESE SAUCE:

½ stick butter
1 (10¾-ounce) can cream of
   mushroom soup

1 soup can of milk
1 cup grated cheese
Pepper and garlic salt to taste

Melt butter in small saucepan over medium heat. Add soup and milk. When warm, add cheese, drippings from rolls, and pepper and garlic salt to taste. Heat through. Serve over chicken rolls.

Heart & Soul

Chicken Savannah!

1 egg
1½ cups bread crumbs
½ teaspoon garlic powder
¼ teaspoon pepper
6 chicken breasts, boneless
and skinless
¼ cup margarine
1 (14-ounce) can artichoke
hearts, drained, cut into
quarters
12 small new red potatoes

1 (6-ounce) jar mushrooms,
drained
1 (10¾-ounce) can cream of
mushroom soup
2 cups sour cream
½ cup dry white wine
2 tablespoons tarragon
¼ cup grated Parmesan
cheese
Paprika to taste

Beat egg in a shallow dish. Combine bread crumbs, garlic powder, and pepper in a shallow dish and mix well. Dip chicken in beaten egg. Dredge in bread crumb mixture. Brown chicken on both sides in margarine in a skillet. Remove chicken and place in a 9x13-inch baking dish.

Arrange artichokes, potatoes, and mushrooms around chicken. Add soup, sour cream, wine, and tarragon to pan drippings and mix well. Pour over chicken and vegetables. Sprinkle with Parmesan and paprika. Bake, covered, at 350° for 45 minutes. Yields 6 servings.

From Black Tie to Blackeyed Peas

Visitors can enjoy a historic tour of Savannah by trolley, revealing over 270 years of rich southern history and hospitality.

Angel Chicken

6 chicken breast halves,
  skinless and boneless
  (about 1½ pounds)
¼ cup butter
1 (10¾-ounce) can golden
  mushroom or cream of
  mushroom soup

½ (8-ounce) tub cream cheese
  with chives and onions
1 (0.7 ounce) package dry Italian
  salad dressing mix
½ cup dry white wine
Hot cooked angel hair pasta

Cut each chicken breast half into 2–3 pieces. Place chicken in a crockpot. Place butter, soup, and cream cheese in a microwave-safe bowl. Microwave on 50% POWER 2–3 minutes, until ingredients soften. Add salad dressing mix and wine; stir to combine. Pour over chicken. Cover and cook on LOW 3–4 hours. Serve chicken and sauce over hot cooked pasta.

Tried & True Recipes–Residents of Wild Timber

Mexican Chicken Casserole

6 chicken breasts, skinned,
  boned, and cut into bite-size
  pieces
Olive oil for sautéing
1 medium pepper, sliced
1 medium onion, chopped
1 (8-ounce) package sliced
  mushrooms

16 ounces tomato sauce
Taco sauce to taste
1½ cups cooked white rice
¼ cup shredded Monterey Jack
  cheese, divided
¼ cup shredded Romano cheese,
  divided

Sauté chicken in olive oil; add pepper, onion, and mushrooms. Add tomato sauce. Add taco sauce to taste. Spread cooked rice on bottom of greased 9x13-inch baking pan; top with half the Monterey Jack and Romano cheeses. Cover with chicken mix; top with remaining cheeses. Bake at 350° for 30 minutes. Serves 6.

It's the People; It's the Food

Sesame Chicken Skewers

½ cup honey
¼ cup ketchup
¼ cup sesame oil
2 cloves garlic
¼ cup sliced green onions
1 tablespoon peeled and
   minced fresh ginger

¾ cup soy sauce
4 skinless, boneless breast
   halves, cut into 4-inch strips
14 wooden skewers (soaked in
   water for 30 minutes)
2 tablespoons sesame seeds

Purée honey, ketchup, sesame oil, garlic, green onions, and ginger in processor until smooth. With machine running, gradually add soy sauce; blend until smooth. Mix chicken with ½ cup of the dressing in zipper bag, and marinate for 1–2 hours. Reserve remaining sauce for dipping. Thread chicken onto skewers and sprinkle with sesame seeds. Grill skewers over medium high heat until chicken is cooked through, about 3–5 minutes per side. Serve with dipping sauce.

Tried & True Recipes–Residents of Wild Timber

Berry College near Rome has the largest campus of any college in the world—close to 30,000 acres. Founded by Martha Berry in 1926, the college was one of several "Berry Schools" that were established to provide poor children in the north Georgia mountains with the opportunity to earn an education. Though the other schools have long closed, the college continues to enjoy a reputation as a respected regional institution.

Sour Cream Chicken Enchiladas

These enchiladas are so delicious and easy, you will never have to order them out again.

5 tablespoons butter or
   margarine, divided
1 medium onion, chopped
   (1 cup)
½ cup chopped green bell
   pepper
2 cups chopped, cooked chicken
1 (4-ounce) can chopped green
   chiles

¼ cup all-purpose flour
1½ teaspoons coriander
¾ teaspoon salt
2½ cups chicken broth
1 (8-ounce) carton sour cream
1½ cups shredded Monterey
   Jack cheese, divided
12 (6-inch) flour tortillas
Salsa for garnish (optional)

Preheat oven to 350°. Melt 2 tablespoons butter in a large skillet. Sauté onion and bell pepper until limp. Remove from skillet and combine with chicken. Add green chiles; set aside. In the same skillet, melt remaining butter; blend in flour, coriander, and salt. Cook over medium-high heat 1 minute, stirring constantly. Slowly stir in chicken broth; bring to a boil; cook until thick and bubbly, stirring constantly. Remove from heat and stir in sour cream and ¾ cup cheese. Stir 1 cup of sauce into chicken mixture. Dip a tortilla into remaining sauce. Spoon ¼ cup chicken mixture on top ⅓ of tortilla. Fold top of tortilla over filling; fold in sides and continue rolling tortilla to totally encase filling. Place seam side down in a lightly greased 9x13-inch baking dish. Repeat with remaining tortillas and filling. Pour any remaining sauce over tortillas. Cover pan with aluminum foil and bake 20 minutes. Remove foil, sprinkle with remaining cheese, and return to oven for 5 additional minutes or until cheese is melted. Serves 6.

Confessions of a Kitchen Diva

Each year Georgia hosts the largest poultry convention in the world, the International Poultry Trade Show. Chickens are the largest agricultural commodity in the state, accounting for almost $2.5 billion in income each year (2002). The state of Georgia is designated as the Poultry Capital of the World.

Chicken Elegante

This chicken dish makes a delicious cream sauce. Complete the meal with a crisp salad and cooked rice.

6 boneless, skinless chicken breasts
1 teaspoon salt
½ teaspoon pepper
2 tablespoons butter or margarine
1 small onion, diced (½ cup)
1 clove garlic, crushed (½ teaspoon)
1 (8-ounce) package sliced mushrooms

½ cup dry white wine (or substitute chicken broth)
1 (10¾-ounce) can cream of chicken soup
1 (8-ounce) container sour cream
2 tablespoons chopped green onion tops or chives (optional)

Pound chicken between 2 sheets of plastic wrap until ½-inch even thickness. Season with salt and pepper. Heat a large skillet over medium-high heat; melt butter. Add chicken breasts; brown (chicken does not have to be cooked all the way through). Remove chicken to a 9x12-inch baking dish that has been lightly greased or coated with a nonstick cooking spray.

Add onion to same skillet and sauté until clear and limp. Stir in garlic and cook for an additional minute, being careful not to burn. Add mushrooms and cook until mushrooms release their liquid. Add wine or broth; stir, scraping the bottom of the pan to release any browned bits. Remove pan from heat; stir in soup and sour cream until mixed thoroughly. Pour sauce mixture over chicken. Cover with aluminum foil and bake at 350° for 20–30 minutes until sauce is bubbly and chicken is done. Sprinkle with chopped green onion tops and serve. Serves 6.

Confessions of a Kitchen Diva

Chicken Casserole

Great for company or family.

2½ cups chicken broth
1 (7-ounce) package curry rice
1 medium onion, chopped
1 chicken fryer, cooked, boned
  and cubed
1 (16-ounce) can seasoned
  French green beans
1 (10¾-ounce) can cream of
  celery soup
1 (2-ounce) jar pimentos
1 cup mayonnaise
1 (8-ounce) can sliced water
  chestnuts

In medium saucepan, bring chicken broth to a boil; add rice and simmer for 20 minutes. Add onion to rice and cook 5 minutes longer. In large casserole dish, combine chicken, rice mixture, and remaining ingredients. Bake at 350° for 40 minutes.

Main Street Winder

Chicken Tetrazzini

1 large hen, or 2 whole chicken
  breasts
1 small onion, sliced thick
1 stalk celery with leaves
Salt to taste
1 (10¾-ounce) can cream of
  mushroom soup
1 (4-ounce) can mushrooms
1 (5-ounce) jar Old English
  Cheese
1 tablespoon Worcestershire
1 (8-ounce) package fine
  spaghetti
Reserved chicken stock
Buttered bread crumbs

Cover chicken with water. Add onion, celery, and salt. Cook until tender, about an hour (2 hours for hen); bone; set meat aside. Combine in saucepan, ¾ cup stock (may substitute some white wine for stock), soup, juice from canned mushrooms, cheese, and Worcestershire. Cook until smooth. Add mushrooms. Cook spaghetti in remaining chicken stock, adding bouillon cube and water, if not enough stock. Drain. Put ½ of spaghetti in a casserole dish; add ½ the chicken, and ½ the sauce. Repeat layers. Top with buttered bread crumbs. Cook 20–30 minutes in 350° oven. Serves 8.

Cook and Love It

Bobby's Chicken Pie with Self Crust

1 (3-pound) fryer (may use chicken breasts)
Salt and pepper to taste
Reserved 2 cups chicken broth
1 (10¾-ounce) can cream of celery
1 (15-ounce) can Veg-All
4 eggs, hard-boiled, sliced

Boil chicken in seasoned water until done. Cut into bite-size pieces. Save the broth. Combine 2 cups broth and soup in saucepan. Heat mixture until boiling. Stir to blend; add Veg-All. Place chicken pieces into lightly greased 9x13-inch casserole dish; add sliced eggs. Pour broth mixture on top. Add extra broth if needed to keep from being dry.

CRUST:
½ stick butter, melted
1 cup self-rising flour
1 cup milk
1 teaspoon pepper
½ cup mayonnaise or sour cream

Mix well and pour over chicken mixture. Do not stir. Bake at 350° for 30–45 minutes.

Red Oak Recipes

Always Requested Chicken Pot Pie

4 chicken breasts
1 cup sour cream
1 (10¾-ounce) can cream of chicken soup
1 (10¾-ounce) can cream of mushroom soup
2 (15-ounce) cans Veg-All
1 tablespoon Salad Supreme seasoning
Salt and pepper to taste
1 (2-crust) pack pie dough

Bake chicken breasts in oven at 350° for one hour. Remove chicken from oven and shred. Preheat oven to 425°. Mix together chicken, sour cream, soups, Veg-All, Salad Supreme, salt and pepper. Place one pie crust in the bottom of a 9-inch pie plate. Pour mixture into crust. Place second crust on top of mixture and seal around edges. Cut several slits in top of pie. Bake at 425° for 40–50 minutes or until crust is golden brown.

Georgia National Fair Blue Ribbon Cookbook

Iced Chicken Breasts

This recipe is one that makes the rounds quite often and is always mighty welcome when it does. I have served it many, many times—even carried it to Lake Sinclair one time to serve at a birthday luncheon on the screened porch of our cabin. I made a notation that I liked it better with Vidalia onions, fresh chives with the cream cheese, and ½ teaspoon curry. Anyway you do it—it is so good, and a wonderful summertime specialty.

4 whole chicken breasts, skinned, boned, and halved
2 (10½-ounce) cans chicken broth
1 (3-ounce) package cream cheese with chives, softened
¼ cup mayonnaise
2 tablespoons lemon juice
½ teaspoon grated lemon peel
¼ teaspoon salt

1 green onion with top, finely chopped
Crisp Bibb lettuce leaves
2–3 large tomatoes, peeled and chilled
Salt and pepper to taste
2 large avocados
½ cup toasted slivered almonds
Pitted ripe olives
Vinegar and oil dressing

Cook chicken breasts in broth until tender. Refrigerate in broth to cool. Thoroughly mix cream cheese, mayonnaise, lemon juice, lemon peel, salt, and onion. Remove chicken from broth. Completely coat the rounded side of each breast with the cream cheese dressing. Arrange lettuce leaves on 8 dinner plates. Cut tomatoes into 8 thick slices and place on lettuce; sprinkle with salt and pepper. Arrange a chicken breast on each tomato slice. Halve and peel the avocados; cut each into 4 slices and arrange beside chicken. Sprinkle chicken with toasted almonds and garnish with ripe olives. Serve with vinegar and oil dressing.

Eating from the White House to the Jailhouse

The locomotive engine popularly known as "The General" is housed in the Big Shanty Museum in Kennesaw. It was stolen in the Andrews Railroad Raid in 1862, and later depicted in *The Great Locomotive Chase*, a popular 1956 movie.

Chicken with Drop Dumplin's

1 (3- to 4-pound) chicken, cut up
2 stalks celery, diced
2 tablespoons chicken bouillon
  granules
1 bay leaf
8 cups water
2 cups all-purpose flour
4 teaspoons baking powder
1 teaspoon salt
¾ cup milk

½ cup chopped green onion
  tops
Pinch of cayenne pepper
½ cup chopped fresh parsley
¼ teaspoon freshly grated
  nutmeg
1 (10¾-ounce) can cream of
  chicken soup
Salt and pepper to taste

Place the chicken pieces, celery, bouillon, and bay leaf in a stockpot. Add the water and bring to a boil over medium-high heat. Reduce the heat and cook for 45–60 minutes, or until the chicken is tender. Remove the chicken and let it cool slightly. Pick the meat off of the bones, discarding the bones and skin; set aside.

Sift the flour, baking powder, and salt into a large bowl. Add the milk and mix well. Add the onions and cayenne; mix. Drop batter by tablespoons into the boiling broth until all the batter is used up. Gently shake the pot. (Never stir dumplings with a spoon, as this will tear them.) Add parsley and nutmeg; shake pot again. Cover, reduce the heat, and simmer gently for about 15 minutes without lifting the lid. While the dumplings are cooking, heat soup with 1 can water in a small saucepan. When the dumplings are done, carefully pour the soup into the dumpling pot. Shake the pot gently. Return the chicken to the pot and again shake the pot, this time in a rotating motion. Season to taste with salt and pepper. Serves 6–8.

The Lady & Sons, Too!

Grilled Thai Chicken Thighs

½ cup mango chutney
⅓ cup pineapple juice
⅓ cup soy sauce or tamari
¼ cup vegetable oil

½ teaspoon bottled, minced
  garlic
2 pounds boneless skinless
  chicken thighs (12–14 pieces)

Combine all ingredients, except chicken, in a blender container; blend until marinade is smooth. Transfer marinade to a large resealable plastic bag. Add chicken thighs; turn to coat with marinade. Refrigerate at least 1 hour or overnight, turning the bag occasionally.

When ready to cook, prepare the grill to medium heat. Place chicken on hot grill and cook 5 minutes on each side, or until desired doneness. Discard remaining marinade. Serves 8.

The One-Armed Cook

Thai Ground Chicken with Basil
Gai Pad Gra Pow

3 tablespoons peanut oil
4 cloves garlic, minced
2 green onion stalks, chopped
2 red chile peppers, seeded and
  finely chopped
1 pound ground chicken

¾ cup roughly chopped fresh
  basil leaves, loosely packed
1 tablespoon granulated sugar
2 tablespoons fish sauce
Steamed jasmine rice

Heat peanut oil in wok over high heat. Add garlic and green onions; stir-fry until onions are wilted, but not browned. Add peppers, stir-fry about 1 minute. Add chicken; fry until browned, stirring to crumble meat. Stir in basil, sugar, and fish sauce; mix well. Cook for about 5 more minutes. Serve over steamed jasmine rice.

Note: Fish sauce and jasmine rice can be found at most Asian markets. Many grocery super centers now carry a wide array of Asian staples as well.

Collard Greens and Sushi

Korokke
Japanese Meat and Potato Croquettes

4 medium white potatoes	Pinch of black pepper
½ medium onion, finely chopped	½ cup flour
2 tablespoons canola oil	2 eggs, beaten
½ pound ground turkey, or ground round	1½ cups panko (Japanese bread crumbs)
½ teaspoon salt	Canola oil for frying
	Shredded cabbage for garnish

Peel potatoes; cut into medium-sized chunks. Boil until soft, about 15 minutes. Drain potatoes in colander; mash well. Sauté onion in oil until slightly translucent. Add ground meat; sauté until browned (if using ground round, drain meat of any fat). Mix mashed potatoes with onion and meat in a large bowl. Add salt and pepper; mix well. Form oval shaped patties, approximately 3 inches long and ½ inch thick. Coat each patty lightly with flour on both sides, dip both sides in beaten egg, then coat each patty with panko. Set aside until all patties are coated. In 1 inch of oil, fry a few patties at a time over medium-high heat, approximately 3 minutes per side, until lightly browned. Drain on paper towels; serve over shredded cabbage.

Collard Greens and Sushi

Turkey Joes

3 tablespoons canola oil
¼ cup finely chopped onion
¼ cup finely chopped green
  bell pepper
1 clove garlic, minced
1 pound ground turkey
1 cup ketchup

2 tablespoons yellow mustard
2 tablespoons Worcestershire
3 teaspoons brown sugar
½ teaspoon garlic powder
1 teaspoon salt
6 hamburger buns

In a medium skillet, heat oil over medium-high heat. Add onion and bell pepper; sauté until onions are slightly translucent. Add garlic and stir. Add ground turkey, stirring to crumble. Continue to sauté until turkey is browned. Add remaining ingredients; mix well. Reduce heat, cover, and simmer for 30 minutes, stirring occasionally. Serve on hamburger buns.

Collard Greens and Sushi

Quail Paprika

10 quail
¾ cup flour
½ teaspoon salt
½ teaspoon black pepper
6 tablespoons butter
6 tablespoons finely chopped
  onion

1 tablespoon sweet paprika
¾ cup dry white wine
1 cup chicken or quail stock
½ cup sour cream
2 tablespoons lemon juice

Remove breast fillets and leg quarters from quail. (Use remaining portions of quail to make quail stock). Mix flour, salt, and pepper; dust breasts and legs lightly. Melt butter in frying pan over low heat and brown quail pieces lightly on both sides. Add chopped onion and sauté until onion starts to take on color. Sprinkle with paprika. Add wine and stock. Bring to a boil and stir up the browned bits from the bottom of the pan. Cover and simmer 5–10 minutes until quail are tender. If gravy is too thick, bring to desired consistency with a little water. Carefully blend in sour cream and lemon juice. Bring to a simmer, but do not boil. Serve promptly with wild rice or white rice.

Note: You can freeze this dish before adding sour cream and lemon juice. Thaw when ready to use; heat slowly, adding a little water, if needed. Carefully stir in sour cream and lemon juice. Bring to a simmer, but do not boil. Serves 6.

A Traveler's Table

SEAFOOD

PHOTO © GEORGIA DEPARTMENT OF ECONOMIC DEVELOPMENT

A drive along Georgia's coastline, which stretches approximately one hundred miles between South Carolina and Florida, offers the perfect opportunity to sample oysters, soft-shelled crabs, scallops, rock shrimp, catfish, hushpuppies, and Low Country boils.

Savannah Crab Cakes

1 pound crabmeat, picked free
   of shell
½ cup crushed Ritz Crackers
3 green onions with tops,
   finely chopped
½ cup finely chopped bell
   pepper
1 teaspoon salt
Dash of cayenne pepper

¼ cup mayonnaise
1 egg
1 teaspoon Worcestershire
1 teaspoon dry mustard
Juice of ½ lemon
¼ teaspoon garlic powder
Flour for dusting
½ cup peanut oil

Mix all ingredients together except flour and peanut oil. Shape into patties and dust with flour. Pan fry in hot peanut oil over medium heat until browned, 4–5 minutes. Flip and pan fry other side until golden brown. Serves 4–6.

TARTAR SAUCE:

½ cup chopped green onion
½ cup chopped dill pickle

1 cup mayonnaise
½ teaspoon House Seasoning

In a bowl, combine chopped onion, pickle, mayonnaise, and House Seasoning; mix well. Serve alongside crab cakes with lemon wedges.

Variation: Substitute ⅓ cup capers for ½ cup pickles; add a dash of cayenne pepper.

HOUSE SEASONING:

1 cup salt
¼ cup pepper

1 cup garlic powder

Mix well. Store in shaker near stove for convenience.

The Lady & Sons Savannah Country Cookbook

Gooey Crab Pizza

Early in my career I received a mailing from a newly opened restaurant announcing that they were the home of the "soon-to-be-famous Crabmeat Gooeys." I nearly dropped dead—this was our internal reference to our beloved "Hot Crab Canapés." I had been making the dish out of leftovers for eight years, since I developed the idea when I was in my early twenties. One of my staff was so enraged that she called the owner to ask how they could base their reputation on "my item" without my permission. They informed her that it had nothing to do with me; they had gotten the idea from Virginia Rainey . . . who they did not know was my general manager! Nevertheless, the concept works in a variety of ways. Crab pizza is one of them that is currently in vogue, and the possibilities of the procedure are endless.—Lee Chadwick

1 (8-ounce) can lump crabmeat, drained
12 ounces cream cheese, softened
3 scallions, white part only, thinly sliced
4 (1-ounce) slices imported Swiss cheese, chopped

½ teaspoon coarsely ground pepper
1 tablespoon grated Parmesan cheese
2 tablespoons Hellmann's mayonnaise
5 English muffins, split

Preheat the oven to 400°. Combine crabmeat, cream cheese, scallions, Swiss cheese, pepper, Parmesan cheese, and mayonnaise in a bowl and mix well. Spread liberally over each muffin half almost to the edge. Place on a baking sheet. Bake 10 minutes or until puffy and starting to brown. Let stand 5 minutes. Cut each muffin half into quarters. Serves 4–5.

Some Assembly Required

Catch of the Day Casserole

1 (6-ounce) box quick wild rice
  mix
⅔ cup sliced fresh mushrooms
¼ cup chopped onion
2 tablespoons olive oil, divided
1 pound crabmeat

Flour
1 pound bay scallops
½ cup milk
½ (10¾-ounce) can cream
  of mushroom soup
2 tablespoons cooking sherry

Cook rice as directed on package, omitting butter; set aside. In large skillet, sauté mushrooms and onion in 1 tablespoon oil for 5 minutes. Add crab and cook 2 more minutes. Remove vegetables and crab from skillet. Add remaining oil to skillet and sauté lightly floured scallops for 2 minutes. Blend together milk, soup, and sherry. Add to scallops along with vegetables and crab mixture. Cook 1 more minute; remove from heat. Combine seafood mixture together with rice, and spoon into a greased 2-quart baking dish. Bake at 350° for 30 minutes. Serves 8.

Traditions

Shrimp, Scallop, and Artichoke Divan

12 tablespoons butter, divided
9 tablespoons flour
1½ cups milk
1½ cups heavy cream
Salt and pepper to taste
1 pound cooked shrimp
1 pound raw scallops
2 (9-ounce) cans artichoke hearts,
  drained

1½ cups sliced mushrooms
½ cup dry sherry
2 tablespoons Worcestershire
1 cup grated Parmesan
Paprika
Parsley for garnish

Preheat oven to 375°. Melt 9 tablespoons butter; stir in flour. Add milk and cream, stirring constantly until thick and smooth. Season with salt and pepper. Arrange shrimp, scallops, and artichoke hearts in bottom of buttered 9x13-inch dish. Cook mushrooms in remaining butter; spoon over shrimp mixture. Add sherry and Worcestershire to cream sauce; pour over shrimp mixture. Sprinkle with cheese and paprika; bake 30 minutes. Garnish with parsley. Serve over rice.

Tried & True Recipes—Residents of Wild Timber

Vic's Seafood Cheese Delight

1 onion, chopped
1 bell pepper, chopped
1 pound ground beef
1 pound turkey, or beef sausage
   links, sliced or diced
1 (14½-ounce) can diced
   tomatoes with chiles
1 (17-ounce) can whole-kernel
   corn

1 (4-ounce) can sliced
   mushrooms
1 pound shrimp, peeled
1 pound imitation crabmeat
1 (10¾-ounce) can cream of
   mushroom soup
1 (8-ounce) jar Cheez Whiz
½–1 cup water
Rice, cooked and separated

In a large pot, sauté onion and bell pepper; brown the ground beef and turkey or sausage until cooked through. Add tomatoes, corn, and mushrooms; heat to a boil. Add shrimp and crabmeat; heat to a boil; reduce heat.

In a separate skillet, combine soup, Cheez Whiz, and water until boiling. (Cheez Whiz comes out easily if you heat the jar in the microwave a few seconds; watch your heat, it can stick.) Pour the cheese mixture over other ingredients; stir well. Serve over rice or add rice to the mixture. Season to taste. Great with garlic bread. Serves 10–12 people.

Note: Ingredients are interchangeable with your favorite meats and veggies.

Culinary Classics

Edie Ferguson's
Bombay Shrimp à la Greyfield

On a very special deep-sea fishing trip, our crowd stayed at the wonderful old Greyfield Inn on Cumberland Island off the coast of Georgia. The inn was the former home of the great philanthropist Andrew Carnegie and was run by his granddaughter, Edie Ferguson, and her husband.

One night at dinner, after a day in the hot sun, we were served this marvelous shrimp dish that I thought was about the best thing I'd ever tasted. I asked Edie for the recipe but got little or no response. As we were saying our final goodbyes and preparing to load the luggage on the ferryboat to go back to the mainland, Edie surreptitiously slipped the recipe into my hand.

I have treasured it ever since and would list it as one of my top ten, all-time favorite recipes. Although the recipe calls for ten pounds of shrimp, I always only use five. It works just as well. I make it in a fish mold and always try to garnish it as beautifully as it deserves.

5 pounds shrimp	**1 bell pepper, finely chopped**
Garlic powder	**1 cup Hellmann's mayonnaise**
Whole cloves	**Curry powder to taste**
3 cups cooked rice	**Quartered tomatoes and**
2 stalks celery, cut small	**cucumber slices for garnish**
1 onion, grated (use juice)	

Cook shrimp 3–4 minutes in boiling water with garlic powder and cloves. Drain, cool, and chop or break into pieces, reserving a few whole shrimp for garnishing. Mix all other ingredients with shrimp. Put into a fish mold or other salad mold and let stand in refrigerator overnight. Turn out onto a bed of lettuce. Garnish with shrimp, tomatoes, and cucumber slices. Makes an excellent main dish for a summer supper.

Eating from the White House to the Jailhouse

Cumberland Island, Georgia's largest and southernmost barrier island, is largely unspoiled. On this National Seashore, the animals rule and people are only visitors. Wild horses run free through the marshes and wind-swept dunes, while the inland forests shelter deer, alligator, armadillo, and mink. There is no bridge to the island; the most convenient access is by ferry from the town of St. Marys. Once privately owned, large areas were deeded to the National Parks Foundation by members or heirs of the Carnegie family in 1971. The ruins of the once magnificent Carnegie Estate "Dungeness" still stand on the south end of the island.

Garlic Shrimp in Lemon-Wine Sauce

2 shallots, finely chopped
4 cloves garlic, minced
4 tablespoons low-calorie or
   low-cholesterol margarine
¼ cup dry white wine
2 tablespoons lemon juice
1 tablespoon chopped fresh
   chives
1 tablespoon chopped fresh
   parsley

1 pound raw shrimp, peeled
   and deveined
½ teaspoon paprika
¼ teaspoon dried whole thyme
3 tablespoons whole-wheat
   bread crumbs
3 tablespoons grated Parmesan
   cheese

In skillet, sauté shallots and garlic in margarine until shallots are softened. Add wine; cook until wine is reduced and almost evaporated. Add lemon juice, chives, parsley, shrimp, paprika, and thyme. Sauté shrimp, tossing and turning over medium-high heat until shrimp are opaque and cooked through. Do not overcook. Sprinkle with bread crumbs and cheese. Cook and toss for another minute. Serve immediately with cocktail forks or on individual plates. Serves 6.

Peachtree Bouquet

Located on Cumberland Island, the stately ruins of Dungeness are all that remain of the original estate built by Thomas and Lucy Carnegie, which burned in 1959.

Marinated Shrimp

4 pounds medium shrimp,
  boiled, shelled, and deveined
4 onions, sliced and ringed
4 lemons, thinly sliced
Juice of 1 lemon
1 cup condensed tomato soup
1½ cups vegetable oil
¾ cup white vinegar

¼ cup sugar
½ teaspoon paprika
1 teaspoon cayenne
1 tablespoon dry mustard
1 tablespoon Worcestershire
2 teaspoons salt
¼ teaspoon Tabasco

Place shrimp, onions, and lemons in large container. Mix remaining ingredients together. Pour over shrimp mixture. Marinate in refrigerator at least 24 hours. Serve in a bowl in marinade with toothpicks, or drain and serve as a salad on a bed of lettuce.

Tea-Time at the Masters®

Stewed Shrimp

1½ pounds shrimp, peeled
  and deveined
3 tablespoons margarine or
  butter
¾ cup chopped celery
½ cup chopped onion
⅓ cup finely chopped green
  bell pepper

2 tablespoons flour or
  cornstarch
1 teaspoon salt
1 teaspoon pepper
2 teaspoons Worcestershire
1 teaspoon light soy sauce
1 cup water
Dash of hot sauce (optional)

Prepare shrimp and set aside. In large skillet, melt margarine or butter over medium heat. Add celery, onion, and green pepper. Sauté until tender. Add flour, salt, pepper, Worcestershire, and soy sauce, stirring until well blended. Add shrimp and cook about 2 minutes, then add water. Cook while stirring until shrimp are bright pink and gravy is smooth. A dash of hot sauce may be added. Makes 4–5 servings.

It's the People; It's the Food

Shrimp Stroganoff

1 (8-ounce) package fettuccine
2 tablespoons butter
2 tablespoons chopped onion
1/2 pound shrimp, peeled
1 (10¾-ounce) can condensed
   cream of shrimp soup
1/2 cup milk
1/2 cup sour cream
1/4 teaspoon paprika
Salt and pepper to taste

Cook fettuccine according to directions on package; drain. Melt butter in pan and sauté onion. Add shrimp and cook until done. Blend in soup and milk; heat. Stir in sour cream and paprika. Be careful not to let mixture boil. Serve over hot fettuccine.

Southern Manna

Daufuskie Island Shrimp Creole

4 green onions, or 1 Vidalia
   onion, chopped
1/2 cup chopped celery
3/4 cup chopped green bell
   pepper
1 garlic clove, minced
2 tablespoons butter or
   margarine
1 (16-ounce) can whole
   tomatoes, or 4 fresh tomatoes,
   chopped
1 (16-ounce) can tomato sauce
1 teaspoon salt
2 teaspoons dried parsley
1/4 teaspoon cayenne
2 teaspoons Worcestershire
2 teaspoons soy sauce
1 teaspoon hot sauce
1 tablespoon lemon juice
2 teaspoons curry powder
   (optional)
3 bay leaves (optional)
1 cup golden raisins (optional)
1 pound shrimp, peeled

Sauté onions, celery, pepper, and garlic in butter in large saucepan until onions are transparent. Add tomatoes, tomato sauce, salt, parsley, cayenne, Worcestershire, soy sauce, hot sauce, lemon juice, curry powder, bay leaves, and raisins; mix well. Bring to a simmer; simmer for 30 minutes. Add shrimp; cook over medium-low heat until shrimp turn pink. Remove the bay leaves. Serve over rice. Yields 4–6 servings.

From Black Tie to Blackeyed Peas

Pickled Shrimp

Must do ahead.

1 (10¾-ounce) can tomato soup
½ cup vinegar
¼ cup sugar
1 cup oil
Salt and pepper to taste
¼ teaspoon cayenne pepper

1 teaspoon Worcestershire
1 (0.18-ounce) box bay leaves
6 small onions, sliced
3 lemons, sliced
2 pounds shrimp, boiled and
   shelled

Mix soup, vinegar, sugar, oil, salt, pepper, cayenne, and Worcestershire in blender; blend 10–15 seconds. Place one layer each of bay leaves, onion slices, lemon slices, and shrimp in large bowl. Pour dressing over layers; marinate 24 hours. Serves 4–6.

Perennials

Scalloped Oysters

Scalloped oysters are delicious with roasted, stuffed turkey on Thanksgiving or Christmas Day.

¾ stick butter, melted,
   divided
2 tablespoons finely chopped
   onion
1½ sleeves saltine crackers,
   coarsely crumbled

1 quart fresh oysters in their
   liquid
4–6 dashes hot sauce
½ teaspoon ground nutmeg
Salt and black pepper to taste
1 cup cream

Butter a shallow casserole dish. In a sauté pan melt remaining butter and sauté onions until limp. In bottom of casserole dish, put a ½-inch layer of saltines; top with oysters. Pour melted butter and onions over oysters; season with hot sauce, nutmeg, salt and pepper. Pour cream over all; top with another ½-inch layer of saltines. Bake immediately in a preheated 350° oven for 45–50 minutes until nicely browned and bubbly. Serves 6–8.

A Traveler's Table

Roasted Grouper
with Sesame Almond Crust

2 tablespoons sesame oil
2 tablespoons vegetable oil
2 tablespoons lemon juice
2 tablespoons water
1 egg, beaten
¼ teaspoon salt
¾ teaspoon freshly cracked
   black pepper, divided
1 teaspoon hot chili sauce
1 cup crushed crisp wheat
   crackers
½ cup (2-ounces) grated
   Asiago cheese

¼ cup chopped toasted
   almonds
2 tablespoons toasted sesame
   seeds
¼ cup minced fresh Italian
   parsley
2 tablespoons minced fresh
   tarragon
6 (6-ounce) black grouper fillets,
   ½ inch thick
2 tablespoons butter, melted
2 tablespoons extra virgin
   olive oil

Preheat oven to 425°. Butter a shallow baking pan. In a medium bowl, combine sesame oil, vegetable oil, lemon juice, water, egg, salt, ½ teaspoon pepper, and chili sauce. Set aside.

In the bowl of a food processor, combine crackers, cheese, almonds, sesame seeds, parsley, tarragon, and remaining pepper; process to crumbs. Set aside.

Dip fish fillets in marinade, then in crumbs. Place on baking pan. Do not allow fillets to touch each other. Combine melted butter and olive oil; drizzle over fish; roast in oven for 20 minutes, until fillets are browned and cooked through. Serves 6.

Savannah Seasons

The Soque River is ranked as one of the top trout fishing streams in the eastern United States. It's the only river in Georgia that begins and ends in its home county.

Pecan-Crusted Grouper

½ cup pecan pieces
½ cup bread crumbs
1 (1-pound) grouper fillet, cut
   diagonally into 4 (4-ounce)
   pieces
Salt and pepper to taste
¼–⅓ cup flour

2 eggs, beaten
¾ cup butter or margarine,
   divided
Juice of 1 lemon
1 bunch Italian parsley,
   chopped

Process pecans and bread crumbs in a food processor just until a coarse mixture forms. Season fillet pieces with salt and pepper. Dredge in flour; dip in egg. Coat with pecan mixture. Melt ¼ cup butter in a nonstick oven-proof skillet over medium-high heat. Sauté fish on one side until brown; turn fish. Place skillet in oven; bake at 400° for 10 minutes or until fillet pieces flake easily. Remove fish to a warm platter; wipe skillet. Add remaining butter to skillet. Cook over high heat until butter is foamy and dark brown, stirring constantly. Add lemon juice and parsley, stirring until combined. Pour over grouper. Serve immediately. Serves 4.

True Grits

Quick Draw's Stuffed Halibut Steaks

3 tablespoons butter, plus
   melted butter for basting
¼ cup chopped onions
½ cup chopped mushrooms
¼ cup finely chopped parsley
¼ teaspoon thyme

½ cup fresh bread crumbs
2 tablespoons heavy cream
2 (2-pound) halibut steaks
Salt and pepper to taste
Lemon wedges

Preheat oven to 400°. In a skillet, heat butter; add onions. Cook until onions are transparent. Add mushrooms, parsley, and thyme; stir in bread crumbs and cream. Oil a baking dish and place one of the fish steaks on the bottom. Cover center with stuffing and top with the other fish steak. Skewer with toothpicks to hold together. Brush the top steak with butter. Sprinkle with salt and pepper. Bake 30–40 minutes or until fish flakes easily when tested with fork. Baste with additional melted butter while cooking. Serve with lemon wedges. Serves 6–8.

Wanted: Quick Draw's Favorite Recipes

Quick Draw's Salmon in a White Wine Sauce

½ cup minced onion
½ cup butter
4½ tablespoons all-purpose flour
1½ cups milk
½ teaspoon salt
½ teaspoon black pepper
½ cup heavy cream
¼ cup sherry
2 tablespoons cognac
2 cups cooked and flaked salmon
1 tablespoon chopped parsley
Toast points

In saucepan, sauté onion in butter until transparent. Using a wire whisk, stir in flour. Bring milk to a boil; add all at once to butter and onion mixture, stirring vigorously with whisk until sauce is thick and smooth. Stir in salt, pepper, cream, sherry, and cognac. Stir in the cooked, flaked salmon. Sprinkle with parsley. Serve with toast points. Serves 4–6 people.

Wanted: Quick Draw's Favorite Recipes

Georgia Mountain Trout in Wine

6 pieces trout
Salt and pepper to taste
Juice of 2 fresh lemons
3 large tomatoes, peeled and sliced
2 medium onions, thinly sliced
½ cup chopped parsley
½ cup dry white wine
¼ cup chicken bouillon

Oil shallow baking dish; place trout in dish; season with salt, pepper, and lemon juice (sprinkle outside and rub inside cavity). Cover trout with sliced tomatoes, then cover tomatoes with sliced onions. Sprinkle with chopped parsley. Pour wine and chicken bouillon over all. Bake uncovered 30 minutes at 400°. Garnish with lemon slices and parsley. Serve with brown rice. Serves 6.

Flavors of the Gardens

Grilled Red Snapper with Lime Marinade

1 tablespoon lime juice
1 scant tablespoon olive oil
1½–2 shallots, minced

1½ teaspoons fresh thyme
1 (4-ounce) snapper fillet
2 (½-inch) slices lime

In shallow dish, combine lime juice, oil, shallots, and thyme. Place red snapper fillet in dish, turning to coat evenly with marinade. Marinate skin side up, covered, in refrigerator for 1 hour. Heat grill (indoor or outdoor). Cook fillet on grill or under broiler, skin side up, for 3 minutes. Turn fillet, baste with marinade, and cook 3–6 minutes. Place lime on grill or under broiler and baste lightly with marinade. Cook 1 minute, turning once. Serve with fillet. Serve with lime marinade reduced to a sauce. Makes 1 serving.

Bread of Life–Chef Curtis Watkins

Tuna Bisque

I really don't know of any recipe that gets rave reviews more than this Tuna Bisque, which is my mother's recipe. I have made it so many times I don't really need to look at the recipe anymore. When I carry it to an older friend of mine, she empties the container, hands it back, and says, "Make me some more." And I do, because it's so delicious I always want to save out a bowl or two for myself.

½ cup finely chopped onion
1 (4-ounce) can button
  mushrooms, drained
2 tablespoons butter
1 (10¾-ounce) can cream of
  mushroom soup
1 soup can filled with milk

1 (7-ounce) can tuna, drained
  and flaked
1 tablespoon chopped parsley
1 teaspoon curry powder
1 (2-ounce) jar chopped
  pimentos
½ teaspoon salt

Sauté onion and mushrooms in butter until tender. Add remaining ingredients. Simmer over low heat for 10 minutes. More milk may be added, if desired. This is delicious served hot immediately or can be refrigerated, heated, and served later.

Eating from the White House to the Jailhouse

CAKES

Savannah is known as America's first planned city. The downtown district, most of which was designed by General James Edward Oglethorpe, is a National Historic Landmark and is considered one of America's most beautiful cities.

Georgia Pecan Cake

½ cup butter
½ cup vegetable shortening
2 cups sugar
5 large eggs, separated
1 teaspoon vanilla

2 cups sifted all-purpose flour
1 teaspoon baking soda
1 cup buttermilk
1¼ cups chopped pecans
1¼ cups flaked coconut

Cream butter and shortening thoroughly. Gradually add sugar. Beat until fluffy. Add egg yolks and vanilla. Sift flour with baking soda 3 times. Add to batter alternately with buttermilk, beginning with flour ending with flour. By hand, stir in nuts and coconut. Beat egg whites until stiff, but not dry. Carefully fold in all the egg whites. Bake at 350° in 3 greased large layer pans about 25 minutes or until done, or for about 1 hour in tube pan.

FROSTING:

1 (8-ounce) package cream
   cheese, softened
¾ stick margarine, softened

1 (1-pound) box powdered sugar
1 teaspoon vanilla
½ cup chopped pecans

Mix together ingredients and spread on cooled cake.

Grandma Mamie Jones' Family Favorites

The Stovall Covered Bridge, built in 1895 near Helen, was featured in the 1951 film, *I'd Climb the Highest Mountain.* The movie, starring Susan Hayward, William Lundigan, and Rory Calhoun, was based on a book of the same title by famed Georgia writer Cora Harris.

Chocolate Bourbon Pecan Cake

This is an unforgettable recipe from my cousin's bakery, Gabriel's Desserts.

8½ (1-ounce) squares semisweet chocolate	½ cup sugar, divided
½ cup (1 stick) butter	¼ cup bourbon
3 jumbo eggs, separated	¼ cup all-purpose flour
	1½ cups chopped pecans

Preheat oven to 325°. Grease and flour a 9-inch springform pan. Melt chocolate and butter in top of a double boiler over slightly simmering water (don't let top pan touch the water). Remove from heat, leaving pot with chocolate over the water; set aside. Whisk egg yolks and half the sugar in a metal mixing bowl; place bowl over slightly simmering water and whisk while heating to 140° (yolks will feel warm to the touch). Remove from heat and beat yolk-sugar mixture with an electric mixer to a ribbon stage. (When you lift the beaters, the mixture will flow back onto the surface like a ribbon.) Add bourbon to chocolate mixture, then fold yolk-sugar mixture into chocolate mixture.

Mix flour with pecans and fold into chocolate mixture. Using an electric mixer, whip egg whites and remaining sugar to form soft peaks, then fold into chocolate mixture. Pour batter into prepared pan and bake for 20–25 minutes (cake should test done with a toothpick but not dry). Allow cake to cool in pan and then place in the freezer for at least 2 hours. Once it is frozen, remove sides of springform pan. Invert cake onto a wire rack and remove bottom of springform pan.

GANACHE:
A ganache is simply a frosting made of chocolate and hot cream.

1 cup heavy cream	1¼ cups semisweet chocolate chips

Prepare Ganache by bringing cream to a boil and pouring over chocolate chips in a bowl. Whisk until completely smooth. Set wire rack containing cake onto a sheet pan with sides. Pour lukewarm Ganache over cake, coating completely. Re-pour if necessary to cover well. Gently jiggle wire rack to help drain excess Ganache. Ganache will lose its shine when set. Remove cake from wire rack with a wide spatula and place on a serving plate. Serves 10–12.

The Lady & Sons Just Desserts

Toasted Butter Pecan Cake

3 tablespoons butter or
   margarine, melted
1⅓ cups chopped pecans,
   divided
¾ cup butter or margarine
   softened
1⅓ cups sugar

1½ teaspoons vanilla
2 eggs
2 cups sifted flour
2 teaspoons baking powder
¼ teaspoon salt
⅔ cup milk

Spread melted butter over pecans, and toast at 350° for 15 minutes; stir occasionally. Cream butter and gradually add sugar; beat until light and fluffy. Add vanilla and beat in eggs, one at a time. Sift together flour, baking powder, and salt; add dry ingredients to creamed mixture alternately with milk. Fold in 1 cup of nuts. Pour batter into 2 greased and floured 8-inch cake pans. Bake at 350° for 30–35 minutes. Cool partially; remove from pans and cool completely.

BUTTER PECAN FROSTING:

4 tablespoons butter or
   margarine, softened
3 cups sifted powdered sugar

2½–3 tablespoons light cream
1 teaspoon vanilla

Combine butter, sugar, cream, and vanilla; beat until smooth and creamy. Frost cake and sprinkle remaining nuts on top.

A Taste of the Holidays

Carrot Walnut Cake

3 cups plain flour	4 large eggs
2 teaspoons baking powder	2 tablespoons orange juice
1 teaspoon baking soda	2 tablespoons grated orange
1 teaspoon cinnamon	peel
½ teaspoon salt	2 tablespoons lemon juice
4 cups grated carrots	2 tablespoons grated lemon
1 cup butter, softened	peel
1 cup packed brown sugar	1 cup chopped walnuts
1 cup white sugar	1 cup raisins

Sift together flour, baking powder, baking soda, cinnamon, and salt. Set aside. Wash and grate carrots; set aside. In large bowl, cream together butter, brown sugar, and white sugar until fluffy. Add eggs one at a time, mixing well after each addition.

In small bowl, combine orange juice, orange peel, lemon juice, and lemon peel; set aside. At low mixing speed, add flour mixture in 4 parts, alternating with orange-lemon mixture, beginning and ending with flour mixture. Fold in carrots, nuts, and raisins; mix well. Spoon mixture into a greased and floured 10-inch tube pan. Bake at 350° for one hour or until toothpick inserted into cake comes out clean. Cool for 20 minutes, then remove from pan; top with glaze. Yields 25–30 slices.

CREAM CHEESE GLAZE:

1 (8-ounce) package cream	1 teaspoon grated lemon peel
cheese, softened	1½ cups powdered sugar
1 tablespoon lemon juice	½ cup chopped walnuts

In small double boiler, heat on low setting, cream cheese, lemon juice, and peel until liquid. Add powdered sugar and walnuts; stir. Pour immediately over cooled cake.

Traditions

The largest state east of the Mississippi River, Georgia is a diverse land of magnolias and moss-draped oaks, pine tress and cypress swamps, mountains, and a 100-mile Atlantic Ocean coastline.

Plum Nutty Cake

Easy and wonderful.

2 cups self-rising flour	1 cup vegetable oil
2 cups sugar	3 eggs
½ teaspoon cinnamon	2 (4-ounce) jars, or 1 (9½-ounce)
½ teaspoon cloves	jar baby food plums, strained
¼ teaspoon nutmeg	1 cup chopped nuts

In large bowl, mix dry ingredients together. Beat in oil, eggs, and plums. Beat with mixer about 4 minutes or until well blended. Fold in nuts. Bake in tube pan in preheated 325° oven for 1 hour or until tests done. Cool cake about 10 minutes. While cake is slightly warm, glaze top with thin frosting using ½ cup confectioners' sugar and lemon juice, if desired.

Note: If using plain flour, add 3 teaspoons baking powder and ½ teaspoon salt. This works fine without a mixer, if beaten well by hand.

My Best to You

Raw Apple Cake

This is one of my mother's favorite recipes. She usually cooked this at Christmastime.

2 cups sugar	1 teaspoon cinnamon
3 medium eggs, well beaten	3 cups cubed and peeled raw
1½ cups vegetable oil	tart apples
3 cups all-purpose flour	1 cup chopped nuts
1 teaspoon baking soda	2 cups flaked coconut
2 teaspoons vanilla	

Cream sugar and eggs until light. Add oil, then dry ingredients. Add apples, nuts, and coconut. (You may add dates that have been rolled in small amount of flour.) Bake in tube pan at 300°–325° until firm when tested, about 1½ hours.

FILLING:

1 cup brown sugar	¼ cup sweet milk
1 stick margarine	

Combine all ingredients in a saucepan. Cook until the bubbles burst. Cool and spread on cooled cake.

My Best to You

Apple Cake
with Cream Cheese Frosting

½ cup margarine, melted
2 cups sugar
2 large eggs
1 teaspoon vanilla
2 cups all-purpose flour
1 teaspoon baking soda
1 teaspoon salt

2 teaspoons ground cinnamon
4 Granny Smith apples, peeled
  and chopped
½ cup chopped walnuts,
  toasted
½ cup golden raisins

Stir together margarine, sugar, eggs, and vanilla in a large bowl. In a separate bowl, combine flour, baking soda, salt, and cinnamon. Add to butter mixture. Stir in apples, walnuts, and raisins. Spread in a greased 9x13-inch baking dish. Bake at 350° for 45 minutes or until center is done. Cool completely in pan.

CREAM CHEESE FROSTING:
1 (8-ounce) package cream
  cheese, softened
3 tablespoons margarine,
  softened

1½ cups powdered sugar
⅛ teaspoon salt
1 teaspoon vanilla

Beat cream cheese and margarine at medium speed with electric mixer until creamy. Gradually add sugar and salt, and beat until blended. Stir in vanilla. Spread frosting on cooled cake. Sprinkle with additional toasted walnuts, if desired. If Frosting is too thin, stir in additional powdered sugar until of spreading consistency.

At the End of the Fork

Cornelia is home to the Big Red Apple Festival each October. The Big Red Apple monument in Cornelia weighs 5,200 pounds and is the largest monument in the world dedicated to the apple growing industry.

Strawberry Cake

2 sticks butter, softened
2 cups sugar
1 (3-ounce) package strawberry
   gelatin
3½ cups sifted cake flour

3 teaspoons baking powder
1 cup milk
½ cup cut-up strawberries
6 egg whites, stiffly beaten

Preheat oven to 350°. Cream together butter, sugar, and gelatin until light and fluffy. Add sifted flour and baking powder alternately with milk. Fold in strawberries. Fold in egg whites. Pour into 3-4 greased and floured 9-inch round cake pans. Bake at 350° approximately 25 minutes or until tests done. Spread Strawberry Icing between layers and on top and sides.

STRAWBERRY ICING:
1 stick butter, softened
½ cup cut-up strawberries

1 (16-ounce) box confectioners'
   sugar

Blend all ingredients well, and spread on cake when cool.

Bevelyn Blair's Everyday Cakes

Wet and Wild Coconut Cake

1 (18¼-ounce) box yellow cake
   mix without pudding
1 (15-ounce) can Coco Lopez
   (cream of coconut)
1 (14-ounce) can Eagle Brand
   condensed milk

1 (7-ounce) bag flaked coconut
1 (16-ounce) container Cool
   Whip

Bake cake in a greased 9x13-inch pan according to directions on box. When cake is almost cooled, poke holes with fork all over the cake. Combine Coco Lopez and condensed milk. Stir until blended. Spoon mixture over cake slowly. Cover with plastic wrap and refrigerate. Mix coconut and Cool Whip together. Store in a separate container in refrigerator. Ice the cake just before serving.

At the End of the Fork

Blackberry Jam Cake
with Buttermilk Icing

I have made this cake so many times that I almost don't need a recipe and I have never had a failure. It takes a while to make but is certainly worth every minute. I never cease to be amazed at the icing. It starts off white as snow and ends up being a lovely caramel color and taste. I have, on a couple of occasions, used strawberry jam when I didn't have any blackberry jam, but I think the blackberry is better.

1¾ cups flour	1 cup sugar
1 teaspoon baking powder	1 cup oil
½ teaspoon salt	3 eggs, beaten
1 teaspoon baking soda	¾ cup buttermilk
1 teaspoon cinnamon	1 teaspoon vanilla
½ teaspoon nutmeg	1 cup blackberry jam
½ teaspoon allspice	1 cup finely chopped pecans
¼ teaspoon ground cloves	

Preheat oven to 325°. Sift and measure all dry ingredients 3 times, except sugar; mix all together. Add sugar to oil; mix well. Add eggs; mix well. Add dry ingredients alternately with buttermilk. Stir in vanilla and blackberry jam; stir nuts in well. Bake in 2 greased and floured 9-inch pans about 30–35 minutes.

BUTTERMILK ICING:

3 cups sugar	1 teaspoon baking soda
1 cup butter	1 cup chopped pecans
1 cup buttermilk	1 teaspoon vanilla
2 tablespoons light corn syrup	

In 4-quart pot over medium heat (be sure to use a 4-quart pot, or this icing will boil over), add all icing ingredients except nuts and vanilla. Boil, stirring constantly. Cook until small amount dropped into cold water forms ball. Pour into large bowl and beat with mixer at high speed for a few minutes. Beat with spoon until it cools; add nuts and vanilla; spread on layers.

Eating from the White House to the Jailhouse

At nearly 150 acres, the Atlanta State Farmer's Market in Forest Park is considered one of the largest of its kind in the world. Besides wholesale and retail sales, it has a garden center, a restaurant, a welcome center, and a USDA Federal-State office. Good prices, too.

Pineapple Upside-Down Cake

This is Mama's recipe —Joyce Day Smith Ramsey

1 stick margarine
1 cup brown sugar
1 (20-ounce) can pineapple
slices
1 (4-ounce) bottle maraschino
cherries

1 (18¼-ounce) box Duncan
Hines Pineapple Supreme
Cake Mix

Melt butter in a 9x13-inch pan. Sprinkle with brown sugar, then layer pineapple slices over brown sugar. Put a red cherry in each pineapple hole. Mix cake as directed on package. Pour over pineapple. Bake in preheated oven at 350° for 45–50 minutes. Cool in pan for 3–5 minutes, then invert onto serving platter or cut in squares in pan.

The Day Family Favorites

Key Lime Cake

1 (18¼-ounce) box lemon
cake mix
1 (6-ounce) box lime Jell-O
¾ cup orange juice

5 eggs
1½ cups vegetable oil
1 lime (optional)

Preheat oven to 325°. In large mixing bowl, stir cake mix and unprepared Jell-O together. Add orange juice, then eggs, one at a time, mixing well after each addition. Add oil and mix thoroughly. Pour into prepared cake pan(s) and bake 20–30 minutes or until done. Cool and frost with Cream Cheese Frosting. Garnish with lime slices.

CREAM CHEESE FROSTING:

1 (8-ounce) package cream
cheese, softened
1 stick margarine, softened

1 (1-pound) box confectioners'
sugar
1 teaspoon vanilla

Soften cream cheese and margarine. Beat cream cheese and margarine together, then add vanilla; blend in sugar in small amounts until of spreading consistency. Spread on cool cake.

Heritage Cookbook

Quick Draw's Lemon Icebox Cake

1 package ladyfingers
1½ tablespoons cornstarch
⅓ cup milk
4 egg yolks
¼ cup granulated sugar
Juice of 1 lemon
Grated zest of 1 lemon

1½ sticks unsalted butter,
 softened
1½ cups confectioners' sugar
1 cup heavy whipping cream
½ cup shredded coconut
 (unsweetened)

Line a 9x3-inch springform pan with ladyfingers. Place them standing up around side of pan. Cover bottom with remaining ladyfingers. Place cornstarch in small bowl. Add milk, stirring until smooth. Place egg yolks and sugar in top of double boiler and beat until lightened in color. Add cornstarch and milk mixture and blend. Cook over simmering water. Whisk constantly until thickened and smooth. Avoid overheating or mixture will curdle. Remove from heat. Add lemon juice and zest; cool.

In small bowl, cream butter and confectioners' sugar. Gradually combine egg and butter mixture, stirring until well blended. Beat whipping cream to soft peaks. Stir 1 cup of whipped cream into egg mixture, then fold in remaining whipped cream. Pour mixture into pan. Refrigerate overnight.

Unhinge pan sides and gently remove. Do not remove cake from pan bottom. Let sit at room temperature 5 minutes. Before serving, sprinkle with coconut. Serve with dollops of whipped cream. Serves 8–10.

Wanted: Quick Draw's Favorite Recipes

Peach-Glazed Almond Cake

2¾ cups all-purpose flour,
  divided
¾ cup plus 2 tablespoons
  sugar, divided
¾ teaspoon salt, divided
½ cup butter
1 tablespoon water
3 eggs, separated
¾ cup peach preserves,
  divided

⅛ teaspoon cream of tartar
½ cup finely chopped
  unblanched almonds
½ cup milk
⅓ cup vegetable oil
1½ teaspoons baking powder
1¼ teaspoons almond extract
1 (28-ounce) can cling peach
  slices, drained

Preheat oven to 350°. In large bowl, mix 1½ cups flour, 2 table-spoons sugar, and ¼ teaspoon salt. With pastry blender or 2 knives used scissor-fashion, cut butter into flour mixture until mixture resembles coarse crumbs. Stir in water and 1 egg yolk. With hands, work dough until smooth. Press dough evenly and firmly on bottom and sides of a 9-inch round cake pan. Brush dough with ¼ cup peach preserves.

In small bowl with mixer at high speed, beat 3 egg whites and cream of tartar until stiff peaks form; set aside. In large bowl with mixer at low speed, beat almonds, milk, oil, baking powder, almond extract, and remaining ½ teaspoon salt, 2 egg yolks, 1¼ cups flour, and ¾ cup sugar until smooth; fold in beaten egg whites. Pour into dough-lined cake pan, spreading batter evenly. Bake 45 minutes, or until cake springs back when touched with finger. Cool cake 20 minutes on wire rack, or until side of cake shrinks from pan. Remove cake from pan and cool completely on rack. Place cake onto platter. Brush top of cake with ¼ cup peach preserves. Arrange peach slices on top of cake; brush with remaining ¼ cup peach preserves. Serves 10.

Peachtree Bouquet

Orange Blooms

Too wonderful to eat just one.

1 (18¼-ounce) yellow cake mix
4 eggs
¾ cup orange juice

1 (3-ounce) package instant
  lemon pudding
¾ cup oil

Mix all ingredients and pour into mini muffin pans sprayed with nonstick vegetable oil. Bake in preheated 350° oven for 8–10 minutes.

GLAZE:

2 tablespoons oil
2 cups powdered sugar

⅓ cup plus 2 tablespoons
  orange juice

Mix all ingredients until smooth. Dip top of cupcakes in Glaze and set on wire rack. Makes 48 cupcakes.

A Southern Collection: Then and Now

Poppy Seed Cake

1 (18¼-ounce) box yellow
  butter cake mix
4 eggs
½ cup oil
1 cup water

1 (5-ounce) package instant
  vanilla pudding
¼ cup poppy seeds
Confectioners' sugar

Preheat oven to 375°. Beat all ingredients together for 10 minutes in electric mixer. Pour batter into generously greased and floured 10-inch tube pan. Bake 55 minutes. Cake will rise very high but will settle when cool. Sprinkle with confectioners' sugar when cool.

Cook and Love It

Cola Cake

2 cups sugar
2 cups all-purpose flour
1 ½ cups small marshmallows
½ cup butter or margarine
½ cup vegetable oil
3 tablespoons cocoa

1 cup Coca-Cola
½ cup buttermilk
1 teaspoon baking soda
2 eggs
1 teaspoon vanilla extract

Preheat oven to 350°. In a bowl, sift sugar and flour. Add marshmallows. In saucepan, mix butter, oil, cocoa, and Coca-Cola. Bring to a boil and pour over dry ingredients; blend well. Add buttermilk, baking soda, eggs, and vanilla; mix well. Pour into a well-greased 9x13-inch pan; bake 45 minutes. Remove from oven and frost immediately.

FROSTING:
½ cup butter
3 tablespoons cocoa
6 tablespoons Coca-Cola
1 (16-ounce) box confectioners' sugar

1 teaspoon vanilla extract
1 cup chopped pecans

Combine butter, cocoa, and Coca-Cola in a saucepan. Bring to a boil and pour over confectioners' sugar, blending well. Add vanilla and pecans. Spread over hot cake. When cool, cut into squares and serve. Serves 12.

Atlanta Cooknotes

Coca-Cola was invented in May 1886 by Dr. John S. Pemberton in Atlanta. The name was suggested by Dr. Pemberton's bookkeeper, Frank Robinson. Frank penned the name in the flowing script that is still famous today. Coca-Cola was first sold at a soda fountain in Jacob's Pharmacy in Atlanta by Willis Venable.

Southern Rum Cake

3 cups sugar
2 cups light or dark rum
8 eggs
1 cup cooked grits
1 (18¼-ounce) box Pillsbury
white cake mix

½ cup vanilla
1 pound butter, softened
Whipped cream
Fresh fruit

Preheat oven to 325° degrees. Combine sugar, rum, eggs, and grits; mix thoroughly. Add cake mix, vanilla, and butter; mix well. Pour batter into 3 greased and floured 9-inch round cake pans. Bake 1½ hours. Top each cake with whipped cream and garnish with fresh fruit. Serves 15–20.

Note: Butter must be added last.

Atlanta Cooknotes

Double Chocolate Gooey Butter Cake

1 (18¼-ounce) package
chocolate cake mix
3 eggs, divided
2 sticks butter, melted, divided
1 (8-ounce) package cream
cheese, softened

3–4 tablespoons cocoa powder
1 (16-ounce) box powdered
sugar
1 teaspoon vanilla
1 cup chopped nuts

Preheat oven to 350°. Lightly butter a 9x13-inch baking pan. In a large bowl, combine cake mix, 1 egg, and 1 stick butter; stir until well blended. Pat mixture into prepared pan and set aside.

With a mixer, beat cream cheese until smooth. Add remaining eggs and cocoa powder. Lower speed of mixer, and add powdered sugar. Continue beating until ingredients are well mixed. Slowly add remaining butter and vanilla, continuing to beat mixture until smooth. Stir in nuts with a rubber spatula. Spread filling over cake mixture in pan. Bake for 40–50 minutes. Be careful not to overcook cake; center should still be a little gooey when finished baking. Let cake partially cool on a wire rack before cutting into pieces.

A Gift of Appreciation

Gooey Butter Chess Cake

1 (18¼-ounce) box yellow
   butter cake mix
2 eggs
½ cup butter or margarine,
   melted
1 cup cooked grits

1 (8-ounce) package cream
   cheese, softened
1 (16-ounce) package
   powdered sugar
2 eggs
1 teaspoon vanilla

Preheat oven to 350°. Combine first 4 ingredients in large mixing bowl. Beat thoroughly.

Spread mixture in well-greased 9x13-inch baking pan. Beat next 4 ingredients until smooth and creamy. Pour over cake batter. Bake for 25–35 minutes. Cool and cut into bars. Topping will be "gooey." Serves 24–36.

Gone with the Grits

Brown Mountain Cake

1 cup butter, softened
2 cups sugar
3 eggs
3 cups flour
1 cup buttermilk

½ cup warm water
3 tablespoons baking cocoa
1 teaspoon baking soda
1 teaspoon vanilla extract

Cream butter and sugar in mixer bowl until light and fluffy. Add eggs one at a time, beating well after each addition. Add flour and buttermilk alternately to creamed mixture, beating well after each addition. Mix water, cocoa, and baking soda in bowl. Add to flour mixture; beat well. Stir in vanilla. Pour into 2 greased and floured 9-inch round cake pans. Bake at 350° for 35–40 minutes or until layers test done. Cool in pans for 10 minutes. Remove to wire rack to cool completely.

ICING:

1 cup butter
2 cups sugar

1 cup evaporated milk
1 teaspoon vanilla extract

Melt butter in saucepan over medium heat. Add sugar and evaporated milk. Cook to soft-ball stage, stirring constantly. Remove from heat. Beat in vanilla. Let stand to cool. Beat until of spreading consistency. Spread between layers and over top and side of cake. Serves 12.

From Our House to Yours

Old-Fashioned German Chocolate Cake

1 (4 ounce) package sweet
  chocolate
½ cup boiling water
1 cup (2 sticks) butter, softened
2 cups sugar
4 eggs, separated

1 teaspoon vanilla
2 cups all-purpose flour
1 teaspoon baking soda
½ teaspoon salt
1 cup buttermilk

Melt chocolate in boiling water; cool. Cream butter and sugar. Beat in egg yolks. Stir in vanilla and chocolate. Set aside. Mix flour, baking soda, and salt. Beat in flour mixture alternately with buttermilk. Beat egg whites until stiff peaks form; fold into batter. Pour batter into 3 greased 9-inch layer pans, lined on bottoms with wax paper. Bake at 350° for 30 minutes or until cake springs back when lightly pressed in center. Cool 15 minutes; remove and cool on rack. Spread frosting between layers and over top of cake.

COCONUT-PECAN FROSTING:
1 cup evaporated milk
1 cup sugar
3 egg yolks, slightly beaten
½ cup butter

1 teaspoon vanilla
1⅓ cups shredded coconut
1 cup chopped pecans

Combine evaporated milk, sugar, egg yolks, butter, and vanilla in saucepan. Cook and stir over medium heat until thickened. Remove from heat. Stir in coconut and pecans. Cool until thick enough to spread. Makes 2½ cups.

Special Treasures

German Chocolate Upside Down Cake

1 cup shredded coconut
1 cup chopped pecans
1 (18¼-ounce) box German
  chocolate cake mix
1 stick butter

1 (8-ounce) package cream
  cheese
1 (16-ounce) box confectioners'
  sugar

Mix nuts and coconut. Place in bottom of greased 9x13-inch pan. Prepare cake mix according to directions. Pour over coconut pecan mix. Place butter and cream cheese in saucepan. Heat mixture until warm enough to stir in confectioners' sugar. Pour over cake mix. Bake 35–40 minutes at 350°. Do not cut until cool.

Tastes for All Seasons

Tunnel of Fudge Cake

¾ pound (3 sticks) butter,
  softened
6 eggs
1½ cups sugar
2 cups all-purpose flour

1 (12½-ounce) can creamy
  double Dutch frosting
2 cups chopped walnuts or
  pecans

Preheat oven to 350°. Cream butter in large bowl on high speed. Add eggs one at a time, beating well. Add sugar gradually, creaming at high speed, until light and fluffy. Gradually add flour. By hand, stir in frosting mix and nuts until well blended. Pour batter in well-greased and floured Bundt pan. Bake for 60–65 minutes. Cool 2 hours before removing from pan. Cake will have a dry, brownie-type crust and a moist center with a tunnel of fudge running through it. Serves 16–20.

The Lady & Sons Savannah Country Cookbook

Wormsloe Éclair Cake

Regular éclairs are very difficult and time-consuming to make. This cake tastes exactly like bakery-quality éclairs without all the fuss!

2 cups water
1 cup margarine
2 cups flour, sifted
8 eggs
2½ cups milk

2 (3-ounce) packages vanilla
    instant pudding mix
6 ounces nondairy whipped
    topping

Combine water and margarine in a saucepan. Bring to a boil. Remove from heat. Add flour and mix well. Add eggs, one at a time, mixing well after each addition. Shape dough into a 12-inch ring on a baking sheet. Bake at 400° for 45–50 minutes. Remove to a wire rack to cool completely.

Beat milk and pudding mix in a mixer bowl at low speed for 2 minutes. Fold in whipped topping. Cut cake into halves. Place bottom half on a serving plate. Spread pudding mixture over bottom half. Place top half over pudding mixture. Drizzle with Chocolate Frosting. Store in refrigerator. Yields 16 servings.

CHOCOLATE FROSTING:
1 cup confectioners' sugar
¼ cup butter
1 (1-ounce) square unsweetened
    chocolate

⅓ cup milk
Pinch of salt
1 teaspoon vanilla extract

Combine confectioners' sugar, butter, chocolate, milk, and salt in a saucepan. Bring to a boil over low beat. Boil for 5–8 minutes or until thick. Stir in vanilla.

From Black Tie to Blackeyed Peas

The Appalachian National Scenic Trail, generally known as the Appalachian Trail or simply the A.T., is a 2,174-mile marked hiking trail in the eastern United States, extending between Springer Mountain in Georgia and Mount Katahdin in Maine. Along the way, the trail also passes through the states of North Carolina, Tennessee, Virginia, West Virginia, Maryland, Pennsylvania, New Jersey, New York, Connecticut, Massachusetts, Vermont, and New Hampshire. There are roughly 75 miles of the 2,174-mile Appalachian Trail in Georgia.

Chocolate Angel Food Cake

1½ cups egg whites
  (12–14 eggs)
1 teaspoon cream of tartar
¼ teaspoon salt

1½ cups sugar
1 teaspoon vanilla
¾ cup flour
¼ cup cocoa

Beat egg whites until foamy. Add cream of tartar and salt; continue beating until stiff. Gradually beat in sugar. Add vanilla. Sift flour and cocoa together 4 times. Sprinkle flour onto egg white mixture and fold in by hand. Pour into an ungreased tube pan and bake at 325° for 1 hour and 15 minutes. Immediately invert cake pan. When cooled, remove from pan.

Holiday Favorites

My Chocolate Cake

1 cup butter, softened
3 cups packed brown sugar
4 eggs
2 teaspoons vanilla
2⅔ cups flour

¾ cup cocoa
1 tablespoon baking soda
½ teaspoon salt
1½ cups sour cream
1½ cups boiling water

In mixing bowl, beat butter and sugar; add eggs one at a time, beating well after each addition. Beat until light and fluffy. Blend in vanilla. Combine flour, cocoa, baking soda, and salt; add to creamed mixture alternately with sour cream, beating well after each addition. Stir in water until well blended. Pour into 3 greased and floured 9-inch round cake pans. Bake at 350° for 35 minutes.

FROSTING:
½ cup butter
3 squares sweet chocolate
3 squares semisweet chocolate

5 cups powdered sugar
1 cup sour cream
2 teaspoons vanilla

In saucepan, melt butter and chocolates over low heat. Cool. In mixing bowl, combine sugar, sour cream, and vanilla. Add chocolate mixture and beat until smooth. Frost cooled cake. Makes 15 servings.

Montezuma Amish Mennonite Cookbook II

Six Flavor Cake

1 stick margarine, softened	1 teaspoon lemon extract
1 cup Crisco shortening	1 teaspoon almond extract
3 cups sugar	1 teaspoon coconut extract
5 large eggs	1 teaspoon rum extract
3 cups all-purpose flour	1 teaspoon vanilla extract
1 teaspoon baking powder	1 teaspoon butter extract
1⅛ cups milk	

Preheat oven to 300°. Cream margarine, Crisco, and sugar at medium speed with electric mixer. Add eggs, one at a time, mixing thoroughly after each addition. Combine flour and baking powder; sift in a bowl. Add alternately with milk, blending well at low speed after each addition. Add extracts one at a time, blending well. Pour in greased and floured 10-inch tube pan. Bake at 300° for 1 hour and 45 minutes. Pierce top with toothpick. If it comes out clean, it is done; if not, bake a little longer. Remove from oven; pierce top with fork and pour Glaze over cake before removing from pan.

GLAZE:

1 cup sugar	½ teaspoon each extract used
½ cup water	in cake above

Cook over low heat until sugar melts. Cool and pour over cake. Let cool completely before removing from pan.

Heavenly Dishes

7-Up Pound Cake

3 sticks butter, softened	3 cups cake flour
3 cups sugar	¾ cup 7-Up
5 eggs	1 tablespoon lemon flavoring

Preheat oven to 300°. Grease and flour a tube pan and set aside. Cream butter and sugar together until light and fluffy; add eggs one at a time to butter and sugar mixture, beating between each addition. Add flour gradually, alternating with 7-Up. Stir in lemon flavoring. Bake until firm and set, about 1 hour. Cool.

Heart & Soul

Caramel Nut Pound Cake

1 cup butter, softened
½ cup shortening
1 (1-pound) package light
  brown sugar
1 cup white sugar
5 eggs

3 cups sifted flour
½ teaspoon salt
½ teaspoon baking powder
1 cup milk
1 tablespoon vanilla extract
1 cup finely chopped pecans

Beat butter, shortening, and brown sugar in mixer bowl until creamy. Add white sugar gradually, beating until light and fluffy. Add eggs one at a time, beating well after each addition. Sift flour, salt, and baking powder together; add alternately with milk, beginning and ending with flour mixture. Stir in vanilla and pecans. Spoon into greased and floured 10-inch tube pan. Bake at 325° for 1½ hours or until cake tests done. Cool in pan for 15 minutes. Invert onto cake plate.

ICING:
½ cup butter or margarine
1 cup packed light brown sugar

¼ cup milk
1¾–2 cups confectioners' sugar

Heat butter in saucepan until melted. Stir in brown sugar. Boil over low heat for 2 minutes, stirring constantly. Add milk; mix well. Bring to a boil, stirring constantly. Remove from heat. Let stand until cool. Add confectioners' sugar gradually, beating until of spreading consistency. Spread over top and side of cake. Makes 18 servings.

Home Sweet Habitat

Cream Cheese Pound Cake

1½ cups margarine, softened
1 (8-ounce) package cream
  cheese, softened
3 cups sugar

2 teaspoons vanilla extract
6 eggs, at room temperature
3 cups flour

Cream first 4 ingredients in mixer bowl until light and fluffy. Add eggs and flour ⅓ at a time, mixing well after each addition. Spoon into greased and floured 10-inch tube pan. Bake at 325° for 1½ hours. Cool on wire rack. Serves 16.

From Our House to Yours

Chocolate Cream Cheese Pound Cake

1 cup butter, room temperature
1 (8-ounce) package cream
   cheese, softened
3 cups sugar

6 eggs, room temperature
2½ cups all-purpose flour
½ cup cocoa powder
2 teaspoons vanilla flavoring

Preheat oven to 325°. Cream butter, cream cheese, and sugar for 3–5 minutes until light and fluffy. Add eggs, one at a time, beating well after each addition. Sift flour and cocoa together. Add to creamed mixture, one cup at a time, scraping down sides after each addition. Add flavoring. Pour into greased and floured tube pan and bake for 1½ hours; test with toothpick. Cool in pan for 10 minutes. Remove from pan and cool completely. Cake can be frozen up to 2 months.

Bread of Life–Salem Baptist Church

Carnival-Style Funnel Cake

Peanut or canola oil for frying
3 large eggs
2¼ cups milk
½ teaspoon lemon extract
4 cups flour
1 cup light brown sugar

1 tablespoon baking powder
½ teaspoon salt
Powdered sugar, with or
   without cinnamon, for
   dusting

Preheat oil to 375°. In a mixing bowl, whisk eggs, milk, and lemon. Whisk well. Sift flour, sugar, baking powder, and salt together. Fold flour mixture into egg mixture. Stir until smooth. Hold your finger over the funnel opening; fill with ¾ cup filling. Place your hand over the oil and carefully remove your finger. Scribble and crisscross the filling into the hot oil. Fry until golden on both sides. Remove from oil and drain on paper towels. Dust with powdered sugar or cinnamon-powdered sugar. Repeat process until all of the batter is used.

Culinary Classics

Almond Cheesecake

CRUST:

1¼ cups vanilla wafer crumbs   ¼ cup sugar
¾ cup finely chopped almonds   ⅓ cup margarine, melted

Stir together crumbs, almonds, and sugar; add margarine; mix well. Press in bottom of an ungreased 10-inch springform pan.

FILLING:

4 (8-ounce) packages cream   4 eggs
   cheese, softened   1 teaspoon vanilla
1¼ cups sugar   1½ teaspoons almond extract

Beat cream cheese and sugar until smooth and creamy. Add eggs, one at a time, beating well after each addition. Beat in vanilla and almond extract just until blended. Pour into Crust. Bake at 350° for 55 minutes or until center is almost set. Remove from oven and allow to stand for 5 minutes.

TOPPING:

1 pint sour cream   1 teaspoon vanilla
¼ cup sugar   ⅛ cup toasted sliced almonds

Mix together sour cream, sugar, and vanilla. Spread over Filling. Return to oven for 5 minutes. When completely cooled, cover and refrigerate overnight. Just before serving, remove sides and decorate top with almonds. Store in refrigerator.

Holiday Delights

Oreo Cheesecake

CRUST:

4 tablespoons butter, melted

2 cups finely crushed Oreo cookies (about 18)

Heat oven to 250°. Wrap the outside of a 10x3-inch springform pan tightly with foil (to prevent water from leaking in). Line bottom with a parchment circle. Set aside. In medium bowl, stir together melted butter and Oreo crumbs. Place in pan and press down firmly and evenly. Bake at 250° for 8–10 minutes. Remove from oven; set aside to cool.

FILLING:

3 pounds cream cheese, softened

2¾ cups granulated sugar

5 eggs

2 teaspoons pure vanilla extract

2 cups Oreo cookie chunks (about 15)

1 (12-ounce) tub whipped topping (optional)

12 Oreo cookies (optional)

Place cream cheese in a mixing bowl and mix on medium speed until soft, 6–8 minutes. Use a rubber spatula to scrape bowl often to ensure even distribution. Add sugar and blend well, scraping bowl just until smooth (no lumps). Reduce mixing speed to low, then slowly add eggs and vanilla; mix until combined. Remove from mixer. With a wooden spoon, stir Oreo chunks into filling. Pour filling into Crust. Place cheesecake pan into large roasting pan with water, leaving 1 inch of space from top of the cheesecake pan. Bake in preheated oven for 2½–3 hours until top of cheesecake is slightly golden. Refrigerate at least 24 hours before serving. Serves 12.

If desired, garnish each slice of cheesecake with 1 ounce of whipped cream and an Oreo cookie.

Bread of Life–Chef Curtis Watkins

Hawkinsville is home to one of the largest harness racing training facilities in the country. The town has had a long history of horse racing, and celebrates the Hawkinsville Harness Horse Festival every spring.

Key Lime Cheesecake
with Strawberry Sauce

CRUST:

2 cups graham cracker crumbs ½ cup butter or margarine,
¼ cup sugar   melted

Stir together all ingredients and firmly press on bottom and 1 inch up sides of a greased 9-inch springform pan. Bake at 350° for 8 minutes; cool.

FILLING:

3 (8-ounce) packages cream   1 (8-ounce) container sour
  cheese, softened   cream
1¼ cups sugar   1½ teaspoons grated lime zest
3 large eggs   ½ cup lime juice

Beat cream cheese at medium speed with an electric mixer until fluffy; gradually add sugar; beat until blended. Add eggs, one at a time, beating well after each addition. Stir in sour cream, zest, and juice. Pour Filling into Crust. Bake at 325° for 1 hour and 5 minutes. Remove from oven and immediately run knife around edge of pan, releasing sides. Cool completely on wire rack. Cover and chill 8 hours. Garnish with strawberries. Serve with Strawberry Sauce.

STRAWBERRY SAUCE:

1¼ cups chopped fresh   ½ cup sugar
  strawberries   1½ teaspoons grated lime zest

Process all ingredients in food processor until smooth.

Strawberries: From Our Family's Field to Your Family's Table

Hartsfield-Jackson Atlanta International Airport is the busiest airport in the world both in terms of number of passengers as well as the number of takeoffs and landings, surpassing Chicago's O'Hare International Airport. It accommodated 980,197 takeoffs and landings in 2005, and handled 88.4 million passengers.

New York Cheesecake

2 cups graham cracker crumbs
½–1 stick butter, melted
1 cup sugar, divided
2 pounds cream cheese, softened

2 large eggs, slightly beaten
1 teaspoon vanilla
2 tablespoons cornstarch
1 cup sour cream

Preheat oven to 450°. Mix graham cracker crumbs, melted butter, and 2 tablespoons sugar; blend well. Reserve 2 tablespoons crumb mix for top. Press into greased 9-inch springform pan. Chill in freezer. Beat cream cheese and remaining sugar in bowl. Add beaten eggs, vanilla, and cornstarch just until blended. Stir in sour cream. Put into prepared crust. Bake for 10 minutes; reduce temperature to 200°. Bake for 45 minutes. Turn oven off, leaving cake in for 3 hours. Take out and sprinkle 2 tablespoons crumb mixture on top. Keep in refrigerator.

The Day Family Favorites

Fabulous Cheesecake

CRUST:
2 cups graham cracker crumbs
2 tablespoons sugar

½ cup butter, softened

Combine crumbs, sugar, and butter. Press into bottom of greased springform pan.

FILLING:
2 (8-ounce) packages cream
   cheese, softened
1 (16-ounce) container cottage
   cheese
1½ cups sugar
4 eggs, slightly beaten

3 tablespoons cornstarch
3 tablespoons flour
2 tablespoons lemon juice
1 teaspoon vanilla extract
½ pound butter, melted
1 pint sour cream

Beat cream cheese and cottage cheese until smooth and creamy. Gradually beat in sugar, then beat in one egg at a time until well combined. With electric mixer at low speed, beat in cornstarch, flour, lemon juice, and vanilla. Add melted butter and sour cream, beating just until smooth. Pour into Crust. Bake at 325° for 1 hour and 10 minutes or until firm around edges. Turn off oven; allow cake to cool completely in oven for 2 hours. Remove from oven; continue cooling; chill 8 hours or overnight.

    Serve with fresh, sweetened berries, peaches, or pineapple, if desired.

Bevelyn Blair's Everyday Cakes

Elegant Cheesecake

CRUST:

¾ cup coarsely ground nuts
¾ cup graham cracker crumbs

3 tablespoons melted butter or
   margarine

Combine nuts, crumbs, and butter; press firmly in bottom of 9-to 10-inch springform pan.

FILLING:

4 (8-ounce) packages cream
   cheese, softened
1¼ cups sugar

4 eggs
1 tablespoon lemon juice
2 teaspoons vanilla (optional)

Beat cream cheese in mixer until light and fluffy. Beat in sugar until smooth. Add eggs, one at a time. Add lemon juice and vanilla and beat well. Spoon Filling over Crust. Set pan on cookie sheet and bake at 350° (10-inch pan) 40–50 minutes, (9-inch pan) 50–55 minutes. Remove from oven; let stand 15 minutes.

TOPPING:

2 cups sour cream
¼ cup sugar

1 teaspoon vanilla

Combine sour cream, sugar, and vanilla; blend well. Spoon over top of Filling; spread to within ½ inch of edge. Return to 350° oven for 5 minutes. Let cake cool completely, then refrigerate at least 24 hours (2 days is better).

GLAZE:

1 pint strawberries
1 (12-ounce) jar strawberry or
   raspberry jelly

1 tablespoon cornstarch
¼ cup water
¼ cup Cointreau

A couple of hours before serving, wash and hull berries; dry. Combine jelly with cornstarch in saucepan and mix well. Add water and Cointreau. Cook over medium heat, stirring until thickened and clear (about 5 minutes); cool. Using kitchen knife, loosen cake from pan; remove springform. Arrange berries on top of cake; spoon glaze over berries to drip down sides. Return to refrigerator.

Best of the Holidays

COOKIES & CANDIES

PHOTO © GEORGIA DEPARTMENT OF ECONOMIC DEVELOPMENT

Centennial Olympic Park made its debut when Atlanta served host to the 1996 Summer Olympics. Granite from each of the five continents represented in the Olympic Games is used in the park. The Fountain of Rings is the world's largest interactive fountain.

Pumpkin Cookies

½ cup margarine, softened
1½ cups sugar
1 egg
1 cup pumpkin (canned or
  cooked)
1 teaspoon vanilla
2½ cups all-purpose flour

1 teaspoon baking powder
1 teaspoon baking soda
½ teaspoon salt
1 teaspoon nutmeg
1 teaspoon cinnamon
½ cup chopped nuts
1 cup (6 ounces) chocolate chips

Cream margarine and sugar until light and fluffy. Beat in egg, pumpkin, and vanilla. Mix and sift flour, baking powder, baking soda, salt, nutmeg, and cinnamon. Add to creamed mixture. Mix well. Add nuts and chocolate chips. Mix well. Drop by teaspoonfuls onto well-greased cookie sheet. Bake at 350° for 15 minutes or until light brown. Makes 5–6 dozen.

A Taste of Georgia, Another Serving

Old-Fashioned Tea Cakes

1 cup butter, softened
2 cups sugar
5 eggs
5½ cups flour

3 teaspoons baking powder
¼ cup milk
1 teaspoon vanilla flavoring

In a large mixing bowl, cream butter and sugar. Add eggs, one at a time. Combine flour and baking powder. Add to butter mixture alternately with milk. Add vanilla; mix well. Knead dough to cutting consistency. Roll ¼–½ inch thick. Cut with cookie cutter. Bake at 350° for 12–15 minutes.

Give Us This Day Our Daily Bread

Lemon Whippersnaps

1 (18¼-ounce) box lemon
  cake mix
2 cups (4½ ounces) frozen
  whipped topping, thawed

1 egg
½ cup powdered sugar

Combine dry cake mix, whipped topping, and egg. Stir until well mixed. Drop by teaspoonfuls into powdered sugar. Roll in powdered sugar to coat. Place on greased cookie sheet 2 inches apart. Bake at 350° for 10–15 minutes.

A Taste of the Holidays

World's Best Cookies

2 sticks margarine, softened
1 cup light brown sugar
1 cup white sugar
1 egg
1 cup salad oil
1 cup regular oats
1 cup Rice Krispies
½ cup flaked coconut
3½ cups plain flour
1 teaspoon salt
1 teaspoon baking soda
2 teaspoons vanilla
½ cup chopped pecans

Cream margarine and sugars. Add egg; mix well. Add oil; continue beating. Add oats, Rice Krispies, and coconut; mix well. Add flour, salt, baking soda, and vanilla. Stir in pecans. Form mixture into small balls. Place on ungreased cookie sheet. Flatten with fork dipped in water. Bake at 325° for 10–12 minutes.

Grandma Mamie Jones' Family Favorites

Peanut Butter Cookies

⅔ cup flour
1 teaspoon baking powder
¼ teaspoon salt
½ cup chunky peanut butter
¼ cup margarine, softened
1 cup brown sugar, packed
1 teaspoon vanilla extract
2 eggs

Sift flour, baking powder, and salt together. Cream peanut butter and margarine in mixer bowl until light and fluffy. Add brown sugar and vanilla; beat well. Beat in eggs. Add dry ingredients; beat well. Spread in greased 8x8-inch baking pan. Bake at 350° for 25–30 minutes or until top looks dry and wooden pick inserted in center comes out clean. Cool in pan on wire rack. Cut into 2-inch squares. Makes 16 servings.

From Our House to Yours

Since Sylvester proudly boasts of being the Peanut Capital of the World, it's only fitting that the Georgia Peanut Festival be held there each year on the third weekend in October. Did you know that the Peter Pan Peanut Butter Company is located in Sylvester?

Crispy Pecan Sticks

½ cup butter, softened
¼ cup powdered sugar, plus extra for rolling
2 cups all-purpose flour
¼ teaspoon salt
1 cup coarsely chopped pecans
1 tablespoon vanilla extract
1 tablespoon ice water

Beat butter with mixer until creamy. Gradually add powdered sugar; beat well. Combine flour and salt; add to butter mixture, beating at low speed until blended. Stir in pecans, vanilla, and ice water. Shape dough into 3-inch sticks. Place sticks on lightly greased baking sheet. Bake 15–18 minutes at 350° or until browned. Roll in powdered sugar. Makes 3 dozen.

Georgia National Fair Blue Ribbon Cookbook

Miss Jamie's Pecan Cookies

Miss Jamie was a teacher at Jefferson and a member of Bethany Methodist Church. She always brought a big box of these cookies to homecomings at Bethany. All the children loved them. This is a very old recipe, as you can tell by the ingredients. It's been a long time since we used lard.

½ cup lard or Crisco
½ cup butter or margarine, softened
2½ cups brown or white sugar, or mixed
2 eggs, beaten
2½ cups flour
¼ teaspoon salt
½ teaspoon baking soda
1 cup chopped pecans

Cream shortening, butter, and sugar; add eggs. Sift flour, salt, and baking soda. Add to cream mixture; add pecans. Drop from spoon onto greased cookie sheet. Bake 11–15 minutes at 375°. Makes 4 dozen.

My Best to You

"The Tree that Owns Itself," is located at the corner of Dearing and Finley Streets in Athens. The large white oak was willed eight feet of land on all sides around its base. Legend holds that Colonel William H. Jackson, a professor at the University of Georgia, owned the land on which the tree stood, and enjoyed its shade and "magnificent proportions" so much that he willed the tree the land around it.

Sugar Cookies

1 cup margarine, softened
1 cup granulated sugar
1 cup cooking oil
2 eggs
1 teaspoon vanilla

4 cups plus 4 tablespoons
    plain flour
1 teaspoon salt
1 teaspoon baking soda
1 teaspoon cream of tartar

Cream margarine, sugar, and oil. Add eggs and vanilla. Add sifted dry ingredients. Drop by teaspoonfuls onto ungreased cookie sheet. Dip small glass in sugar and gently press each cookie. Bake at 350° for 10 minutes.

Heavenly Dishes

Too-Good-To-Be-True Cookies

Every ingredient you love in a cookie all stirred into one.

2 sticks butter, softened
¾ cup light brown sugar,
    packed
¾ cup granulated sugar
1 teaspoon vanilla extract
1 egg
1½ cups rolled oats

1½ cups self-rising flour
1 cup dried cranberries,
    chopped
1 (8-ounce) package toffee bits
1 cup semisweet chocolate
    chips

Preheat oven to 350°. Beat butter, brown sugar, and granulated sugar until light and fluffy. Add vanilla and egg; stir to mix well. Stir in oats, flour, cranberries, toffee bits, and chocolate chips. Drop by teaspoonfuls onto greased baking sheet. Bake for 10 minutes. Remove to wire rack and let cool before removing from baking sheet. Makes 3 dozen cookies.

Par 3: Tea-Time at the Masters®

Rosalynn Carter's
Raisin Oatmeal Cookies

1 cup flour, sifted
½ teaspoon baking soda
¼ teaspoon cinnamon
1½ cups quick-cooking oats
2 egg whites, lightly beaten

1 cup packed brown sugar
⅓ cup vegetable oil
½ cup skim milk
1 teaspoon vanilla extract
1 cup seedless raisins

Sift flour, baking soda, and cinnamon into bowl; stir in oats. Combine egg whites, brown sugar, oil, milk, vanilla, and raisins; mix well. Add to flour mixture; mix well. Drop by teaspoonfuls onto greased cookie sheet. Bake at 375° for 12–15 minutes or until light brown. Increase baking time for crisp cookies or decrease baking time for chewy cookies. Makes 36 servings.

Home Sweet Habitat

Jimmy Carter was born October 1, 1924, in Plains. In 1975, when Jimmy Carter began his race for the presidency, the small rural town of Plains had a population of only 653. Many Americans marveled at how a man from such an isolated, small-town upbringing came to broaden his horizons to eventually become the 39th president of the United States (1977–1981). In 2002, Carter won the Nobel Peace Prize for his efforts to find peaceful solutions to international conflicts, to advance democracy and human rights, and to promote economic and social development.

Christmas Cookies

1 cup margarine, softened
1 cup light brown sugar
3 eggs
3 cups plain flour
½ cup milk
1 teaspoon cinnamon
1 teaspoon salt
1 teaspoon baking soda

3 teaspoons vanilla
1 box white raisins
6 slices crystallized pineapple, chopped
½ pound crystallized cherries, chopped
1 pound dates, chopped
7 cups chopped pecans

Cream margarine and sugar. Add eggs, one at a time. Add flour, milk, cinnamon, salt, baking soda, and vanilla. Combine fruits and nuts in separate bowl; pour dough over fruit-nut mixture. Mix well. Drop by spoonfuls onto cookie sheet. Bake 25 minutes at 300°.

Grandma Mamie Jones' Family Favorites

Macadamia Nut White Chocolate Chunk Cookies

¾ cup firmly packed brown sugar
½ cup butter, softened
1 egg
1½ teaspoons vanilla
1⅓ cups all-purpose flour
½ teaspoon baking powder

½ teaspoon baking soda
½ teaspoon salt
2 (3-ounce) bars white chocolate, cut into ½-inch pieces
1 (3½-ounce) jar (¾ cup) salted macadamia nuts, coarsely chopped

Heat oven to 350°. In a large bowl, mix brown sugar, butter, egg, and vanilla. Beat at medium speed until creamy. In a medium bowl, mix flour, baking powder, baking soda, and salt with a wire whisk. Combine both mixtures by hand. Add white chocolate chunks and macadamia nuts. Drop by rounded tablespoonfuls 2 inches apart onto ungreased cookie sheet. Bake for 9–12 minutes or until light golden brown. Makes 2 dozen cookies.

A Gift of Appreciation

Chocolate Mint Thumbprints

½ cup unsalted butter
⅓ cup sugar
1 egg
½ teaspoon vanilla extract
¾ cup all-purpose flour
¼ cup cocoa powder
¾ cup chopped pecans, lightly
    toasted

¼ cup mint jelly
1 tablespoon finely chopped
    fresh mint
Powdered sugar

Cream together butter, sugar, and egg. Stir in vanilla. Sift flour and cocoa together; stir into creamed mixture. Stir in pecans. Chill dough 30 minutes or until firm. Roll dough into balls ¾ inch in diameter, and place on ungreased baking sheet. Make a deep depression in each ball with the end of a wooden spoon handle. Bake for 10 minutes at 350°. Cool 5 minutes.

Stir jelly and mint together with a fork. Spoon ¼ teaspoon into each cookie. Dust lightly with powdered sugar. Makes 3 dozen cookies.

Cooking with Herbs Volume I

Easy Peppermint Cookies

1 pound dark chocolate candy
    coating

8 drops peppermint oil
Ritz Crackers

Melt chocolate on LOW in microwave. Stir in peppermint oil. Dip crackers in chocolate; tap off excess. Lay on wax paper until set.

Georgia National Fair Blue Ribbon Cookbook

Cornflake Crinkles

1 cup butter, softened
1 cup sugar
1½ cups sifted flour
1 teaspoon cream of tartar
½ teaspoon salt

1 teaspoon baking soda
1 teaspoon vanilla
4 cups cornflakes cereal
1 cup chopped pecans

Combine butter and sugar. Beat until smooth and creamy. Combine flour, cream of tartar, salt, and baking soda; gradually add to butter mixture. Add vanilla; beat until smooth and well blended. Gently fold in cornflakes and nuts so as not to crush cereal. Drop by teaspoonfuls onto ungreased cookie sheet. Bake at 300° for 12–15 minutes or until lightly browned.

Holiday Delights

Savannah Cheesecake Cookies

These are a favorite among Savannahians.

CRUST:
1 cup all-purpose flour
½ cup packed light brown
   sugar

1 cup chopped pecans
½ cup (1 stick) butter, melted

Preheat oven to 350°. Combine flour, brown sugar, pecans, and butter in a bowl. Press dough into ungreased 9x13x2-inch pan. Bake for 12–15 minutes or until lightly browned.

FILLING:
2 (8-ounce) packages cream
   cheese, softened
1 cup granulated sugar
3 eggs

1 teaspoon pure vanilla or
   almond extract
Fresh berries and mint leaves
   for garnish

Beat cream cheese and granulated sugar together in a bowl until smooth, using a handheld electric mixer; add eggs and extract; beat well. Pour over Crust. Bake 20 minutes. Cool completely. Cut into squares before serving. Decorate tops with berries and mint leaves. Makes 24 squares.

The Lady & Sons Just Desserts

Six Layer Cookies

Easy. No mixing. Super!

1 stick margarine
1½ cups graham cracker
  crumbs
1 (3⅓-ounce) can flaked
  coconut

1 (12-ounce) package chocolate
  chips
1 cup chopped nuts
1 (14-ounce) can condensed milk
  (not evaporated milk)

Melt margarine in 9x13x2-inch pan or casserole dish. Sprinkle graham cracker crumbs evenly in bottom of pan on melted margarine. Follow with a layer of coconut, a layer of chocolate chips, and a layer of nuts. Pat down each layer. Top with condensed milk. Bake at 350° for 25 minutes. Cool before cutting.

Out On Our Own

Chocolate Toffee Bars

Graham crackers
1 cup margarine
1 cup brown sugar

1 cup finely chopped pecans
12 ounces milk chocolate chips
  or candy bars

Break crackers apart and arrange on a 10x15-inch foil-lined jelly-roll pan; cover entire pan. Melt margarine and sugar; bring to a boil. Boil 2 minutes. Remove from heat and stir in nuts. Pour boiling mixture over crackers and bake for 10–12 minutes at 350°. Remove from oven and sprinkle chocolate chips or candy bar pieces over top at once. As chocolate melts, spread evenly over top. Cool and cut. Makes approximately 6 dozen bars.

Best of the Holidays

Lavonda's Brownies

½ cup shortening or butter
1 cup sugar
2 eggs, beaten
2 squares (2-ounces)
  unsweetened chocolate,
  melted

¾ cup sifted cake flour
¼ teaspoon baking powder
¼ teaspoon salt
¾ cup chopped nuts

Work shortening with a spoon until fluffy and creamy; add sugar gradually. Continue to work with a spoon until light. Add eggs and melted chocolate. Mix and sift the flour, baking powder, and salt. Add nuts. Combine mixtures. Turn into a greased pan and bake in oven at 350° for 30–35 minutes. Immediately cut into squares.

Red Oak Recipes

Neiman Marcus Brownies

1 (18¼-ounce) box butter
  pecan cake mix

1 stick butter, melted
1 egg, beaten

Mix ingredients together; dough will be stiff. Press into a floured and greased 9x13-inch pan.

TOPPING:
1 (8-ounce) package cream
  cheese, softened
1 stick butter, softened
2 eggs, beaten

1 (1-pound) box confectioners'
  sugar
1½ cups pecans, chopped

Mix together all ingredients except pecans. Pour over the brownie layer. Top with pecans. Bake at 300° for 50–55 minutes.

Home Run Recipes

Atlanta has more shopping center space per capita than any other city except Chicago.

Brownie Decadence

I made this recipe on Calling All Cooks *on TV's Food Network.*

1 cup (2 sticks) butter or
   margarine
4 squares (4-ounces)
   unsweetened baking chocolate
2 cups sugar
4 large eggs

2 teaspoons vanilla
1½ cups all-purpose flour
1 teaspoon baking powder
1 teaspoon salt
1 bar (4-ounces) premium white
   chocolate, chopped

Preheat oven to 350°. Lightly grease or coat a 9x13-inch baking pan with nonstick cooking spray. In a large saucepan, melt butter and unsweetened chocolate over low heat. Remove from heat and mix in sugar. Add eggs and vanilla, stirring until well blended. Add flour, baking powder, and salt; stir just until mixed. Gently stir in chopped white chocolate. Spread mixture in prepared pan. Bake 25–30 minutes until brownies begin to pull away from sides of pan and center is slightly puffed. Remove from oven and cool completely. While brownies are baking, prepare Ganache Topping. Makes 24 squares.

GANACHE TOPPING:

1 cup heavy cream
2 cups semisweet chocolate
   chips

1½ cups pecans, toasted
   and chopped

In a medium saucepan, bring heavy cream just to a boil. Remove from heat and add chocolate chips. Let set for a few minutes to soften chocolate. Stir until mixture is smooth. Set aside; let chocolate mixture cool and thicken, stirring occasionally, 30–45 minutes. Spread onto brownies. Sprinkle with nuts. When Ganache Topping has hardened, cut into 24 squares. Cut squares into 48 triangles, if desired. Carefully remove from pan. (Can be tightly covered and frozen up to 3 weeks.)

Confessions of a Kitchen Diva

Praline Brownies

Extra moist and chewy. We defy anyone to guess that these scrumptious brownies come from a mix. Must do ahead.

1 (22½-ounce) package
  brownie mix
¾ cup firmly packed light
  brown sugar

3 tablespoons margarine,
  melted
¾ cup chopped pecans

Prepare brownie mix according to package directions; do not add nuts. Place in greased 9x13x2-inch pan. In small mixing bowl, combine remaining ingredients. Sprinkle over brownie batter. Bake at 350° for 25–30 minutes. Cut when thoroughly cooled. These freeze well or can be stored in a tin. Makes 2 dozen.

Perennials

Pecan Brittle

1 cup sugar
½ cup white corn syrup
1 tablespoon water

2 cups chopped pecans
1 teaspoon baking soda

Combine sugar, corn syrup, and water, and cook on low heat 5 minutes. Add pecans and cook 10 minutes or until tan in color. Take off heat, and add baking soda. Stir, then pour out onto greased jellyroll pan. Crack into large pieces when hard.

Down Through the Years

Established in 1918, Fort Benning (named for Major General Henry L. Benning) is the world's largest infantry training center. Known as the Home of the Infantry, the installation spreads over 182,000 acres and is home to the U.S. Army Infantry Training Brigade, U.S. Infantry School, Ranger Training Brigade, Airborne School, and School of the Americas. It has an active duty population of 34,834.

Peanutty Balls

12 ounces crunchy peanut
  butter
1 cup margarine
2 cups graham cracker crumbs
1 pound powdered sugar

1 teaspoon vanilla
12 ounces chocolate chips
4 ounces paraffin
1 cup finely chopped nuts

Combine peanut butter, margarine, crackers crumbs, powdered sugar, and vanilla; mix until blended. Form into small balls and chill. Melt chocolate and paraffin in a double boiler. Using a pick, dip each ball into chocolate and sprinkle with nuts.

Holiday Favorites

Martha's Kisses

2 egg whites
Pinch of salt
½ cup sugar
½ teaspoon vanilla

1 (6-ounce) package butterscotch
  bits
½ cup chopped nuts

Preheat oven to 375°. Beat egg whites and salt until soft peaks form. Slowly add sugar and continue beating until stiff peaks form. Add vanilla. Fold in butterscotch bits and nuts. Cover cookie sheet with brown paper or aluminum foil. Drop by teaspoonfuls onto cookie sheet. Put in oven, close door, and turn off heat. Let Kisses remain in oven until oven cools to room temperature about 3 hours. Makes approximately 36.

Tea-Time at the Masters®

Atlanta was briefly named Marthasville from 1843–1844, after the daughter of Georgia's governor at that time. However, the business community was concerned that such a name wouldn't attract commerce, and so a new name, "Atlanta," was chosen in 1845 as being much more marketable.

Chocolate Creams

2 (1-pound) boxes powdered sugar	1 tablespoon butter, melted
1 (14-ounce) can condensed milk	1 teaspoon vanilla
	1/4 teaspoon salt
	2 cups finely chopped nuts

Combine all ingredients and mix well. Roll into small balls and let stand in refrigerator overnight.

CHOCOLATE COATING:

4 squares chocolate	1/4 cake paraffin

Melt chocolate and paraffin in top of double boiler. Spear each ball with pick and dip into chocolate, allowing excess to drip over pan. Place on wax paper.

Best of the Holidays

The Best Fudge Ever

A little more trouble, but oh, so good!

3/4 cup evaporated milk	2 tablespoons light corn syrup
2 (1-ounce) squares unsweetened chocolate, grated	1 tablespoon butter or margarine
2 cups sugar	1 teaspoon vanilla
Pinch of salt	3/4–1 cup chopped nuts

Heat milk; add grated chocolate and stir until melted. Combine sugar and salt in a heavy kettle or saucepan. Pour milk over sugar; add syrup and cook over low heat. Stir vigorously until sugar is dissolved. Increase heat and stir only until mixture boils. Boil gently. Occasionally dip to bottom and use a folding motion. Cook until it reaches 234° on candy thermometer, or until it forms a soft ball when dropped into a cup of cold water. Remove from heat, add butter, and set aside until it cools to room temperature. Beat vigorously with a spoon. Add vanilla and continue beating until it loses its shine and gloss and begins to thicken. Add nuts and pour onto buttered wax paper or buttered 8x12-inch pan. Cut when completely cool.

A Taste of the Holidays

Cheesy Fudge

4 (1-pound) boxes confectioners' sugar
1 cup Hershey's cocoa
1 pound butter
1 pound Velveeta cheese
3 cups chopped nuts
1 tablespoon vanilla flavoring

Sift sugar and cocoa together in an extra large bowl. Melt butter and cheese in a double boiler, but do not let the mixture come to a boil. Pour into sugar and cocoa mix, stirring as you pour. Add nuts and vanilla. After you pour it all into the sugar and cocoa mix, you will have to use your hands to knead and mix all of the sugar and nuts in. Pat into buttered pan or glass dish. Makes 7 pounds.

Note: This can be frozen in aluminum foil up to one year.

Bread of Life–Salem Baptist Church

Quick Draw's Key Lime Fudge

1 (12-ounce) can evaporated milk
3½ cups sugar
1 teaspoon salt
1 (10.5-ounce) bag miniature marshmallows
4 cups white chocolate morsels
½ cup grated lime zest (about 6 limes)
4 tablespoons Key lime juice

Line a 9x13x2-inch pan with aluminum foil. Grease foil with margarine. Combine milk, sugar, and salt in a heavy 6-quart saucepan over medium heat. Bring to boiling; boil 8 minutes, stirring constantly. Remove from heat. Add marshmallows, chocolate morsels, lime zest, and lime juice to milk mixture. Stir until marshmallows and chocolate are melted and smooth. Pour fudge into prepared pan. Cool completely. Cut into 1-inch squares. Makes about 2 pounds.

Note: If you can't find Key lime juice, use the same amount of fresh-squeezed lime juice. The fudge will be slightly sweeter.

Wanted: Quick Draw's Favorite Recipes

PIES & OTHER DESSERTS

Beautiful Brasstown Bald Mountain, rising 4,784 feet above sea level, is Georgia's highest point. On clear days, the spectacular panoramic view from atop the mountain allows you to see four states: Georgia, Tennessee, North Carolina, and South Carolina.

Strawberry Splendor Mile High Pie

The crust complements the delicious strawberry taste!

CRUST:

1 cup all-purpose flour
¼ cup firmly packed light
  brown sugar

½ cup butter, melted
½ cup finely chopped pecans

Preheat oven to 350°. In a large mixing bowl, combine all Crust ingredients until blended. Spread thinly onto an ungreased baking sheet. Bake 15 minutes, stirring occasionally. Cool slightly. Stir to crumble. Reserve ½ cup crumb mixture for garnish. Press remaining warm crumb mixture into a lightly buttered 9-inch glass pie plate. Cool.

FILLING:

1 (10-ounce) package frozen
  strawberries with syrup,
  thawed
1 cup granulated sugar
2 teaspoons freshly squeezed
  lemon juice

2 egg whites
1 (8-ounce) carton whipping
  cream, whipped

Using an electric mixer, combine strawberries, sugar, lemon juice, and egg whites. Beat on high speed 15 minutes until mixture is very stiff (beating is the secret!). Fold in whipped cream by hand. Turn Filling into prepared Crust. Sprinkle reserved crumb mixture over top. Freeze overnight before serving; serve frozen.

Bevelyn Blair's Everyday Pies

Million Dollar Pie

1 (14-ounce) can sweetened
  condensed milk
¼ cup freshly squeezed lemon
  juice
1 cup pared, sliced, ripe
  peaches

1 cup pineapple, well drained
1 (8-ounce) container frozen
  whipped topping, thawed
2 (9-inch) graham cracker
  crumb pastry shells

In a large mixing bowl, combine milk and juice, stirring until slightly thickened. Gradually fold in peaches and pineapple. Lightly fold in whipped topping until mixed together thoroughly. Divide mixture and turn into shells. Chill 3 hours before serving.

Bevelyn Blair's Everyday Pies

Company's Coming Peach Pie

1 (8- or 9-inch) pie shell,
  unbaked
1 tablespoon butter, melted
2 teaspoons vanilla extract
1 (8-ounce) package cream
  cheese, softened
¼ cup sugar

¼ cup sour cream
½ cup apricot preserves,
  divided
1 (16-ounce) can sliced red
  freestone peaches, drained

Brush pie shell with butter. Bake according to package directions; let stand until cool. Process vanilla, cream cheese, sugar, sour cream, and ¼ cup preserves in blender or food processor until smooth. Pour into baked pie shell. Arrange peaches artfully in a spoke pattern over top. Drizzle remaining ¼ cup preserves (may have to heat slightly) over peaches. Chill in refrigerator. Serves 6.

Some Assembly Required

Cloister Lemon Meringue Pie

Recipe given to me by a long time baker for the Cloister Resort Hotel on St. Simons Island.

1½ cups sugar
7 tablespoons cornstarch
Dash of salt
1½ cups water
3 egg yolks, beaten

1 teaspoon grated lemon peel
2 tablespoons butter or
 margarine
½ cup lemon juice
1 (9-inch) pie shell, baked

In a saucepan, combine sugar, cornstarch, and salt. Stir in water. Bring to boiling over medium heat and cook, stirring constantly until thick, about 5 minutes. Remove from heat, stir small amount of hot mixture into egg yolks, then return to remaining mixture in pan. Bring to a boil and cook 1 minute, stirring constantly. Remove from heat. Add lemon peel and butter. Slowly stir in lemon juice. Cool to lukewarm. Pour into cooled pie shell; top with Meringue.

MERINGUE:
3 egg whites
1 teaspoon lemon juice

6 tablespoons sugar

Beat egg whites with lemon juice until soft peaks form. Gradually add sugar, beating until stiff. Spread Meringue over filling; seal to edges of pastry. Bake at 350° for 12–15 minutes or until Meringue is golden brown. Cool thoroughly before serving. Serves 6–8.

Southern Manna

Blueberry Sky Pie

1 (8-ounce) package cream
 cheese, softened
1 (6-ounce) can frozen
 lemonade
1 (14-ounce) can sweetened
 condensed milk

1 (21-ounce) can blueberry pie
 filling, divided
2 graham cracker pie crusts

Beat cream cheese until creamy; add lemonade and condensed milk. Mix till well blended. Fold together ¾ of cream cheese mixture and ⅔ of blueberry pie filling. Spread into crusts; chill. Garnish with remaining cream cheese mixture and remaining pie filling. Makes 2 pies.

Culinary Classics

Grapefruit Grand Meringue Pie

A wonderful pie to make with a light and unusual flavor!

FILLING:

2 cups granulated sugar
6 tablespoons cornstarch
½ cup water
2 cups freshly squeezed
  grapefruit juice

3 eggs yolks, well beaten
1½ tablespoons butter
1 (9-inch) single plain pastry
  shell, baked and cooled

In a large saucepan, combine sugar, cornstarch, water, and juice; stir until blended and smooth. Cook over medium heat 5 minutes or until thickened, stirring constantly. Remove from heat. Quickly stir ⅓ cup hot mixture into beaten egg yolks; return to saucepan. Cook and stir for 2 minutes. Remove from heat. Add butter, stirring until melted. Spread evenly into shell; set aside to cool.

MERINGUE:

3 egg whites
⅛ teaspoon salt
¼ teaspoon cream of tartar

6 tablespoons granulated sugar
1 teaspoon grated grapefruit
  zest for garnish

Preheat oven to 375°. Using an electric mixer, beat egg whites until foamy. Gradually add salt, cream of tartar, and sugar, beating until stiff and shiny. Quickly spread over Filling to the edge. Sprinkle zest evenly over top. Bake 10 minutes or until light golden brown. Cool 3 hours on a wire rack before serving.

Bevelyn Blair's Everyday Pies

The setting for generations of pirate lore and tales of buried treasure, coastal Georgia's Blackbeard Island was named for Edward Teach, best known as "Blackbeard," a pirate who conducted raids on merchant shipping in the region in the early 18th century.

Peanut Butter Pie

Peanut butter pie is fundamental to the serious dessert repertoire of the South, and that is especially true in the peanut-rich state of Georgia. This creamy peanut butter pie is on the dessert table every day at Blue Willow Inn. A guest once asked, "Who made the peanut butter pie? I want to marry her."

1 (8-ounce) package cream
  cheese, softened
1 cup confectioners' sugar
¾ cup crunchy peanut butter

2 (12-ounce) cartons whipped
  topping, divided
2 graham cracker pie crusts

In a large bowl, mix cream cheese, confectioners' sugar, and peanut butter together. Fold in 1 carton of whipped topping. Divide mixture between pie crusts and chill for several hours. Top each pie with half the remaining whipped topping. Makes 16 servings.

The Blue Willow Inn Bible of Southern Cooking

Egg Custard Pie

Easy and our favorite.

1 frozen pie shell, thawed
3 eggs
⅓ cup plus 2 tablespoons
  sugar

2 cups milk
½ teaspoon vanilla
Pinch of salt

Thaw pie shell. When soft, pinch top edge of crust up off the flat lip of the pie pan so it is easier to get out of oven when baked. Preheat oven to 350°. Beat eggs in medium bowl until mixed well. Add sugar and mix. Add milk, vanilla, and salt; beat lightly. Pour into unbaked pie shell. Bake for 10 minutes; reduce heat to 325° and bake 30–40 minutes longer or until custard is set and firm. To test, insert knife in center of pie and remove slowly. If custard sticks to knife, it needs more cooking.

Note: In order to prevent the bottom crust from being soggy, put pie on bottom shelf of oven for first 10 minutes; carefully move to the middle shelf for the remaining time. This will bake the bottom faster and prevent "the soggies." Do not forget to reduce heat. You can use more sugar if you like your custard really sweet; I do not. Some use a whole cup of sugar.

Out On Our Own

Chocolate Fudge Pie

A family favorite and so easy to make!

1½ (1-ounce) squares
   unsweetened baking chocolate
¼ cup butter
1½ cups granulated sugar
½ cup evaporated milk

2 eggs, lightly beaten
½ teaspoon pure vanilla extract
1 (9-inch) single plain pastry
   shell, unbaked

Preheat oven to 350°. In a medium saucepan over low heat, melt chocolate and butter, stirring until mixture is smooth. Remove from heat. Gradually add sugar; blend until smooth. Slowly add milk until combined. Gradually add eggs and vanilla, stirring until blended thoroughly. Spread evenly into shell. Bake 55 minutes or until firm, but soft in the center. Remove from oven. Delicious served warm with sweetened whipped cream.

Bevelyn Blair's Everyday Pies

Four-Minute Brownie Pie

2 eggs
1 cup sugar
½ cup butter or margarine,
   softened
½ cup flour

4 tablespoons cocoa
1 teaspoon vanilla
Dash of salt
½ cup chopped pecans or
   walnuts

Place eggs, sugar, butter, flour, cocoa, vanilla, and salt in small mixer bowl; beat 4 minutes. Stir in nuts. Pour into greased 8-inch pie pan. Bake at 325° for 30 minutes or until done. Pie will settle like a meringue when cool. Cut in wedges and serve with whipped cream or ice cream.

Family Collections

In 1836, Wesleyan College in Macon became the first college in the world chartered to grant degrees to women.

Coffee Angel Pie

MERINGUE SHELL:

4 egg whites
¼ teaspoon cream of tartar
¼ teaspoon salt

1 cup sugar
1 tablespoon instant coffee
   crystals

Preheat oven to 275°. Combine egg whites, cream of tartar, and salt. Beat until soft peaks form. Gradually add sugar, 1 tablespoon at a time, beating well after each addition. Add coffee with last of sugar until stiff glossy peaks form. Spread ½ of meringue on bottom of 10-inch pie plate. Swirl or pipe remaining around sides and rim. Bake for 1 hour.

FILLING:

1 (14-ounce) can condensed milk
1 cup strong coffee, chilled

1½ cups heavy whipping cream
1 cup finely chopped pecans

Mix condensed milk with coffee. Add stiffly beaten cream. Pour mixture into Meringue Shell, sprinkle generously with pecans, and freeze. Serves 6–8.

Montezuma Amish Mennonite Cookbook I

Frozen Crème de Menthe Pie
(Grasshopper Pie)

24 Oreo cookies, finely crushed,
   divided
¼ cup butter, melted
¼ cup crème de menthe

1 (7-ounce) jar marshmallow
   crème
2 cups whipping cream

In medium bowl, toss cookie crumbs with butter, reserving ½ cup for top of pie. Press remaining in bottom of 9-inch springform pan. Gradually add crème de menthe to marshmallow crème, mixing well until blended. Whip cream until it holds its shape. Fold into marshmallow mixture. Pour into crumb-lined pan. Sprinkle reserved crumbs over top of pie. Freeze until firm. Serves 6.

Cook and Love It

Macaroon Pie

3 eggs, separated
1 cup sugar, divided
1 cup graham cracker crumbs
1½ cups chopped pecans
1 teaspoon vanilla extract
1 teaspoon almond extract
½ teaspoon salt

Beat egg whites until slightly stiff; add ½ cup sugar. Beat egg yolks and remaining sugar. Beat two egg mixtures together. Add cracker crumbs, nuts, vanilla extract, almond extract, and salt. Pour into a well-greased pie pan. Bake at 350° for 35 minutes. If using glass pie plate, bake at 325°. Serve with whipped cream or ice cream.

Holiday Favorites

Coconut Pie

5 large eggs
7 ounces shredded coconut
2 cups sugar
¾ stick butter, melted
1 teaspoon vanilla
¾ cup buttermilk

Slightly beat eggs, then add other ingredients; mix well. Pour into 2 (9-inch) pie shells. Bake at 350° degrees for 30–40 minutes.

Tastes for All Seasons

Run for the Roses

3 tablespoons bourbon
1 cup chopped English walnuts
1 cup sugar
1 cup white corn syrup
4 eggs
1 stick butter, melted
1 cup chocolate chips
1 teaspoon vanilla extract
2 (8- or 9-inch) pie shells,
   unbaked

Pour bourbon over nuts and set aside. Beat sugar, syrup, and eggs together. Add butter, chocolate chips, and vanilla extract. Add bourbon and nuts. Pour into shells. Bake 45 minutes at 350°. Makes 2 (8- or 9-inch) pies.

A Taste of Georgia

Pecan Pie

½ cup (1 stick) butter, melted
1 cup sugar
1 cup light corn syrup
4 eggs, beaten

1 teaspoon vanilla extract
¼ teaspoon salt
1 (9-inch) pie shell, unbaked
1 cup chopped pecans

Combine the butter, sugar, and corn syrup in a saucepan; mix well. Cook over low heat until sugar is dissolved, stirring constantly. Remove from heat; cool. Add eggs, vanilla, and salt; mix until well blended. Pour into pie shell and top with pecans. Bake at 325° for 50–55 minutes or until set.

Variation: For a Rum Pecan Pie, prepare as directed above, adding 3 tablespoons rum with the eggs.

Mother's Finest: Southern Cooking Made Easy

Best Ever Sweet Potato Pie

1 cup whole milk, scalded
1 cup evaporated milk
1 cup cooked, mashed sweet
   potatoes
¾ cup white sugar
¾ cup brown sugar

3 tablespoons flour
½ teaspoon nutmeg
½ teaspoon cinnamon
½ teaspoon salt
3 eggs, separated
2 (9-inch) unbaked pie crusts

Scald whole milk. Mix together both milks, sweet potatoes, sugars, flour, spices, and salt. Add egg yolks. Whip egg whites until stiff and fold in last. Pour into pie crusts. Bake at 400° for 10 minutes, then 350° for 45 minutes. Makes 2 pies.

Variation: For crumb topping, mix 1 cup flour, 1 cup brown sugar, 1 cup oatmeal, and 1 stick softened butter. Add to top of pies before baking.

Montezuma Amish Mennonite Cookbook II

Zucchini "Apple" Pie

6 cups sliced zucchini	2 teaspoons cream of tartar
1¾ cups sugar	2 tablespoons flour
2 teaspoons cinnamon	2 tablespoons cornstarch
Dash of nutmeg	2 (9-inch) pie crusts
Dash of salt	Butter
3 tablespoons lemon juice	

Use large zucchini, but still tender enough that you can pierce the skin easily with your thumbnail. Peel and cut in quarters lengthwise. Remove the seeds and slice crosswise; cook until tender.

Mix sugar, spices, lemon juice, cream of tartar, flour, and cornstarch in a bowl. Add zucchini and mix well. It will be runny, but that's okay. Place filling in pie crust and dot with butter. Add top crust and bake at 400° for 40 minutes or until golden brown.

Cooking with Watkinsville First Christian Church

Golden Delicious Apple Streusel Pie

An easy dessert to prepare, yet elegant and delicious!

FILLING:

2 cups granulated sugar	10 cups pared, thinly sliced
2 cups water	Golden Delicious apples

In a large saucepan, combine sugar and water. Bring to boiling point. Remove from heat and stir until sugar is dissolved; set aside. Layer apple slices in a 9x13x2-inch glass baking dish. Pour sugar-water mixture over top; set aside.

TOPPING:

1¾ cups all-purpose flour	1 teaspoon ground cinnamon
⅛ teaspoon salt	1 cup granulated sugar
2 teaspoons baking powder	½ cup cold butter

Preheat oven to 350°. In a large mixing bowl, sift together flour, salt, baking powder, cinnamon, and sugar. Cut in butter with a pastry blender until mixture resembles coarse crumbs. Sprinkle over apple mixture. Bake 50 minutes or until golden brown. Remove from oven; cool on wire rack. Serve warm or cold.

Bevelyn Blair's Everyday Pies

Pavlova

BAKED MERINGUE SHELL:

4 egg whites

1 cup sugar

¼ cup cornstarch

1½ teaspoons white vinegar

½ teaspoon vanilla extract

Grease baking sheet; line with greased wax paper. Draw 8-inch circle on wax paper using skewer or wooden pick. Beat egg whites in mixer bowl until soft peaks form. Add sugar gradually, beating constantly until stiff peaks form. Beat in cornstarch, vinegar, and vanilla until blended. Spread meringue with rubber spatula over circle on prepared baking sheet, building up sides to form 2-inch rim. Bake at 225° for 2 hours or until surface is dry but not brown. Turn off oven. Let stand in oven with door slightly ajar until cool. May store baked meringue, loosely covered, at room temperature for up to 3 days.

1 Baked Meringue Shell

1½ cups whipping cream

3 tablespoons sugar

½ teaspoon vanilla extract

2 cups strawberry halves

1 (8-ounce) can pineapple
  tidbits, drained

1 star fruit, sliced

1 kiwi, cut into halves
  lengthwise, sliced

Arrange Baked Meringue Shell on serving plate. Beat whipping cream in mixer bowl until soft peaks form. Add sugar and vanilla; mix well. Spread shell with whipped cream. Decorate with strawberries, pineapple, star fruit, and kiwi. Serve immediately. Makes 12 servings.

Home Sweet Habitat

People pay a lot for famous signatures. Among the famous men who signed the Declaration of Independence are Thomas Jefferson, John Hancock, and Ben Franklin, but it is Georgia's own Button Gwinnett who nets the highest price for a signature, mostly because only eight are known to exist.

Peach Viennese Torte

A beautiful dessert!

¼ cup butter, softened
¼ cup confectioners' sugar
1 cup sifted flour
1 cup granulated sugar
2 tablespoons cornstarch

1 cup water
4 tablespoons cherry-flavored
  gelatin
8–10 large fresh peaches
1 cup whipping cream, whipped

Cream butter and gradually add confectioners' sugar. Add flour to mix, and form a soft dough. Pat on bottom and up sides of a 12-inch pizza pan. Bake at 325° for 20 minutes. Cool.

Combine sugar, cornstarch, and water. Cook over low heat, stirring constantly, until thick and clear. Stir in gelatin; allow to cool.

While cooling, peel and slice peaches; arrange in a single layer over the baked shell. Spread the cooled gelatin glaze over the peaches; chill. When ready to serve, top with whipped cream.

Our Best Home Cooking

Boarding House Trifle

1 large box vanilla instant
  pudding mix
1 pound cake or sponge cake
1 teaspoon sherry extract or
  sherry to taste

⅔ cup whipped cream
1 (10-ounce) jar cherries
  (candied or maraschino),
  cut up

Make pudding as directed on box. Let stand while breaking cake into crumbs. Add sherry to pudding and pour over crumbs. Stir whipped cream through the mixture and garnish with cherries. Makes 8 servings.

Famous Recipes from Mrs. Wilkes' Boarding House

Georgia Blackberry Cobbler

3–4 cups blackberries	1½ cups water
¾ cup sugar	1 tablespoon lemon juice
3 tablespoons all-purpose flour	

Place berries in a lightly greased shallow 2-quart baking dish. Combine sugar and flour; stir in water and lemon juice. Pour mixture over berries; bake at 425° for 15 minutes.

CRUST:

1¾ cups all-purpose flour	¼ cup plus 2 tablespoons
2 teaspoons baking powder	whipping cream
¾ teaspoon salt	¼ cup plus 2 tablespoons
2–3 tablespoons sugar	buttermilk
¼ cup shortening	2 tablespoons butter, melted

Combine first 4 ingredients. Cut in shortening with pastry blender until mixture resembles coarse meal; stir in whipping cream and buttermilk. Knead dough 4–5 times; roll out on a lightly floured surface. Cut dough to fit baking dish. Place Crust over hot berries; brush with butter. Bake at 425° for 20–30 minutes or until golden brown. Serve warm with ice cream, if desired. Makes 6–8 servings.

Our Best Home Cooking

Simple Summer Cobbler

The name says it all. Make the most of summer's bounty without spending a long time in the kitchen.

¾ cup margarine	¾ cup milk
1½ cups sugar, divided	1 tablespoon lemon juice
¾ cup flour	3 cups fruit (blueberries,
1½ teaspoons baking powder	peaches, apples, etc.)
1 teaspoon salt	Vanilla ice cream (optional)

Preheat oven to 350°. Melt margarine in 9x11-inch pan in pre-heating oven. In separate bowl, mix ¾ cup sugar, flour, baking powder, and salt. Stir in milk, blending well. Add remaining sugar and lemon juice to fruit. Place fruit in pan over margarine; pour batter over all. Do not stir. Bake for 30 minutes. Top each serving with a scoop of ice cream. Serves 6–8.

Perennials

My Favorite Peach Cobbler

CRUST:

2 cups flour	½ teaspoon salt
1½ cups sugar	1½ cups milk
4 teaspoons baking powder	1 teaspoon vanilla

Combine flour, sugar, baking powder, and salt. Stir in milk and vanilla; set aside.

FILLING:

2 quarts peach slices, drained	3 tablespoons cornstarch
½ stick butter	or clear gel
2 teaspoons lemon juice	¾ cup water
½ cup sugar	

In saucepan, bring first 4 Filling ingredients to a boil. Mix together cornstarch and water to make a paste; gradually add to Filling mixture. Pour into 3-quart baking dish and put Crust mixture on top.

TOPPING:

1 stick butter	1 teaspoon cinnamon
¼ cup sugar	

Melt butter and pour over Crust. Mix together sugar and cinnamon; sprinkle over top. Bake at 350° for 40 minutes. Serve warm with milk. Serves 10.

Montezuma Amish Mennonite Cookbook I

The Seven Natural Wonders
of Georgia

- The farmers who scratched out a hard living growing mainly cotton out of the soil 170 years ago didn't know about soil conservation practices such as contour plowing, crop rotation, and cover crops. They would be astounded if they could see today's massive gullies that were started with their mule-drawn plows. Poor farming practices, along with the extremely soft soils, led to the land that is now **Providence Canyon State Park**, near Lumpkin—also known as the Little Grand Canyon of Georgia.

- **Warm Springs** maintains a constant 88-degree temperature year-round and flows at approximately 914 gallons per minute. It was the late former President Franklin Delano Roosevelt who first gave national recognition to Warm Springs when, in 1924, he visited the town's naturally heated mineral springs as treatment for his polio-related paralysis. Roosevelt was so enchanted with Warm Springs that he built a modest, six-room cottage called the Little White House which served as a relaxing, comfortable haven for him during his regular visits. It was here where he died on April 12, 1945, while posing for the "Unfinished Portrait." The structure and grounds, including a museum, now serve as a memorial in his honor.

Little White House, Warm Springs

- Covering approximately 700 square miles of south Georgia and north Florida is a bowl-shaped depression in the coastal plain called the **Okefenokee Swamp**. Twenty-five miles across and forty miles long, Okefenokee is a primitive wetland that harbors hundreds of birds, mammals, reptiles, and amphibians, many of which are endangered or threatened. The name Okefenokee is derived from an Indian word meaning the "trembling earth."

Okefenokee Swamp

Tallulah Gorge

- **Tallulah Gorge** is a dramatic natural area with grand views. It is the oldest natural gorge in the United States and second in depth only to the Grand Canyon. It is the only quartzite-walled gorge in the southern Appalachian Mountains. The gorge, often called the Niagara of the South, ranges in depth from 200—1200 feet and is nearly two miles long.

- Cascading 729 feet, **Amicalola Falls** in Dawson County is the highest waterfall east of the Mississippi River. Amicalola is Cherokee for "tumbling water."

- **Stone Mountain**, located about ten miles northeast of downtown Atlanta, is one of the largest single masses of exposed granite in the world. It is 825 feet tall and covers 583 acres. The top of the mountain is 1,683 feet above sea level. Carved into the mountain are the figures of three

Stone Mountain

Confederate heroes of the Civil War: Stonewall Jackson, Jefferson Davis, and Robert E. Lee. Designed as a memorial to the heroic struggle of the South during the Civil War, the Memorial Carving towers 400 feet above the ground, measures 90x190 feet, and is recessed 42 feet into the mountain. In 1958, Georgia bought 1,613 acres (including Stone Mountain) to establish a state park. DeKalb County donated another 400 acres. Stone Mountain State Park, Georgia's #1 tourist attraction, now totals 3,200 acres.

- **Radium Springs** is the largest natural spring in Georgia. The deep blue waters of Radium Springs flow at 70,000 gallons per minute and empty into the Flint River. Prior to the discovery of radium in the water in 1925, the site was known as Blue Springs. The water temperature is 68 degrees year-round.

Dutch Oven Peach Cobbler

Campers from other sites come driving over to see what's cooking when they smell this cinnamon peach cobbler. Sometimes, Mr. English adds fresh blueberries. Be sure to share! It's the southern thing to do!

2 (16-ounce) cans sliced peaches in heavy or light syrup, or in fruit juice, your choice	½ cup Bisquick baking mix
	⅓ cup sugar
	Ground cinnamon
1 pint fresh blueberries (optional)	

Spray a Dutch oven with vegetable oil cooking spray. Drain 1 can of peaches. Combine both cans of peaches, including the juice from the undrained can, the blueberries, if using, the Bisquick, sugar, and a sprinkling of cinnamon. Place this mixture into the Dutch oven.

TOPPING:

2¼ cups Bisquick baking mix	½ cup milk
¼ cup sugar	Cinnamon sugar
¼ cup (½ stick) butter, melted	

Combine the Bisquick, sugar, butter, and milk in a resealable plastic bag. Using your fingers, drop bits of Topping on top of the peaches. Sprinkle with cinnamon sugar. Place the Dutch oven over about 12 coals, then cover with lid; place about 12 coals on top. Check in 10 minutes; if the dough is brown, there are too many coals on top. If it is not brown at all, add a few coals. The cobbler usually cooks in 30 minutes. Serves about 10 hungry campers.

Paula Deen & Friends

Baseball legend Ty Cobb, nicknamed the "Georgia Peach," was born on December 18, 1886, in Narrows. Ty grew up in Royston. In 1936, he was first player elected into the National Baseball Hall of Fame. Ty's lifetime batting average of .367 is the highest in baseball history. In 1905, the Detroit Tigers purchased Ty Cobb from Augusta of the South Atlantic League for $500.

Strawberry Creamy

FRENCH CREAM:

16 ounces sour cream
2 cups whipping cream
1½ cups powdered sugar
2 (¼-ounce) envelopes
   unflavored gelatin

½ cup cold water
2 (8-ounce) packages cream
   cheese, softened
2 teaspoons vanilla

In a medium saucepan, whisk together sour cream and whipping cream; gradually add sugar, blending well after each addition. Cook over low heat, continuously whisking until just warm. In small saucepan, sprinkle gelatin over cold water; allow to stand 1 minute. Cook over medium heat until gelatin is dissolved. Add to sour cream mixture and whisk until thoroughly combined.

In separate bowl, beat cream cheese with electric mixer until fluffy. Gradually pour in sour cream mixture and blend well. Add vanilla and blend until smooth. Pour into lightly greased 8-cup mold or 2-quart bowl; chill until firm. Will keep up to 2 days. Unmold onto serving platter. Spoon into dishes and spoon sauce over before serving.

STRAWBERRY SAUCE:

4 cups strawberries
1 cup sugar

2 tablespoons thawed orange
   juice concentrate

Purée strawberries in blender. Add sugar and orange juice; blend well. Place in covered bowl and refrigerate until ready to serve.

Optional presentation: Beat one cup whipping cream until foamy; add 1 tablespoon sugar; beat until soft peaks form.

Strawberries: From Our Family's Field to Your Family's Table

Strawberry Pizza I

CRUST:

2 sticks butter, melted

2 cups flour

1 cup chopped pecans

Mix and bake in a pizza pan at 350° for 20 minutes. Cool.

FILLING:

1 (8-ounce) package cream cheese, softened

1 cup confectioners' sugar

1 teaspoon vanilla

1 (16-ounce) container Cool Whip

2 pints strawberries, sliced

Mix cream cheese and powdered sugar together; add vanilla and Cool Whip. Layer Filling on top of Crust after it cools. Put strawberries then Glaze on top.

GLAZE:

1 cup strawberries

1 cup water

½ cup sugar

2 tablespoons cornstarch

Cold water

Crush strawberries; add water; strain through sieve. Combine sugar with strawberry juice in saucepan; stir and heat to boiling. Mix cornstarch with small amount of cold water. Add to boiling berry juice. Stir until thick. Cool; spoon carefully over strawberry Filling.

Strawberries: From Our Family's Field to Your Family's Table

From the mountains to the coast, pick-your-own strawberry farms dot the Georgia landscape. Strawberries rank third in Georgia's small fruit sales, trailing muscadine grapes and top-ranked blueberries.

Strawberry Frenzy

BROWNIE:

1 (19.8-ounce) package fudge
   brownie mix
½ cup oil

¼ cup water
2 eggs

Heat oven to 350°. Grease bottom and sides of 10-inch spring-form pan, or a tiara dessert pan. Combine all Brownie ingredients. Beat 50 strokes. Spread batter in pan. Bake for 25–35 minutes. Cool 30 minutes. Remove from pan. Cool another 30 minutes.

FILLING:

1 cup plus 1 tablespoon sugar,
   divided
1 (10-ounce) package frozen
   strawberries, thawed

1 tablespoon cornstarch
1 cup chopped fresh
   strawberries

Purée 1 cup sugar and strawberries in blender. In a small saucepan, combine remaining sugar and cornstarch. Gradually add strawberry purée: mix well; bring to a boil. Cool 5 minutes. Spread over brownie layer to ½ inch of sides. Arrange fresh strawberries over purée. Refrigerate 45 minutes.

TOPPING:

1 (8-ounce) package cream
   cheese, softened
⅓ cup powdered sugar
1 cup vanilla chips, melted
1 cup Cool Whip

1 tablespoon grated chocolate
   for garnish
Halved strawberries for garnish
Chocolate ants (made from a
   mold) for garnish

Combine cream cheese and powdered sugar; beat until smooth. Add melted chips; beat until smooth. Fold in Cool Whip. Cover and refrigerate 45 minutes.

Stir topping mixture until smooth. Spread 1½ cups of topping over strawberries; pipe on remaining topping. Refrigerate at least 1 hour. Garnish before serving with grated chocolate, halved strawberries, and chocolate ants.

Strawberries: From Our Family's Field to Your Family's Table

Chocolate Lush

1 stick margarine, melted
1 cup flour
1 cup powdered sugar
1 (8-ounce) package cream
 cheese, softened
1 cup Cool Whip
2 (3-ounce) packages instant
 chocolate pudding mix
3 cups milk
Chopped nuts (optional)

Mix melted margarine and flour; press into greased 9x13-inch pan. Bake 15 minutes at 375°. Mix powdered sugar and cream cheese; fold in 1 cup Cool Whip. Mix pudding with milk in separate bowl. Combine with cream cheese mixture. Pour into prepared crust. Top with remaining Cool Whip and, if desired, nuts.

A Gift of Appreciation

Callaway Shortbread
with Georgia Peaches Flambé

⅓ cup granulated sugar
2 cups all-purpose flour
2½ teaspoons baking
 powder
½ teaspoon salt
6 tablespoons butter
1¼ cups heavy cream
8 fresh peaches
1 cup honey
¼ cup Jack Daniels
 bourbon

In a bowl, combine sugar, flour, baking powder, and salt. Cut butter into small pieces and mix in with a fork. Make sure butter is incorporated, then add cream. Do not overwork the dough; the process should take less than 2 minutes. Let the dough rest for 10–15 minutes with a cloth on top to prevent drying. On floured surface, roll out dough to about ½-inch thickness and use a biscuit cutter to cut the dough. Bake on a greased cookie sheet at 350° for 10–15 minutes.

Peel and cut peaches into wedges. Pour honey in a pan and bring to a boil; add peaches. Stir for 3–4 minutes and flambé with Jack Daniels. To serve, place shortbread on a dish and scoop peaches on top. Serves 8.

Editor's Extra: Flambé is French for "flamed" or "flaming." It's the process of sprinkling certain foods with liquor, which, after warming, are ignited just before serving. (Be careful!)

Fine Dining Georgia Style

Lemon Mousse #2

1 (12-ounce) can evaporated
  milk
1 (5-ounce) can evaporated
  milk

1¼ cups sugar
Juice of 3 lemons
Rind of 2 lemons, grated
1 cup graham cracker crumbs

Chill milks in mixing bowl in freezer until ice forms around edge (around 15 minutes). Beat with mixer until tripled in size. Add sugar, lemon juice, and lemon rind; mix well. Spread graham cracker crumbs in bottom of serving dish. Pour mixture over crumbs. Chill in freezer for several hours before serving. Must be stored in the freezer.

Give Us This Day Our Daily Bread

Cocoa Cappuccino Mousse

1 (14-ounce) can sweetened
  condensed milk
⅓ cup cocoa
3 tablespoons margarine

2 teaspoons instant coffee
  granules
2 teaspoons hot water
1 pint whipping cream

Combine milk, cocoa, and margarine in a medium saucepan. Dissolve coffee in hot water; add to saucepan; cook over low heat, stirring constantly, until margarine melts and mixture is smooth. Remove from heat; cool. In a large mixer bowl, beat cream until stiff. Gradually fold chocolate into whipped cream. Spoon into individual dishes. Refrigerate for about 2 hours.

Holiday Delights

Granny's Banana Pudding

1 (8-ounce) package cream
  cheese, softened
2¼ cups milk, divided
1 (3½-ounce) package vanilla
  instant pudding mix

1 (12-ounce) box vanilla wafers,
  divided
2 cups banana slices, divided

Combine cream cheese and ½ cup milk, mixing at medium speed until well blended. Add remaining milk and pudding mix; beat at low speed for 1 minute. Layer ⅓ pudding mixture, ½ wafers and ½ bananas in 1½-quart serving bowl; repeat layers. Top with remaining pudding. Cover, chill, and garnish with banana slices and wafers.

Bread of Life–Salem Baptist Church

Debbie's Disappearing Banana Pudding

CUSTARD:

½ cup sugar
⅓ cup flour
Dash of salt
3 eggs, separated (save whites
   for meringue)
1 cup milk

1 cup half-and-half
½ teaspoon vanilla
1 ounce white chocolate
1 (16-ounce) box vanilla wafers
6 really ripe bananas

Mix sugar, flour, and salt in top of double boiler. Blend in egg yolks, milk, and half-and-half. Cook, uncovered, over boiling water, stirring constantly until smooth and thickened with no flour clumps. Remove from heat; stir in vanilla and white chocolate. Spread small amount of custard on bottom of casserole; cover with layer of wafers and a layer of sliced bananas. Pour about ⅓-½ of custard over bananas. Continue to layer wafers, bananas, and custard, ending with the custard.

MERINGUE:

3 egg whites   ¼ cup sugar

Beat egg whites until soft peaks form. Gradually add sugar, beating until peaks are stiff, but not dry. Spoon on top of Custard, spreading to cover entire surface and sealing well to edges. Bake at 350° for 15-20 minutes or until the peaks are browned. Cool slightly and then refrigerate several hours until chilled. Makes about 8 servings.

Note: Once you've mastered the custard part, you can add coconut instead of bananas or leave out the bananas and have egg custard.

Culinary Classics

Dr. Crawford W. Long introduced painless surgery in Jefferson in 1842 by using ether as an anesthetic. He removed a cyst from the neck of James Venable. The Crawford W. Long Medical Museum in Jefferson documents this medical discovery and the advancement of the use of anesthesia.

The Best Bread Pudding

On September 20, 2000, Joanie Duke, one of the cutest little older ladies that I've had the pleasure of meeting, bounded into the restaurant (and when I say "bounded in," I really mean it). She told me how much she enjoyed my recipes and that she had one of hers to share with me and shoved something into my hand, wrapped in plastic wrap. It was the best bread pudding I had ever wrapped my lips around. This quickly became the favorite bread pudding recipe for The Lady & Sons.

2 cups granulated sugar
5 large eggs, beaten
2 cups milk
2 teaspoons pure vanilla extract
3 cups cubed Italian bread, cut
   and allowed to stale overnight
   in a bowl

1 cup packed light brown sugar
¼ cup (½ stick) butter,
   softened
1 cup chopped pecans

Preheat oven to 350°. Grease a 9x13x2-inch pan. Mix together granulated sugar, eggs, and milk in a bowl; add vanilla. Pour over cubed bread and let sit for 10 minutes. In another bowl, mix and crumble together brown sugar, butter, and pecans. Pour bread mixture into prepared pan. Sprinkle brown sugar mixture over the top and bake for 35–45 minutes, or until set. Remove from oven.

SAUCE:
1 cup granulated sugar
½ cup (1 stick) butter, melted
1 egg, beaten

2 teaspoons pure vanilla extract
1 cup brandy

Mix together granulated sugar, butter, egg, and vanilla in a saucepan. Over medium heat, stir together until sugar is melted. Add brandy, stirring well. Pour over bread pudding. Delicious served warm or cold.

The Lady & Sons Just Desserts

Bread Pudding with Rum Sauce

4 cups milk
2 cups sugar
4 eggs, beaten
1 tablespoon vanilla extract
1–1½ cups chopped peeled
  apples

1 cup raisins
1 (16-ounce) loaf dry French
  bread, torn into bite-size
  pieces

Beat milk, sugar, and eggs in mixer bowl until blended. Stir in vanilla, apples, and raisins. Pour over bread in bowl; mix well. Let stand until bread absorbs milk, stirring occasionally. Spoon into greased 9x9-inch baking pan. May chill at this point and bake just before serving. Bake at 350° for 30–40 minutes or until pudding tests done.

RUM SAUCE:

2 eggs
¼ cup rum

1 cup confectioners' sugar
1 cup whipping cream, whipped

Beat eggs in saucepan. Add rum and confectioners' sugar; mix well. Cook over low heat until of desired consistency. Remove from heat; fold in whipped cream. Serve warm bread pudding with Rum Sauce or vanilla ice cream. May substitute rum extract for rum. Makes 10 servings.

Home Sweet Habitat

In 1996, a statue of Athena, the Greek goddess of war and the personification of wisdom, was dedicated in front of the Athens Classic Center to commemorate the 1996 Olympic Games, when Athens hosted women's soccer, rhythmic gymnastics, and volleyball competitions.

Krispy Kreme Bread Pudding with Butter Rum Sauce

2 dozen Krispy Kreme donuts
1 (14-ounce) can sweetened condensed milk (not evaporated)
2 (14.5 ounce) cans fruit cocktail, undrained
2 eggs, beaten
1 (9-ounce) box raisins
Pinch of salt
1–2 teaspoons ground cinnamon

Preheat oven to 350°. Cube donuts into a large bowl. Combine other ingredients and pour on top of donuts; let soak for a few minutes. Mix all together until donuts have soaked up the liquid as much as possible. Pour into large greased roasting pan. Bake for about 1 hour until center has jelled. Top with Butter Rum Sauce.

BUTTER RUM SAUCE:
1 stick butter
1 (1-pound) box confectioners' sugar
Rum to taste

Melt butter and slowly stir in confectioners' sugar. Add rum and heat until bubbly. Pour some over each serving of Krispy Kreme Bread Pudding.

Tried & True Recipes from Covington, Georgia

A Little Touch of Heaven

⅔ cup chopped almonds
6 tablespoons butter, melted
2 cups crushed vanilla wafers
2 teaspoons almond extract
3 pints vanilla ice cream, softened, divided
1 (10- to 20-ounce) jar apricot preserves, divided

Combine almonds, butter, wafers, and almond extract. Cover bottom of 8-inch square pan with half the crumb mixture. Cover with ½ of ice cream, and ½ of preserves. Add another thin layer of crumbs, remaining ice cream, and remaining preserves. Top with remaining crumbs. Freeze. Remove from freezer 15 minutes before serving. Cut into squares. Makes 10–12 servings.

Second Round: Tea-Time at the Masters®

Homemade Peach Ice Cream

3 cups sugar
4 eggs, beaten
1 quart milk
1 tablespoon vanilla
1 (14-ounce) can sweetened
   condensed milk
2 (12-ounce) cans evaporated
   milk

1 quart sweetened sliced
   peaches
Sugar to taste
Whole milk
Ice
Rock salt

Combine first 4 ingredients and cook on top of stove until it thickens some. Take off heat and cool. Add condensed milk and evaporated milk. Blend peaches in blender and add sugar to taste. Add to milk mixture. Pour into 6-quart ice cream churn and finish filling with whole milk. Fill churn with ice and rock salt, and churn.

Red Oak Recipes

Sherry Custard Sauce

1 cup sugar
2 tablespoons cornstarch
½ teaspoon salt

3 egg yolks, or 3 whole eggs
1 quart milk, divided
Pale dry sherry

Mix dry ingredients. Beat eggs with part of milk; add to dry mixture. Scald remaining milk. Pour slowly into egg mixture, beating constantly. Cook in double boiler until mixture coats spoon. Remove from heat. Add sherry to taste. Makes 1 quart.

Note: Serve over angel food cake, pound cake, ice cream, or fresh fruit.

The South's Legendary Frances Virginia Tea Room Cookbook

CATALOG *of*
CONTRIBUTING COOKBOOKS

The walls are covered with murals at the Road to Tara Museum in Jonesboro—the setting for Margaret Mitchell's acclaimed novel and film, Gone with the Wind. *The museum contains original props, costume reproductions, and other memorabilia associated with the movie.*

CATALOG of
CONTRIBUTING COOKBOOKS

All recipes in this book have been selected from the cookbooks shown on the following pages. Individuals who wish to obtain a copy of any particular book may do so by sending a check or money order to the address listed by each cookbook. Please note the postage and handling charges that are required. State residents add tax only when requested. Prices and addresses are subject to change, and the books may sell out and become unavailable. Retailers are invited to call or write to same address for discount information.

AT THE END OF THE FORK

by Barbara Roberts   Phone 770-338-1184 or 770-760-0337
4511 Cotton Trail   Fax 770-338-1936
Snellville, GA 30039   barbara@countryplacetravel.com

My family and friends cookbook includes recipes that have been handed down for generations. It also includes some low-fat recipes. The recipes are simple, yet delicious. There are 325 recipes with 134 pages to read for your enjoyment.

$10.00 Retail price   Visa/MC/Amex accepted
  $2.00 Postage and handling

Make check payable to Barbara Roberts

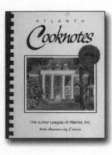

ATLANTA COOKNOTES

Junior League of Atlanta   Phone 678-916-3100
3154 Northside Parkway, NW   Fax 404-814-0656
Atlanta, GA 30327   www.jlatlanta.org
                      cookbooks@jlatlanta.org

A collection of traditional favorites, including 20 recipes from their original cookbook, the *Cotton Blossom,* first published in 1947. Full of cooking basics, including measurements, menu, helpful hints, heart-smart recipes, and a "Cooking with Mom" section. Illustrated by Jack Shields.

$19.95 Retail price
  $1.60 Tax for GA residents   ISBN 0-960-79142-6

Make check payable to Junior League of Atlanta

BEST OF THE HOLIDAYS

by Dot Gibson   Phone 912-285-2848
Dot Gibson Publications   Fax 912-285-0349
P. O. Box 117   www.dotgibson.com
Waycross, GA 31502   info@dotgibson.com

This book, with a striking cover and fantastic recipes, has combined the best, most often bragged-about recipes from *A Taste of the Holidays, Holiday Delights,* and *Holiday Favorites,* and put them all in one book for you. Mouth-wateringly delicious!

$9.95 Retail price
  $.70 Tax for GA residents   ISBN 0-941162-23-0
  $2.00 Postage and handling

Make check payable to Dot Gibson Publications

BEVELYN BLAIR'S EVERYDAY CAKES

by Bevelyn Blair   Phone 706-561-1144
P. O. Box 7852   bevblair@earthlink.net
Columbus, GA 31908

Everyday Cakes is a revised edition of the best-selling *Country Cakes* cookbook. A treasured collection of over 500 tested cake and frosting recipes including family and heirloom ones. The 282-page cookbook is a classic reference guide for cake bakers.

$22.50 Retail price
  $1.58 Tax for GA residents   ISBN 1-892514-61-3
  $4.00 Postage and handling
Make check payable to Bevelyn Blair

BEVELYN BLAIR'S EVERYDAY PIES

by Bevelyn Blair   Phone 706-561-1144
P. O. Box 7852   bevblair@earthlink.net
Columbus, GA 31908

Everyday Pies includes over 300 delectable pies to complement any meal—from casual picnics, parties, and buffets to elegant dinners during holidays and special occasions. Perfect pastry shells and pastry making tips are included in this 311-page cookbook.

$22.50 Retail price
  $1.58 Tax for GA residents   ISBN 1-892514-90-7
  $4.00 Postage and handling
Make check payable to Bevelyn Blair

THE BLUE WILLOW INN BIBLE OF SOUTHERN COOKING

by Louis and Billie Van Dyke   Phone 770-464-2133
Blue Willow Inn Restaurant   Fax 770-464-0599
294 North Cherokee Road   www.bluewillowinn.com
Social Circle, GA 30025   patsy@bluewillowinn.com

The most extensive collection of southern recipes ever in one book, with over 600 recipes that southerners have enjoyed for generations. Now you can re-create the Blue Willow Inn experience in your own kitchen.

$24.99 Retail price   Visa/MC/Disc accepted
  $1.74 Tax for GA residents   ISBN 1-4016-0227-4 (hardcover)
  $4.00 Postage and handling
Make check payable to Blue Willow Inn

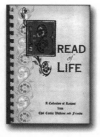

BREAD OF LIFE

by Curtis Watkins
6875 Parkway Drive, Box 98
Douglasville, GA 30135   cwatkins102@yahoo.com

Bread of Life has 150 recipes covering 65 pages, plus two pages of health information on heart disease and diabetes. Includes fifteen pages of nutritional information exclusive of the 65 pages of recipes. Each section has a relative scripture at the beginning.

  $7.00 Retail price
   $.42 Tax for GA residents
  $1.52 Postage and handling
Make check payable to Curtis Watkins

BREAD OF LIFE

Salem Baptist Church Youth   Phone 478-452-6633
126 Salem Church Road
Milledgeville, GA 31061

The *Bread of Life* cookbook is a collection of recipes from the members of Salem Baptist Church. From appetizers to desserts, and from old classics to new favorites, these cherished recipes are sure to find a special place in your kitchen.

$10.00 Retail price
  $3.00 Postage and handling

Make check payable to Salem Baptist Church

BREADS AND SPREADS

by Edward C. Rees   Phone 912-285-2848
Dot Gibson Publications   Fax 912-285-0349
P. O. Box 117   www.dotgibson.com
Waycross, GA 31502   info@dotgibson.com

Edward Rees brings you a no-nonsense approach to breadmaking. Bread recipes for the beginner as well as the experienced cook, plus recipes for delicious jams, jellies, and spreads. Nothing beats the aroma of breads baking or the taste of fresh homemade bread!

$9.95 Retail price
 $.70 Tax for GA residents   ISBN 0-929271-02-5
$2.00 Postage and handling

Make check payable to Dot Gibson Publications

COLLARD GREENS AND SUSHI

by Tamara Patridge   Phone 404-702-9117
6173 Pinedale Court   www.tipiworks.com
Morrow, GA 30260   patridge@bellsouth.net

Honoring ancestors of Japanese, American Indian, and West African descent, the author has captured a diverse collection of recipes that run the gamut from southern favorites to Asian fare. Beautiful family photos that tell a unique story!

$10.00 Retail price
 $.70 Tax for GA residents
 $4.00 Postage and handling

Make check payable to Tamara Patridge

CONFESSIONS OF A KITCHEN DIVA

by Claudine Destino
Happicook, Inc.
P. O. Box 769122   www.akitchendiva.com
Roswell, GA 30076   kitchendiva2003@yahoo.com

Perfect for kitchen novices and seasoned chefs alike, this 300-page cookbook includes timesaving tips, entertaining and party-planning ideas peppered with a splash of humor reflective of its animated author. The recipes are impressive, but simple to follow.

$24.95 Retail price
 $1.75 Tax for GA residents   ISBN 0-9728462-0-4
 $4.00 Postage and handling

Make check payable to Claudine Destino

COOK AND LOVE IT

Lovett Parent Association
4075 Places Ferry Road
Atlanta, GA 30327

Phone 404-262-3032, ext. 1266
Fax 404-261-1967
www.lovett.org
cookbook@lovett.org

These recipes bring the charm of southern hospitality into today's fast-paced lifestyle. Recipes include "loving touches," gifts from the kitchen, menus for special occasions, buffets, picnics, and parties, and easy children's recipes. 304 pages. 600+ recipes.

$16.95 Retail price
 $2.97 Tax for GA residents
 $5.00 Postage and handling

Visa/MC accepted
ISBN 0-9610846-3-4

Make check payable to Lovett Parent Association

COOKING WITH HERBS VOLUME I

The Garden Patch Company
893 Beaver Pond Road
Carrollton, GA 30117

Phone 770-832-6743
Fax 678-547-2525
gpatchco@aol.com

This 150-page cookbook contains 200 recipes from appetizers through desserts. From a small window garden to a moor of heather, herbs make a meal an epicurean creation. A major emphasis in these recipes is to lower salt and fat content in one's cooking without sacrificing flavor and taste.

$11.00 Retail price
 $2.50 Postage and handling

ISBN 0-9651762-1-5

Make check payable to The Garden Patch Company

COOKING WITH HERBS VOLUME II

The Garden Patch Company
893 Beaver Pond Road
Carrollton, GA 30117

Phone 770-832-6743
Fax 678-574-2525
gpatchco@aol.com

A 160-page book filled with a complete variety of recipes featuring herbs and their distinctive flavors. This book has a great section on menu planning using compatible herbs. It has sections on preserving your homegrown herbs, and making interesting craft projects using herbs.

$13.00 Retail price
 $2.50 Postage and handling

ISBN 0-9651762-2-3

Make check payable to The Garden Patch Company

COOKING WITH WATKINSVILLE FIRST CHRISTIAN CHURCH

Christian Women's Fellowship
Watkinsville First Christian Church
P. O. Box 287
Watkinsville, GA 30677

Phone 706-769-2328
(Pat McLure)
www.firstchristianwatkinsville.com
watfirst@bellsouth.net

Our cookbook is a treasured collection of 343 recipes from members and friends, passed down from generation to generation. Includes 119 pages of recipes, food safety, and food quantities for banquet planning. Ann Breelove Powers designed the cover.

$10.00 Retail price
 $.70 Tax for GA residents
 $2.00 Postage and handling

Make check payable to Watkinsville First Christian Church CWF

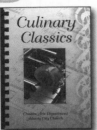

CULINARY CLASSICS

Atlanta City Church's Creative Arts Dept.   Phone 770-964-2138
3355 Old Jonesboro Road   Fax 770-964-6135
Fairburn, GA 30213   www.atlantacitychurch.org/store
info@acitychurch.com

Culinary Classics is a masterpiece for the cookbook collector. Its 136+ pages are filled with 300 recipes, cooking tips, helpful hints, and many extras. Whether a spin on the original, new-found delight or simple kid's fun recipe, you'll be intrigued.

$15.00 Retail price   Visa/MC/Amex accepted
  $2.50 Postage and handling

Make check payable to Atlanta City Church (CAD in memo)

THE DAY FAMILY FAVORITES

Joyce S. Ramsey   Phone 478-456-7199
129 High Hill Street   joyce31042@yahoo.com
Irwinton, GA 31042

The Harvey-Ruby Day Family consisted of fifteen siblings. All living siblings live within the middle Georgia area. This cookbook is a collection of family favorites that have been passed down through the generations. It consists of 152 pages with 350 recipes.

$15.00 Retail price (Includes postage)

Make check payable to Joyce S. Ramsey

DELIGHTFULLY SOUTHERN

by Dot Gibson   Phone 912-285-2848
Dot Gibson Publications   Fax 912-285-0349
P. O. Box 117   www.dotgibson.com
Waycross, GA 31502   info@dotgibson.com

Dot Gibson brings you four generations of outstanding southern recipes in this best-selling cookbook. From appetizers like Cheese Straws and Elegant Crab Dip to desserts like Ice Cream Truffles and Chocolate Seduction, they're all *Delightfully Southern.*

$13.95 Retail price
  $.95 Tax for GA residents   ISBN 0-941162-16-8
$2.00 Postage and handling

Make check payable to Dot Gibson Publications

DOWN THROUGH THE YEARS

Clyo Homemakers Club   Phone 912-754-6953
853 Ralph Rahn Road   juexra@aol.com
Rincon, GA 31326

Our cookbook has 163 pages of recipes, 3 pages of interesting writings by members, 2 pages of blessings to be offered before starting your meals, 38 pages of helpful hints, and an alphabetized index of the 8 categories of recipes.

$10.00 Retail price
  $5.00 Postage and handling

Make check payable to Clyo Homemakers Club

EATING FROM THE WHITE HOUSE TO THE JAILHOUSE

by Louise Dodd   Phone 478-474-8294
776 Middlesex Drive
Macon, GA 31210

Over 350 of the author's favorite recipes (each with a little story) from a lifetime of good eating, including at the White House and the jailhouse. Author is a newspaper and magazine food writer.

$25.00 Retail price   Visa/MC/Amex/Disc accepted
  $1.50 Tax for GA residents   ISBN 0-9752965-0-7
  $2.25 Postage and handling
Make check payable to Louise Dodd

FAMILY COLLECTIONS

St. Matthew's Episcopal Church Woman   Phone 770-979-4210
1520 Oak Road   Fax 770-979-4211
Snellville, GA 30087   www.stmattspeople.us
                                 stmatts@bellsouth.net

Family Collections presents a cornucopia of tried and true recipes used in the homes of St. Matthew's members. Many have stood the test of several generations of good cooks. 222 pages. 600 recipes. Currently out of print.

FAMOUS RECIPES FROM MRS. WILKES' BOARDING HOUSE

by Sema Wilkes   Phone 912-232-5997
Mrs. Wilkes' Dining Room
107 West Jones Street
Savannah, GA 31401

Our book includes original recipes cooked and served by Mrs. Wilkes to her boarders and to the world. It also contains many newspaper and magazine articles written during our years of business.

$14.95 Retail price
   $.90 Tax for GA residents   ISBN 0-939114-72-0
  $3.50 Postage and handling
Make check payable to Wilkes Trading Company

FINE DINING GEORGIA STYLE

by John Bailey   Phone 800-343-1583
Quail Ridge Press   Fax 800-864-1082
P. O. Box 123   www.quailridge.com
Brandon, MS 39043   info@quailridge.com

This cookbook features more than 250 signature recipes from 60 of the finest chefs, restaurants, and bed and breakfast inns in Georgia. Now with detailed instructions, these spectacular dishes can be prepared and enjoyed in your own home.

$24.95 Retail price   Visa/MC/Amex/Disc accepted
  $1.75 Tax for MS residents   ISBN 1-893062-66-X
  $4.00 Postage and handling
Make check payable to Quail Ridge Press

FIRST COME, FIRST SERVED...IN SAVANNAH

St. Andrew's School PTO   Phone 912-897-4941
P. O. Box 30693   Fax 912-897-4943
Savannah, GA 31410   www.saintschool.com
                                 cookbook@saintschool.com

First Come, First Served...In Savannah has earned a reputation as "the" cookbook to have. This treasured book is a culinary travelogue highlighting all the firsts in Savannah's history and provides information, stories, and history about Savannah.

$19.95 Retail price   Visa/MC accepted
  $5.00 Postage and handling   ISBN 0-9713159-0-6
Make check payable to St. Andrew's School Cookbook

FLAVORS OF THE GARDENS

Callaway Gardens   Phone 1-800-CALLAWAY (225-5292)
P.O. Box 2000   Fax 706-663-6812
Pine Mountain, GA 31822-2000   www.callawaygardens.com
                                 info@callawaygardens.com

With more than 400 delicious recipes, this book offers something for every taste. In addition to great recipes, there is a tip, food fact, or quotation on every page! Callaway Gardens is proud to share their wonderful cookbook with food-lovers and cookbook collectors.

$19.95 Retail price   Visa/MC/Amex/Disc accepted
  $4.50 Postage and handling   ISBN 0-9674125-0-1
Make check payable to Callaway Gardens

THE FOXFIRE BOOK OF APPALACHIAN COOKERY

Edited by Linda Garland Page and Eliot Wigginton
The University of North Carolina Press   Phone 800-848-6224
116 South Boundary Street   Fax 800-272-6817
Chapel Hill, NC 27514

More than simply a cookbook, *The Foxfire Book of Appalachian Cookery* combines unpretentious, delectable recipes with the wit and wisdom of those who have prepared and eaten such foods for generations.

$19.95 Retail price   Visa/MC accepted
  $5.00 Postage and handling   ISBN 0-8078-4395-4
Make check payable to UNC Press

FROM BLACK TIE TO BLACKEYED PEAS

by Dr. Irving Victor, M.D.   Phone 912-355-7054
4602 Sussex Place   Fax 912-355-7054
Savannah, GA 31405   www.bonaventture.com
                                 bonaventture@aol.com

This wonderful cookbook epitomizes good food, good tested recipes, and "good food for thought." A great help to the occasional cook, as well as the seasoned chef. Includes heart-healthy recipes and notes on the history of Savannah.

$20.00 Retail price
  $1.20 Tax for GA residents   ISBN 0-9671621-0-6
  $5.00 Postage and handling
Make check payable to Bonaventure Books

FROM OUR HOUSE TO YOURS

Habitat for Humanity International
Habitat Gift Shop   Phone 800-422-5914
20 Constitution Boulevard South   www.habitat.org
Shelton, CT 06484   customerservice@habitatgiftshop.com

Collection of recipes from affiliates and campus chapters of Habitat for Humanity International. 238 pages.

  $4.00 Retail price   Visa/MC/Amex/Disc accepted
   $.28 Tax for GA residents   ISBN 0-87197-384-7
  $3.00 Postage and handling

Make check payable to Habitat for Humanity International

GEORGIA NATIONAL FAIR BLUE RIBBON COOKBOOK

Georgia National Fair / Lora Arledge   Phone 478-988-6553
GNF   Fax 478-988-6514
P. O. Box 1367   www.georgianationalfair.com
Perry, GA 31069   larledge@gnfa.com

This 2004 edition is a collection of over 600 winning recipes with categories ranging from appetizers to vegetables. Compiled from the culinary competitions spanning five fairs—1999 to 2003. 326 pages. Hardcover. Easy to use. Spiral bound.

  $12.00 Retail price   Visa/MC/Amex accepted
    $.84 Tax for GA residents
  $3.95 Postage and handling

Make check payable to Georgia National Fair

A GIFT OF APPRECIATION

Dixie Aerospace Employees   Phone 404-348-8100
560 Atlanta South Parkway, Suite 100   Fax 404-348-8181
Atlanta, GA 30349   www.dixieaerospace.com
                                    mjohns@dixieaerospace.com

Compiling this book was a labor of love. Included are treasured favorites passed down for generations, as well as new favorites that will be passed on for generations. This cookbook is a must-have for your favorite cook's kitchen.

  $10.00 Retail price
   $1.50 Postage and handling

Make check payable to Dixie Aerospace - Company Cookbook

THE GINGERBREAD HOUSE COOKBOOK

Janet Galloway   Phone 912-234-7303
1921 Bull Street   www.thegingerbreadhouse.net
Savannah, GA 31401   gngrbreadhouse@comcast.net

The Gingerbread House, built in 1899, is a favorite site for weddings, parties, and other special events. This cookbook contains recipes created for these functions, along with sample menus and information about Savannah's most photographed home. 160 pages. 187 recipes.

  $15.95 Retail price
    $.96 Tax for GA residents   ISBN 0-9679170-0-6
  $3.50 Postage and handling

Make check payable to The Gingerbread House

GIVE US THIS DAY OUR DAILY BREAD

Rehoboth Baptist Church   Phone 706-274-3315
2737 Bartram Trace Road
Rayle, GA 30660

Contains 399 recipes from members and friends of a small country church. Recipes have been tried and tested many times at our church socials. Spiral bound, laminated front and back cover, index, and sixteen pages of helpful hints.

$10.00 Retail price
  $3.00 Postage and handling
Make check payable to Rehoboth Baptist Church

GLORIOUS GRASS

by Gladys Baldwin Wallace   Phone 404-351-5549
136 Peachtree Memorial Drive N.W. #NC6
Atlanta, GA 30309

This cookbook is a collection of 124 recipes devoted to asparagus. The recipes were collected over the years from family, friends, and a variety of cookbooks. Includes a brief history of asparagus in my family and helpful information for growing asparagus.

  $8.00 Retail price (Includes postage)
Make check payable to Gladys Baldwin Wallace

GONE WITH THE GRITS

by Diane Pfeifer   Phone 800-875-7242
P. O. Box 52404   Fax 404-841-9586
Atlanta, GA 30355

Not just for breakfast anymore, grits lend a nonfat creaminess to dips and sauces, a sponginess to breads, and chewy volume to bar cookies. There's even a fun chapter that puts this once laughed-at grain in your favorite foreign dishes.

$9.95 Retail price   Visa/MC accepted
$3.95 Postage and handling   ISBN 0-9618306-9-7
Make check payable to Strawberry Patch

GRANDMA MAMIE JONES' FAMILY FAVORITES

by Marilyn B. Jones   Phone 229-246-3700
4214 Thomasville Road
Climax, GA 39834

This cookbook is composed of 338 recipes donated by all of Grandma Mamie's children and grandchildren, and some of her great grandchildren.

$7.00 Retail price
  $.49 Tax for GA residents
$2.50 Postage and handling
Make check payable to Marilyn B. Jones

HEART & SOUL
Clinch Chapel
White Oak, GA

This cookbook includes 150 recipes that were collected from friends and family. The book was sponsored by the Youth Department. It has favorite recipes and photos of the youth and a dedication page and expression of appreciation. 70 pages. Currently out of print.

HEAVENLY DISHES
Compiled and edited by Betty Heathman
Central Baptist Church   Phone 770-718-9552
4520 Railroad Street   beheathman@hotmail.com
Oakwood, GA 30566

Wonderful recipes gathered from the good cooks at Central Baptist Church and their friends. It has a shopping list for each recipe. Also has easel back.

$10.00 Retail price
  $2.00 Postage and handling

Make check payable to Central Baptist Church

HERITAGE COOKBOOK
Oak Mountain Village Assisted Living
921 Old Newman Road
Carrolton, GA 30116   cmourey@mindspring.com

Submitted by current and past residents and their families, our cookbook contains 350 heritage recipes that have been passed down through generations. We have a section called "This and That" that contains a lot of unique home remedies and other around-the-house hints.

  $8.00 Retail price
  $2.00 Postage and handling

Make check payable to Cathie Mourey

HOLIDAY DELIGHTS
by Dot Gibson   Phone 912-285-2848
Dot Gibson Publications   Fax 912-285-0349
P. O. Box 117   www.dotgibson.com
Waycross, GA 31502   info@dotgibson.com

A neat little book with a price that makes it a great stocking stuffer or pick-up item. Includes excellent recipes for cakes, pies, cookies, and finer foods. It's a must-have for your holiday celebrations!

  $4.95 Retail price
   $.35 Tax for GA residents   ISBN 0-941162-17-6
  $2.00 Postage and handling

Make check payable to Dot Gibson Publications

HOLIDAY FAVORITES

by Dot Gibson
Dot Gibson Publications
P. O. Box 117
Waycross, GA 31502

Phone 912-285-2848
Fax 912-285-0349
www.dotgibson.com
info@dotgibson.com

A delightful holiday book that's loaded with outstanding recipes for cakes, cookies, pies, and gifts from the kitchen. Includes menus and recipes for entertaining during the holidays. Eye-catching cover and a great price for a gift.

$6.95 Retail price
$.49 Tax for GA residents   ISBN 0-941162-10-9
$2.00 Postage and handling

Make check payable to Dot Gibson Publications

HOME RUN RECIPES

Harris County Diamond Club (2005)
Attn: Arlene Doyle
120 Waterfall Way
Cataula, GA 31804

Phone 706-320-9699
or 706-573-6669
baedoyle@mchsi.com

This 98-page cookbook is filled with 245 of Georgia's most scrumptious recipes. The families, friends, and community of Harris County have submitted their secret recipes of past generations to support our local high school baseball team.

$10.00 Retail price
$.70 Tax for GA residents
$2.50 Postage and handling

Make check payable to Harris County Diamond Club

HOME SWEET HABITAT

Habitat for Humanity International
Habitat Gift Shop
20 Constitution Boulevard South
Shelton, CT 06484

Phone 800-422-5914
www.habitat.org
customerservice@habitatgiftshop.com

Favorite dessert and sweets recipes collected by Habitat for Humanity International affiliates. 238 pages.

$4.00 Retail price   Visa/MC/Amex/Disc accepted
$.28 Tax for GA residents   ISBN 1-887921-00-1
$3.00 Postage and handling

Make check payable to Habitat for Humanity International

IT'S THE PEOPLE; IT'S THE FOOD

St. Matthew's Episcopal Church Women
1520 Oak Road
Snellville, GA 30078

Phone 770-979-4210
Fax 770-979-4211
www.stmattspeople.us
stmatts@bellsouth.net

An eclectic mix of recipes reflecting the diversity of St. Matthew's Parish. Proceeds support a girl at Our Little Roses Home for girls in San Pedro Sula, Honduras, as well as other mission and outreach projects. 219 pages. Over 550 recipes.

$15.00 Retail price (Includes postage)

Make check payable to St. Matthew's Episcopal Church Women

THE LADY & SONS, TOO!

by Paula H. Deen   Phone 912-233-2600
The Lady and Sons   Fax 912-233-8283
102 W. Congress Street   www.ladyandsons.com
Savannah, GA 31401

The Lady & Sons, Too! is a delightful collection of recipes from
Paula Deen, owner of The Lady & Sons restaurant in Savannah.
In addition to featuring 315 southern recipes, this book has 32
helpful kitchen hints from "the Lady."

$19.95   Retail price   Visa/MC/Amex/Disc accepted
  $4.00   Postage and handling   ISBN 0-375-75836-4

Make check payable to The Lady & Sons

THE LADY & SONS JUST DESSERTS

by Paula H. Deen   Phone 912-233-2600
The Lady and Sons   Fax 912-233-8283
102 W. Congress Street   www.ladyandsons.com
Savannah, GA 31401

This cookbook is a seriously sweet southern dessert extravaganza!
Paula Deen shares the down-home recipes that made her famous,
including her signature Gooey Butter Cake, Peach Cobbler, Turtle
Cake, Sweet Baby Carrot Cake, and Pecan Dreams.

$16.95   Retail price   Visa/MC/Amex/Disc accepted
  $4.00   Postage and handling   ISBN 0-7432-2484-1

Make check payable to The Lady & Sons

THE LADY & SONS SAVANNAH COUNTRY COOKBOOK

by Paula H. Deen   Phone 912-233-2600
The Lady and Sons   Fax 912-233-8283
102 W. Congress Street   www.ladyandsons.com
Savannah, GA 31401

From one of the most frequently visited restaurants in Savannah,
The Lady & Sons, comes this collection of down-home southern
family favorites.   Paula Deen has created a friendly cookbook
filled with hundreds of quick and easy recipes.

$15.95   Retail price   Visa/MC/Amex/Disc accepted
  $4.00   Postage and handling   ISBN 0-375-75111-4

Make check payable to The Lady & Sons

MAIN STREET WINDER

Winder Woman's Club   Phone 770-867-5965
c/o Dora Fleming   Fax 770-307-0897
27 Deer Run Trail   dfleming1@earthlink.net
Winder, GA 30680

Published in 1987, this is the fourth cookbook produced since our
first one in 1938. Good cooks in northeast Georgia go first to a
Winder Woman's Club cookbook for authentic, tested, southern
recipes. 239 pages. 350 recipes.

$10.00   Retail price
  $2.00   Postage and handling

Make check payable to Winder Woman's Club

MONTEZUMA AMISH MENNONITE COOKBOOK

by Mrs. Ruth Yoder   Phone 478-472-8921
4336 Mennonite Church Road
Montezuma, GA 31063

This cookbook was put together by the ladies in our Mennonite community sharing their best recipes. It is two books in one. Over 800 recipes plus 416 household hints. We receive lots of compliments on our cookbook saying it's their favorite!

$16.95 Retail price   ISBN 0-9630704-0-1
  $3.00 Postage and handling

Make check payable to *Montezuma Amish Mennonite Cookbook Volume I*

MONTEZUMA AMISH MENNONITE COOKBOOK II

by Mrs. Ruth Yoder   Phone 478-472-8921
4336 Mennonite Church Road
Montezuma, GA 31063

Amish Mennonite Cookbook I was so popular, people were asking me to put together another one. The recipes are from our Mennonite community and from my husband's Amish kinfolks from Kentucky. Everyone shared their ten best recipes.

$17.95 Retail price   ISBN 0-9630704-0-1
  $3.00 Postage and handling

Make check payable to *Montezuma Amish Mennonite Cookbook Volume II*

MOTHER'S FINEST: SOUTHERN COOKING MADE EASY

by Wilma N. Ashcraft   Phone 770-944-9277
P. O. Box 1765   Fax 770-944-6500
Mableton, GA 30126   www.mothersfinestcatering.com
                                james@mothersfinestcatering

A collection of old southern traditional recipes that are simple to reproduce using ingredients found in everyday kitchens. This is a must-have cookbook for collectors and cooks! 185 pages/347 recipes/hard cover.

$19.95 Retail price   Visa/MC/Amex accepted
  $1.20 Tax for GA residents   ISBN 0-9712749-0-8
  $3.50 Postage and handling

Make check payable to Mother's Finest Cookbooks

MOUNTAIN FOLK, MOUNTAIN FOOD

by Betsy Tice White
Recovery Communications, Inc.
4100 Paces Walk SE, #3205
Atlanta, GA 30339   betsytw@mindspring.com

Folksy stories and old-time favorites and comfort foods—a perfect gift book for anyone who enjoys cooking or even just reading about it. Like a kitchen-table visit with a cozy friend.

$8.00 Retail price   ISBN 0-9615995-3-7
$2.00 Postage and handling

Make check payable to Betsy T. White

MY BEST TO YOU

by Carolyn Jackson   Phone 770-867-9309
866 Lakeshore Drive
Winder, GA 30680

Today's busy wives, mothers, and career women need all the help
in the kitchen they can get. Most of these tried-and-true favorite
recipes are quick and easy—perfect for those who want to spend
less time in the kitchen.

$8.00   Retail price
$1.50   Postage and handling

Make check payable to Carolyn Jackson

THE ONE-ARMED COOK

by Cynthia Stevens Graubart and   Phone 770-393-2997
    Catherine Fliegel, RN, CCE   Fax 770-393-1288
660 Spindlewick Drive   www.theonearmedcook.com
Atlanta, GA 30350   cynthia@theonearmedcook.com

How to cook with a baby on your hip! More than 120 recipes prepared in 30 minutes or less—everything from appetizers to
desserts. Lots of tips on stocking up, freezing ahead, and even
dining out. A perfect baby shower gift.

$19.95   Retail price   Visa/MC/Disc/Amex accepted
 $1.40   Tax for GA residents   ISBN 0-696-22682-0
 $5.95   Postage and handling

Make check payable to Cynthia Graubart

OUR BEST HOME COOKING

by Judith C. Dyer
P. O. Box 921722   www.dyer-consequences.com/cookbook.html
Norcross, GA 30010   info@dyer-consequences.com.html

Our Best Home Cooking includes 500 delicious recipes for home-
cooked meals for your family and friends. Family favorites, heirloom recipes, quick and easy dishes, international dishes, plus
recipes for children, our next generation of cooks. From our family to yours.

$10.00   Retail price   Visa/MC/Paypal accepted
  $.60   Tax for GA residents
 $5.00   Postage and handling

Make check payable to Judith C. Dyer

OUR FAVORITE RECIPES

The Garden Patch Company   Phone 770-832-6743
893 Beaver Pond Road   Fax 678-574-2525
Carrollton, GA 30117   gpatchco@aol.com

Includes 150 traditional southern recipes spanning four generations of our family. In light of current research, we have been able
to modify cholesterol levels and fat grams in these recipes. The
memories and value of friends and family sharing good food
remains constant.

$10.00   Retail price   ISBN 0-9651762-0-7
 $2.50   Postage and handling

Make check payable to The Garden Patch

OUT ON OUR OWN

by Gil, Rees, and Mark Gibson
Dot Gibson Publications
P. O. Box 117
Waycross, GA 31502

Phone 912-285-2848
Fax 912-285-0349
www.dotgibson.com
info@dotgibson.com

Excellent recipes—all easy to prepare and ideal for college students, singles, brides, or anyone starting out on their own. Cooking can be fun. Start with some simple recipes and before you know it, you'll be a pro!

$7.95 Retail price
$.56 Tax for GA residents
$2.00 Postage and handling

ISBN 0-941162-19-2

Make check payable to Dot Gibson Publications

PAR 3: TEA-TIME AT THE MASTERS®

Junior League of Augusta
363 Highland Avenue
Augusta, GA 30909

Phone 1-888-JLT-Time
or 706-733-9098
Fax 706-736-6526

www.jlaugusta.org • jlaugustaga@bellsouth.net

Beginning with a foreword by Barbara Nicklaus, this cookbook is divided into eighteen menus with party tips for planning ahead—the key to relaxed entertaining. Filled with gorgeous photography, golf highlights, and information about Augusta.

$21.95 Retail price
$1.54 Tax for GA residents
$4.00 Postage and handling + $3.00 each additional book

Visa/MC accepted
ISBN 0-9621062-5-9

Make check payable to Tea-Time Publications

PAST & PRESENT

Rincon United Methodist Church
115 Shaw Street
Rincon, GA 31326

This cookbook is filled with recipes from our members, past and present. We take great pride in presenting some of the best recipes from our good cooks throughout the years. Enjoy!

$10.00 Retail price
$5.00 Postage and handling

Make check payable to Rincon United Methodist UMW

PAULA DEEN & FRIENDS

by Paula Deen with Martha Nesbit
The Lady and Sons
102 W. Congress Street
Savannah, GA 31401

Phone 912-233-2600
Fax 912-233-8283
www.ladyandsons.com

Paula Deen and her friends are the experts when it comes to creating delightful meals that are easy to prepare. Each chapter is filled with tips and time-saving techniques, as well as memorable cooking stories. More than 150 delicious recipes included.

$25.00 Retail price
$4.00 Postage and handling

Visa/MC/Amex/Disc accepted
ISBN 0-7432-6722-2

Make check payable to The Lady & Sons

PEACHTREE BOUQUET

Junior League of DeKalb County
P. O. Box 183
Decatur, GA 30031

Phone 404-378-4536
Fax 404-378-4185
www.jldekalb.org jdekalb@bellsouth.net

Peachtree Bouquet, published in 1986 and with 60,000 copies in print, features over 600 recipes, including celebrity recipes from Atlanta notables, as well as gift recipes and kid-friendly recipes. All this plus an easy-to-read format makes this book a must-have!

$14.95   Retail price
 $1.05   Tax for GA residents
 $3.00   Postage and handling

Visa/MC/Disc/Amex accepted
ISBN 0-9618508-1-7

Make check payable to JLD

PERENNIALS

Gainesville-Hall County Junior League
P. O. Box 1472
Gainesville, GA 30501

Phone 770-535-1951
Fax 770-536-3616
www.gainesvillehalljuniorleague.org
info@gainesvillehalljuniorleague.org

Perennials is a southern celebration of foods and flavors. 417 pages, over 200 recipes. In the South, food is a part of the celebration of events and of feelings. It is central to all our gatherings.

$27.00   Retail price
 $5.00   Postage and handling

Visa/MC accepted
ISBN 0-942407-32-6

Make check payable to Junior League of Gainesvill-Hall

PUTTIN' ON THE PEACHTREE

Junior League of DeKalb County
P. O. Box 183
Decatur, GA 30031

Phone 404-378-4536
Fax 404-378-4185
www.jldekalb.org
jdekalb@bellsouth.net

This Walter S. McIllhenny Hall of Fame winner contains 346 pages with more than 650 recipes. Includes microwave and cooking tips throughout, and a bonus section with international fare. Over 135,000 copies in print. 20th Anniversary Edition.

$16.95   Retail price
 $1.18   Tax for GA residents
 $3.00   Postage and handling

Visa/MC/Disc/Amex accepted
ISBN 0-9618508-2-5

Make check payable to JLD

RED OAK RECIPES

by Frances G. Womack
519 Cromer Road
Tifton, GA 31794

Phone 229-382-4088

Down-home recipes, very easy-to-make southern recipes that were used in the 40s and 50s. Food I grew up with and I am 81 years old.

$10.00   Retail price
 $.70   Tax for GA residents

Make check payable to Frances G. Womack

SAVANNAH SEASONS

by Elizabeth Terry with Alexis Terry   Phone 912-236-5547
Elizabeth on 37th   Fax 912-232-1095
105 E. 37th Street   www.elizabethon37th.com
Savannah, GA 31401   e37@ix.netcom.com

A modern classic of southern cooking by Elizabeth Terry. Enjoy marvelous recipes and personal stories from Elizabeth on 37th even when you're not in Savannah. Includes artwork and beautiful photos.

$32.50   Retail price   Visa/MC/Disc/Diner's accepted
  $1.95   Tax for GA residents   ISBN 0-385-48236-1
  $5.00   Postage and handling

Make check payable to Elizabeth on 37th

SECOND ROUND: TEA-TIME AT THE MASTERS®

Junior League of Augusta   Phone 1-888-JLT-Time
363 Highland Avenue   or 706-733-9098
Augusta, GA 30909   Fax 706-736-6526
         www.jlaugusta.org • jlaugustaga@bellsouth.net

In 1988, *Second Round* sold more than 20,000 copies in the first year. This cookbook sports a golf theme with restaurant recipes, member and golfer recipes, and Masters® Tournament highlights.

$26.95   Retail price   Visa/MC accepted
  $1.19   Tax for GA residents   ISBN 0-9621062-0-8
  $4.00   Postage and handling + $5.00 each additional book

Make check payable to Tea-Time Publications

SHERMAN DIDN'T BURN OUR RECIPES, BARTOW'S STILL COOKING

Bartow Community Club   Phone 478-364-7905
Walter's Publishing   Fax 478-364-7905
P. O. Box 251   mancin2@pineland.net
Bartow, GA 30413

Contains 160 pages of good southern recipes, including a section of favorites handed down from past generations. A short history of the town is featured. Although Sherman came through Bartow, he didn't burn our recipes—just our cotton bales.

$15.00   Retail price
  $2.50   Postage and handling + $1.00 for each additional book

Make check payable to Bartow Community Club

SIMPLE DECENT COOKING

Habitat for Humanity International
Habitat Gift Shop   Phone 800-422-5914
20 Constitution Boulevard South   www.habitat.org
Shelton, CT 06484   customerservice@habitatgiftshop.com

Quick and easy recipes from Habitat for Humanity International homeowners, volunteers, board members, and staff. 206 pages.

$4.00   Retail price   Visa/MC/Amex/Disc accepted
 $.28   Tax for GA residents   ISBN 1-887921-29-X
$3.00   Postage and handling

Make check payable to Habitat for Humanity International

SOME ASSEMBLY REQUIRED

by Lee Chadwick   Phone 678-527-2000
Meridian International Publishing   Fax 678-527-2001
5895 Windward Parkway, Suite 100   www.stylishfood.com
Alpharetta, GA 30005   eventsjh@meridianpublishing.net

Recipes and style tips by seasoned caterer, travel writer, special event facility proprietor, Lee Chadwick. Lee's no-nonsense, step-by-step approach to cooking and entertaining is peppered with her own life lessons.

$19.95 Retail price   Visa/MC/Amex accepted
$1.40 Tax for GA residents   ISBN 0-9718186-8-1
$3.95 Postage and handling

Make check payable to Meridian International Publishing

THE SOUTH'S LEGENDARY FRANCES VIRGINIA TEA ROOM COOKBOOK

by Millie Coleman   Phone 404-351-1313
2065 Spring Lake Drive NW   Fax 404-351-1359
Atlanta, GA 30305   milliecoleman@comcast.net

This favorite tells old Atlanta stories for tea room fans and history buffs—a collector's delight. Makes a perfect gift for grandmothers or newcomers to the South. Refer to the quantity section with easy recipes for club luncheons or family reunions.

$18.95 Retail price
$1.52 Tax for GA residents   ISBN 0-9653416-0-7
$3.50 Postage and handling

Make check payable to Mildred Coleman

SOUTHERN BREAD WINNERS

by Linda G. Hatcher   Phone 912-285-2848
Dot Gibson Publications   Fax 912-285-0349
P. O. Box 117   www.dotgibson.com
Waycross, GA 31502   info@dotgibson.com

A delightful book to answer all the family's bread needs, from biscuits to yeast breads—cinnamon buns, fritters, cornbreads, muffins, sweet breads, and more. Delicious and easy recipes for every occasion.

$9.95 Retail price
$.70 Tax for GA residents   ISBN 0-941162-12-5
$2.00 Postage and handling

Make check payable to Dot Gibson Publications

A SOUTHERN COLLECTION: THEN AND NOW

Junior League of Columbus, Georgia   Phone 706-327-4207
700 Broadway   www.jlcolumbus.com
Columbus, GA 31901   jlcga1@charter.net

This cookbook presents contemporary recipes and elegant meal ideas with a taste of classic southern cooking. Take a tour of the "Old South" through color photographs, and sample southern traditions with special menus and wine suggestions.

$22.95 Retail price   Visa/MC accepted
$1.61 Tax for GA residents   ISBN 0-9606300-1-5
$4.00 Postage and handling

Make check payable to Junior League of Columbus, GA

SOUTHERN MANNA

by First United Methodist Church   Phone 912-285-2848
Dot Gibson Publications   Fax 912-285-0349
P. O. Box 117   www.dotgibson.com
Waycross, GA 31502   info@dotgibson.com

From delicious appetizers to delectable desserts, and of course great casseroles, this beautiful cookbook is loaded with mouth-watering recipes perfect for family and special company. Recipes submitted by three generations of outstanding cooks.

$16.95   Retail price
   $.35   Tax for GA residents   ISBN 0-941162-07-9
  $2.00   Postage and handling

Make check payable to Dot Gibson Publications

SPECIAL TREASURES

Carol Corley   Phone 770-474-3087
35 Pinecrest Court   Fax 770-474-3087
Stockbridge, GA 30281   carolsspecialtreasures@yahoo.com

Nourish the body as well as the soul and spirit. This book includes 293 recipes from the past as well as scripture and wisdom principles. Beautifully written, this book is a treasured keepsake for yourself or as a gift.

$12.95   Retail price
   $.52   Tax for GA residents
  $2.00   Postage and handling

Make check payable to Carol Corley

STRAWBERRIES: FROM OUR FAMILY'S FIELD TO YOUR FAMILY'S TABLE

Calhoun Produce, Inc.   Phone 229-273-1887
5075 Hawpond Road   Fax 229-273-0082
Ashburn, GA 31714   www.calhounproduce.com
    sheilar@planttel.net

This cookbook is filled with 275 wonderfully delicious strawberry recipes. Winners from our strawberry cook-off are added each year. All your favorite strawberry recipes in one book!

$7.95   Retail price
  $.56   Tax for GA residents
$3.00   Postage and handling

Make check payable to Calhoun Produce

A TASTE OF GEORGIA

Newnan Jr. Service League   Phone 770-251-0113
P. O. Box 1433
Newnan, GA 30263

A Taste of Georgia offers insights into the delights and traditions that make Georgia a place of hospitality and fine cooking. Featuring culinary hints, food presentations, napkin folding, and table settings.

$18.95   Retail price   Visa/MC accepted
  $1.33   Tax for GA residents   ISBN 0-9611002-2-2
  $3.00   Postage and handling

Make check payable to NJSL

A TASTE OF GEORGIA, ANOTHER SERVING

Newnan Jr. Service League   Phone 770-251-0113
P. O. Box 1433
Newnan, GA 30264

A fresh innovative companion to our first cookbook, *A Taste of Georgia*. We have added a child's section and easy reference pages for low-fat, microwave, and grill recipes. A collection of carefully selected, treasured recipes from southern kitchens.

$14.95   Retail price   Visa/MC accepted
  $1.05   Tax for GA residents   ISBN 0-9611002-1-4
  $3.00   Postage and handling

Make check payable to NJSL

A TASTE OF THE HOLIDAYS

by Dot Gibson   Phone 912-285-2848
Dot Gibson Publications   Fax 912-285-0349
P. O. Box 117   www.dotgibson.com
Waycross, GA 31502   info@dotgibson.com

A holiday best seller—this book includes terrific recipes for that special time of the year. Perfect for a stocking stuffer, teacher's gift, or holiday happy. Make someone happy today with a gift that will be appreciated for years to come.

$4.95   Retail price
  $.35   Tax for GA residents   ISBN 0-941162-07-9
 $2.00   Postage and handling

Make check payable to Dot Gibson Publications

TASTES FOR ALL SEASONS

Central Christian Church Ladies Aux.   Phone 404-349-6440
2873 Rockwood Road   Fax 404-466-8355
East Point, GA 30344

Simple, easy recipes for beginners and everyday cooks. Great for busy moms and new cooks alike. 50 pages.

$7.00   Retail price
  $.49   Tax for GA residents
 $1.95   Postage and handling

Make check payable to Central Christian Church, Ladies Auxiliary

TEA-TIME AT THE MASTERS®

Junior League of Augusta   Phone 1-888-JLT-Time
363 Highland Avenue   or 706-733-9098
Augusta, GA 30909   Fax 706-736-6526
       www.jlaugusta.org • jlaugustaga@bellsouth.net

Published in 1977, this cookbook has sold more than 300,000 copies. It is a highly recognizable, comprehensive book with triple-tested recipes from members' and golfers' wives. *Tea-Time* was honored with the McIlhenny Hall of Fame Cookbook Award.

$18.95   Retail price   Visa/MC accepted
  $1.33   Tax for GA residents   ISBN 0-918544-38-6
  $4.00   Postage and handling + $3.00 for additional books

Make check payable to Tea-Time Publications

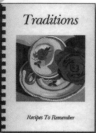

TRADITIONS

by Tina Salser Rees
Dot Gibson Publications
P. O. Box 117
Waycross, GA 31502

Phone 912-285-2848
Fax 912-285-0349
www.dotgibson.com
info@dotgibson.com

An outstanding collection of traditional family recipes, plus up-to-date, time-saving tips for today's busy cooks. This book will appeal to everyone from brides to expert gourmets. Eye-catching cover, and easy-to-follow instructions. 232 pages.

$13.95 Retail price
  $.98 Tax for GA residents   ISBN 0-929271-01-7
  $2.00 Postage and handling

Make check payable to Dot Gibson Publications

A TRAVELER'S TABLE

by John Izard
Sarah Izard Pariseau
807 S. Newport Avenue
Tampa, FL 33606

Fax 813-258-6601
spariseau@tampabay.rr.com

Georgia resident John Izard brings us an unusual selection of especially good recipes that exude smells and flavors of the American South and many foreign countries. Beautiful color illustrations, culinary discussions, and personal anecdotes. Perfect for kitchen shelf or coffee table alike. 264 pages. 250 recipes.

$24.95 Retail price
  $1.75 Tax for FL residents   ISBN 0-9723815-0-3
  $4.95 Postage and handling

Make check payable to *A Traveler's Table*

TRIED & TRUE RECIPES

Covington, Georgia, East Metro
   Christian Women's Connection
Sponsored by Christian Women's Stonecroft Ministries
Conyers, GA

A compilation of "down home" southern cooking, these "tried and true" recipes are just that, having been used time and time again over the years. It is with great pleasure we present this cookbook of treasured favorites.   170 pages.   350 recipes. Currently out of print.

TRIED & TRUE RECIPES

Wild Timber Social Committee
222 Beech Tree Hollow
Sugar Hill, GA 30518

Our cookbook is comprised of about 206 pages containing nearly 400 beloved family recipes and all-time neighborhood favorites. We've covered everything from easy weeknight dishes to a more complicated fare for the seasoned palate. Hope you enjoy!

$12.75 Retail price
  $.77 Tax for GA residents
  $5.00 Postage and handling

Make check payable to Wild Timber Social Committee

TRUE GRITS

Junior League of Atlanta
3154 Northside Parkway, NW
Atlanta, GA 30327

Phone 678-916-3100
Fax 404-814-0656
www.jlatlanta.org
cookbooks@jlatlanta.org

A collection of contemporary recipes from well-known Atlanta chefs, restaurants, and caterers such as Bacchanalia, Pano's & Paul's, and the Dining Room at the Ritz-Carlton Buckhead. Hardbound, illustrated, with full-color photography. A great gift for brides, secretaries, clients, mothers, cookbook collectors, etc.

$26.95   Retail price
  $2.16   Tax for GA residents   ISBN 0-87197-425-8
Make check payable to Junior League of Atlanta

VIDALIA SWEET ONION LOVERS COOKBOOK

Bland Farms
Glennville, GA   www.vidaliabrands.com

Enjoy this compilation of the best sweet Vidalia onion recipes in the South. Thanks to their valued customers, Bland Farms can now share these favorite customer recipes with Vidalia onion lovers all over the world. Currently out of print.

WANTED: QUICK DRAW'S FAVORITE RECIPES

Harold "Quick Draw" Finch   Phone 770-957-5319
1434 Hwy 81 E
McDonough, GA 30252

All 153 recipes in this delightful 81-page cookbook were developed by "Quick Draw" Finch in his over 65 years as a chef. Finch retired from acting and commercials, and has owned several restaurants in his lifetime.

$17.00   Retail price
  $4.00   Postage and handling
Make check payable to Quick Draw Finch

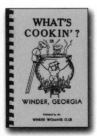

WHAT'S COOKIN'? IN WINDER, GEORGIA

Winder Woman's Club
c/o Dora Fleming
27 Deer Run Trail
Winder, GA 30680

Phone 770-867-5965
Fax 770-307-0897
dfleming1@earthlink.net

What's Cookin'? is the first of four cookbooks published by Winder Woman's Club. It is treasured locally for the inclusion of recipes that date back through five generations of great southern cooks. 100 pages. Over 200 recipes.

$10.00   Retail price
  $2.00   Postage and handling
Make check payable to Winder Woman's Club

Masters® Golf Tournament Trivia

- In 1934, Bobby Jones and Clifford Roberts decided to hold an annual golf tournament and invite the country's best players to attend. The event was originally called the Augusta National Invitation, but in 1939, the name was officially changed to the Masters® Golf Tournament.

- The first Tournament was held March 22, 1934.

- Beginning in 1940, the Masters® was scheduled each year during the first full week in April.

- Horton Smith won the very first Tournament.

- In 1935, Gene Sarazen hit "the shot heard 'round the world" scoring a double eagle on the par 5, 15th hole, tying Craig Wood and forcing a playoff. Sarazen won the 36-hole playoff the following day by 5 strokes.

- The Tournament was not played for three years (1943, 1944, and 1945) due to World War II.

- The tallest Masters® Golf champion was George Archer (6'5") and the shortest Ian Woosnam (5'4½").

- The widest margin of victory came in 1997 with twelve strokes by Tiger Woods. Tiger was the youngest Champion at 21 years, 3 months, and 14 days.

- Jack Nicklaus has the most Tournament victories, having won six times: 1963, 1965, 1966, 1972, 1975, and 1986.

- Next to Jack Nicklaus, Arnold Palmer (1958, 1960, 1962, 1964) and Tiger Woods (1997, 2001, 2002, 2005) are tied for the most victories, having both won four times.

- The tradition of the winner of the Masters® being presented with the famous "green jacket" at Augusta National Golf Club dates to 1937. That year, members of the club wore green jackets during the Tournament so that fans in attendance could easily spot them if they needed to ask questions.

Equivalents, Substitutions, Etc.

EQUIVALENTS:

Apple: 1 medium = 1 cup chopped

Banana: 1 medium = ⅓ cup

Berries: 1 pint = 1¾ cups

Bread: 1 slice = ½ cup soft crumbs = ¼ cup fine, dry crumbs

Broth, beef or chicken: 1 cup = 1 bouillon cube dissolved in 1 cup boiling water

Butter: 1 stick = ¼ pound = ½ cup

Cabbage: 2 pounds = 9 cups shredded or 5 cups cooked

Cheese, grated: 1 pound = 4 cups; 8 ounces = 2 cups

Chicken: 1 large boned breast = 2 cups cooked meat

Chocolate, bitter: 1 square or 1 ounce = 2 tablespoons grated

Coconut: 3½-ounce can = 1⅓ cups

Cool Whip: 8 ounces = 3 cups

Cornmeal: 1 pound = 3 cups

Crabmeat, fresh: 1 pound = 3 cups

Crackers, graham: 15 = 1 cup crushed

Crackers, saltine: 23 = 1 cup crushed

Cream, heavy: 1 cup = 2–2½ cups whipped

Cream cheese: 3 ounces = 6⅔ tablespoons

Egg whites: 8–10 = 1 cup

Eggs: 4–5 = 1 cup

Evaporated milk: 5⅓-ounce can = ⅔ cup; 12-ounce can = 1¼ cups

Flour: 1 pound = 4½ cups

Flour, self-rising: 1 cup = 1 cup all-purpose + 1½ teaspoons baking powder + ½ teaspoon salt

Garlic powder: ⅛ teaspoon = 1 average clove

Gingerroot: 1 teaspoon = ¾ teaspoon ground

Grits: 1 cup = 4 cups cooked

Herbs, fresh: 1 tablespoon = 1 teaspoon dried

Lemon: 1 medium = 3 tablespoons juice

Marshmallows: ¼ pound = 16 large; ½ cup = 4 large

Mushrooms: ¼ pound fresh = 1 cup sliced

Mustard, dry: 1 teaspoon = 1 tablespoon prepared

Noodles: 1 pound = 7 cups cooked

Nuts, chopped: ¼ pound = 1 cup

Onion: 1 medium = ¾–1 cup chopped = 2 tablespoons dried chopped (flakes)

Orange: 3–4 medium = 1 cup juice

Pecans: 1 pound shelled = 4 cups

Potatoes: 1 pound = 3 medium

Rice: 1 cup = 3 cups cooked

Spaghetti: 1 pound uncooked = 5 cups cooked

Spinach, fresh: 2 cups chopped = 1 (10-ounce) package frozen chopped

Sugar, brown: 1 pound = 2½ cups

Sugar, powdered: 1 pound = 3½ cups

Sugar, white: 1 pound = 2¼ cups

Vanilla wafers: 22 = 1 cup fine crumbs

Whole milk: 1 cup = ½ cup evaporated + ½ cup water

SUBSTITUTIONS:

1 slice cooked **bacon** = 1 tablespoon bacon bits

1 cup **buttermilk** = 1 cup plain yogurt; or 1 tablespoon lemon juice or vinegar + plain milk to make 1 cup

1 cup sifted **cake flour** = 7/8 cup sifted all-purpose flour

1 ounce **unsweetened chocolate** = 3 tablespoons cocoa + 1 tablespoon butter or margarine

1 ounce **semisweet chocolate** = 3 tablespoons cocoa + 1 tablespoon butter or margarine + 3 tablespoons sugar

1 tablespoon **cornstarch** = 2 tablespoons flour (for thickening)

1 cup **heavy cream** (for cooking, not whipping) = 1/3 cup butter + 3/4 cup milk

1 cup **sour cream** = 1/3 cup milk + 1/3 cup butter; or 1 cup plain yogurt

1 cup **tartar sauce** = 6 tablespoons mayonnaise or salad dressing + 2 tablespoons pickle relish

1 cup **tomato juice** = 1/2 cup tomato sauce + 1/2 cup water

1 cup **vegetable oil** = 1/2 pound (2 sticks) butter

1 cup **whipping cream**, whipped = 6–8 ounces Cool Whip

1 cup **whole milk** = 1/2 cup evaporated milk + 1/2 cup water

MEASUREMENTS:

3 teaspoons = 1 tablespoon

1 tablespoon = 1/2 fluid ounce

2 tablespoons = 1/8 cup

3 tablespoons = 1 jigger

4 tablespoons = 1/4 cup

8 tablespoons = 1/2 cup or 4 ounces

12 tablespoons = 3/4 cup

16 tablespoons = 1 cup or 8 ounces

3/8 cup = 1/4 cup + 2 tablespoons

5/8 cup = 1/2 cup + 2 tablespoons

7/8 cup = 3/4 cup + 2 tablespoons

1/2 cup = 4 fluid ounces

1 cup = 1/2 pint or 8 fluid ounces

2 cups = 1 pint or 16 fluid ounces

1 pint, liquid = 2 cups or 16 fluid ounces

1 quart, liquid = 2 pints or 4 cups

1 gallon, liquid = 4 quarts or 8 pints or 16 cups

OVEN-TO-CROCKPOT CONVERSIONS:

15–30 minutes in the oven = 1½–2½ hours on HIGH or 4–6 hours on LOW

35–45 minutes in the oven = 2–3 hours on HIGH or 6–8 hours on LOW

50 minutes–3 hours in the oven = 4–5 hours on HIGH or 8–10 hours on LOW

PHOTO © GEORGIA DEPARTMENT OF ECONOMIC DEVELOPMENT

The town of Helen is the most popular destination in north Georgia, and third in the state behind Atlanta and Savannah. The main attractions of Helen are the re-created Alpine Village and Oktoberfest, a six-week party that runs from mid-September to early November.

Georgia Timeline

Presented below is a brief chronology of historical Georgia events.

1540: Hernando de Soto's Spanish expedition enters Georgia.

1566: Spaniard Pedro Menéndez de Avilés builds a fort on St. Catherine's Island.

1732: King George II grants a charter to settle the colony of Georgia.

1733: James Oglethorge arrives with English settlers and establishes the first town, Savannah.

1742: The Battle of Bloody Marsh on St. Simon's Island ends the Spanish influence.

1752: Georgia becomes a royal colony.

1778: Savannah is captured by British troops when they invade Georgia during the Revolutionary War.

1785: America's oldest state-chartered university, University of Georgia, receives its charter.

1788: Georgia becomes the fourth state after ratifying the U.S. Constitution.

1836: Georgia Female College in Macon receives state charter and becomes the world's first female college.

1861: Georgia secedes from the Union.

1862: Union forces overtake Pulaski and close the Savannah seaport.

1863: Confederates defeat Union forces at Battle of Chickamauga.

1864: Union General Sherman burns Atlanta, and occupies Savannah.

1870: Georgia is readmitted to the Union.

1877: Atlanta becomes the permanent capital of Georgia.

1897: Atlanta University and Tuskegee Institute compete together in the first black collegiate football game.

1920: Martin Luther King is born in Atlanta.

1943: Georgia is the first state to allow 18 year olds to vote.

1961: University of Georgia desegregates.

1977: Former Georgia governor Jimmy Carter is elected as the 39th U.S. president.

2000: 2000 Federal Census: state population = 8,186,453; white population = 5,329,380; African-American population = 2,349,512; Hispanic population = 443,882; all others = 63,679.

Collect the Series!

Best of the Best State Cookbook Series

Cookbook collectors love this Series! The forty-two cookbooks, covering all fifty states (see next page for listing), contain over 15,000 of the most popular local and regional recipes collected from approximately 3,000 of the leading cookbooks from these states. The Series not only captures the flavor of America, but saves a lot of shelf space.

To assist individuals who wish to collect the Series, we are offering a **Collect the Series Discount Coupon Booklet.** With the Booklet you get:

Collect the Series!
BEST OF THE BEST STATE COOKBOOK SERIES
With this Special *Collect the Series* Discount Coupon Booklet

OVER 3 MILLION STATE COOKBOOKS SOLD!

continued inside...

Call **1-800-343-1583** to order a free, no-obligation Discount Coupon Booklet.

- **25% discount off the list price ($16.95 minus 25% = $12.70 per copy)**
- **With a single order of five copies, you receive a sixth copy free. A single order of ten cookbooks, gets two free copies, etc.**
- **Only $4.00 shipping cost for any number of books ordered (within contiguous United States).**

Recipe Hall of Fame Cookbook Collection

is also included in the
Collect the Series Discount Coupon Booklet.

| 304 pages • $19.95 | 304 pages • $19.95 | 304 pages • $19.95 | 240 pages • $16.95 |

The four cookbooks in this collection consist of over 1,200 of the most exceptional recipes collected from the entire
BEST OF THE BEST STATE COOKBOOK SERIES.
The Hall of Fame Collection can be bought as a four-cookbook set for $40.00.
This is a 48% discount off the total individual cost of $76.80.

QUAIL RIDGE PRESS
P. O. Box 123 • Brandon, MS 39043 • 1-800-343-1583
E-mail: info@quailridge.com • www.quailridge.com

BEST OF THE BEST STATE COOKBOOK SERIES

ALABAMA
ALASKA
ARIZONA
ARKANSAS
BIG SKY
Includes Montana, Wyoming
CALIFORNIA
COLORADO
FLORIDA
GEORGIA
GREAT PLAINS
Includes North Dakota, South Dakota, Nebraska, and Kansas

HAWAII
IDAHO
ILLINOIS
INDIANA
IOWA
KENTUCKY
LOUISIANA
LOUISIANA II
MICHIGAN
MID-ATLANTIC
Includes Maryland, Delaware, New Jersey, and Washington, D.C.

MINNESOTA
MISSISSIPPI
MISSOURI
NEVADA
NEW ENGLAND
Includes Rhode Island, Connecticut, Massachusetts, Vermont, New Hampshire, and Maine
NEW MEXICO
NEW YORK
NO. CAROLINA
OHIO
OKLAHOMA

OREGON
PENNSYLVANIA
SO. CAROLINA
TENNESSEE
TEXAS
TEXAS II
UTAH
VIRGINIA
VIRGINIA II
WASHINGTON
WEST VIRGINIA
WISCONSIN

All Best of the Best Cookbooks are 6x9 inches, are comb-bound, contain over 300 recipes, and total 288–352 pages. Each contains illustrations, photographs, an index and a list of contributing cookbooks, a special feature which cookbook collectors enjoy. Scattered throughout the cookbooks are short quips that provide interesting information about each state, including historical facts and major attractions along with amusing trivia. Retail price per copy $16.95.

To order by credit card, call toll-free **1-800-343-1583**, visit **www.quailridge.com**, or use the Order Form below.

Q Order Form

Send check, money order, or credit card info to:
QUAIL RIDGE PRESS • P. O. Box 123 • Brandon, MS 39043

Name _____

Address _____

City_____

State/Zip _____

Phone # _____

Email Address _____

❏ Check enclosed

Charge to: ❏ Visa ❏ MC ❏ AmEx ❏ Disc

Card # _____

Expiration Date _____

Signature _____

Qty.	Title of Book (State) or HOF set	Total

Subtotal _____

Mississippi residents add 7% sales tax _____

Postage ($4.00 any number of books) + $4.00

TOTAL _____